From

TULIP

to

ROSES

An Invitation to Complete the Reformation's Bloom

By Rev. Dr. Peter A. Kerr

An A DEO LUMEN publication.

A DEO LUMEN

All Bible verses are quoted from the New American Standard Bible

From TULIP to ROSES
Copyright © 2025 Peter A. Kerr
All rights reserved.
An A DEO LUMEN publication
www.PeterAKerr.com

Library of Congress Cataloging-in-Publication Data
Kerr, Peter A.
From TULIP to ROSES/ Peter A. Kerr —First Edition
"An A DEO LUMEN publication."
ISBN-13: 978-0-9899698-2-6 (Softcover and e-book)
    1.   Theology—Non Fiction.

A DEO LUMEN books are available at Amazon.com in print and
Kindle format
First Edition: November 2025
Printed in the United States of America

Cover image by ©iStockphoto.com
Cover design by Peter A. Kerr

Dedication

This book is dedicated to my faithful brothers and sisters who have believed even without the full historic revelation of God's love. I pray you release past beliefs and feel embraced by an even greater God whose sovereignty grants us all freedom and relationship.

"But thanks be to God, who always leads us in His triumph in Christ, and manifests through us the sweet aroma of the knowledge of Him in every place. For we are a fragrance of Christ to God among those who are being saved and among those who are perishing; to the one an aroma from death to death, to the other an aroma from life to life. And who is adequate for these things? For we are not like many, peddling the word of God, but as from sincerity, but as from God, we speak in Christ in the sight of God." 2 Cor. 2:14-17, NASB

PETER A. KERR

Contents

From

TULIP

to

ROSES

An Invitation to Complete the Reformation's Bloom

Foreword

How doctrine has evolved since the first three centuries of Christianity is truly amazing. We have marveled at this pearl of great price that is God's Word, uncovered much more of the depth of God's love, and constructed fulsome systematic theologies in an attempt to understand God's nature and plan for humanity. Unfortunately, some of our constructs conflict.

James Orr in his 1901 book *The Progress of Dogma* called theology the "science of revealed religion," claiming it to be stable, coherent, and testable. He wrote, "The test of a sound theological development is not its independence of what has gone before, but the degree of its respect for it, the depth of its insight into it, and its capacity of uniting itself with it, and of carrying it a stage further towards completion" (19-20). Genuine development in doctrine is marked by continuity with the past, not radical breaks from it; it builds upon earlier results, respects prior theological insight, and extends past wisdom rather than repudiating it.

While many attempts have been made to unite the multifarious splinters of Christian theology, the best way forward is to join the prophet in saying "come now, let us reason together" as did the early Church Councils (Is 1:18). Unity without truth makes union itself an idol. However, if truth can be obtained and fearlessly championed, if Christ can be lifted up, He will draw all men unto Him (John 12:32).

The fractured state of Christianity is such that it would be impossible to get everyone into a room to discuss their differences. Even if we had such a gathering, we'd need a direction. That direction should at least be looking for ways we broke from the past rather than built upon it.

I propose the best possible direction is a return to the Bible as understood by the first three hundred years of Christian thought.

Theologians back then spoke the Greek of the Bible, could often trace their spiritual lineage directly to an Apostle of Jesus, and were persecuted for their faith ensuring their thinking was less influenced by avarice.

Since we cannot gather everyone at once, maybe we can start a movement of clumping. At first individual doctrines are discussed, then denominations and other fractions can reconcile, creating clumps of believers uniting in truth that eventually narrows the topics needing to be discussed. Larger and larger theological clumps could continue to coalesce ultimately resulting in the reunification of God's Church family. Small drops of truth merge forming streams, then rivers, then the united ocean itself. In the end we can say as Paul does "Now you are Christ's body, and individually members of it" (I Cor. 12:27, NAS).

This process will undoubtedly also leave some disenfranchised groups along the way, but it seems a far better plan than our current union without agreement or widespread disagreement with little union.

This book is hopefully a small step in the right direction as it invites readers to look in-depth at the doctrine of determinism and invites all to come to a resolution on the matter. I serve at a university that is broadly evangelical, inviting all who confess salvation is by faith through grace, and who have a high regard for the Bible, to share in our community. Many doctrines rub against each other in our hallways, but few are so obviously variant but collegially coexistent, making this question a great starting place to seek truth and hopefully come to doctrinal unity.

Littleton, Colorado, 2025

Chapter 1: Common Ground: Evidence from Creation

❦

"Father, glorify Me in Your presence with the glory I had with You before the world existed." John 17:5

"If your concept of God is radically false, then the more devout you are, the worse it will be for you." Anglican Archbishop William Temple (1881-1944)

Few questions have divided Christians more deeply—or revealed more about God's heart—than whether His love is freely offered to all or reserved for a few. Some of my best friends are ardent five-point (TULIP) believing Calvinists. They are faithful men, firmly believing the Bible teaches predestination and so no amount of reason or history or verbal argument can sway them from their position. I admire their tenacity and I praise and share their trust in the Word of God. I also agree with them that how we answer this question does not determine our salvation. While my Calvinist brothers understand election as God predetermining individual salvation before time, I understand it as God seeing His Church that will respond to His call—but we both seek to honor God's gracious initiative and reverence His Word.

My first disagreement with most Calvinists and many in the Free Will camp too is whether God left the question of how God's will and human will interact as a "mystery" to ponder rather than clarifying it in His Word. If left to our own intellect nearly every question would go unanswered, but our God has promised to reveal Himself and thus the truth. God strongly desires to reveal Himself: So much so He even became incarnate, taking the form of man so as to explain His purpose, live as our exemplar, and die to set the captives of sin free. He also trained disciples who went forth after His death to share the truth about God.

Everywhere in Scripture we see God encouraging us to seek, to knock, and to understand His will and purpose. Jesus sent the Holy Spirit to lead us into *all* truth, as we read:

> *But when He, the Spirit of truth, comes, He will guide you into all the truth; for He will not speak on His own initiative, but whatever He hears, He will speak; and He will disclose to you what is to come. He shall glorify Me; for He shall take of Mine, and shall disclose it to you. All things that the Father has are Mine; therefore I said, that He takes of Mine, and will disclose it to you.* (John 16:13-15, NAS).

This firm belief in God's Word and how He reveals His will is at the heart of this book. We cannot tolerate poor doctrine, because it sets us up for failure. When we have a misunderstanding of God, we wonder why He does not behave the way we expect. This leads us to doubt, and doubt leads to sin.

We also become like the thing we worship, so we must know the character of God that we may be conformed to His image instead of an image of Him that is tarnished by untruths. C. S. Lewis warned that neglecting theology is not humility—it is apathetic peril. He wrote, "Everyone reads, everyone hears things discussed. Consequently, if you do not listen to Theology, that will not mean that you have no ideas about God. It will mean that you have a lot of wrong ones—bad, muddled, out-of-date ideas" (*Mere Christianity*, Chapter 1).

This book aims to represent the issues accurately and not to slay straw-man arguments. From the outset we can recognize there are doctrinal abuses on both sides of the determinist question. Some people use Calvinism as an excuse for apathy in evangelism, despair in prayer, and abdication to sin instead of seeking holiness. In the worst cases people misunderstand the Calvinist teaching on election and think "once saved always saved" means they have eternal security despite having no heart change and no life that testifies to God's work of grace.

On the other end of the spectrum, some hyper-Arminians teach we lose our salvation every time we sin, creating a frenetic works-based religion of fear. More often, free will is used as a license to sin, as Arminians fall into the world's extreme individualism and humanistic values. Taken to an extreme it can even lead to the error of universalism (saying everyone will be saved). They often do not make the distinction that believers are set apart from the world, imputed with God's very nature of holiness, and that we are destined to be the sons and daughters of God. We are the Church God elected and purposed to salvation from the beginning, and so this world has no hold upon us.

While I am not making up straw-man arguments, many people reading this who think themselves "Calvinists" will disagree with elements that describe Calvinism. I constantly talk to people who think they are Calvinists when in fact they deny many of its teachings and so are much closer to the Wesleyan perspective that believes in Free Will energized by God's grace. My explanation of Calvinism here attempts to be true to what is taught in Reformed seminaries rather than what actually appears in Reformed pulpits or is believed among the laity. Indeed, I hope many readers discover they are much closer to Free Will (synergism) than they thought.

Common Ground

It is important to recognize practicing Calvinists and Wesleyans/Arminians stand on a lot of common ground. Both firmly testify God is deserving of all glory and that He is the sole author of salvation as there is no other way to God except through Jesus (Act 4:12).

In the "Minutes of Some Late Conversations" (1745) Rev. John Wesley said he saw predestination (apart from foreknowledge) as a "dangerous mistake" but he went on to explain his free will view is only "a hair's breadth" away from Calvin on justification. He said his followers come to the "very edge of Calvinism" because they ascribe all good to the free grace of God, deny all natural free will and all power antecedent to grace (it is God who calls us and empowers us to accept His calling), as well as exclude all merit from humankind even if it is done by God's grace.

Some esteemed modern Calvinist theologians also see a lot of agreement rather than only stark contrast. When it is not being bandied about like the theological version of a curse word, "Pelagianism" is a doctrine that denies the necessity of divine grace for human salvation and moral obedience. Augustine said we require God's grace for salvation, and Calvinists took up a similar cry during the reformation to combat the Catholics who had elevated works rather than grace. However, somewhat evolving from the Calvinists were the Free Will Protestants who agreed grace was essential but who said God loved everyone and so gave grace to everyone so that everyone could repent. Because Wesleyans and others recognize grace as essential, Peterson and Williams in their book *Why I Am Not An Arminian* wrote, "Arminianism is closer to Semi-Augustinianism than it is to Semi-Pelagianism or Pelagianism" (39)[1].

Most importantly, both sides believe the Bible is the bedrock of truth, the infallible/inerrant[2] Word of God, the final arbiter of all

---

[1] Robert A. Peterson and Michael D. Williams, *Why I Am Not an Arminian* (Downers Grove, IL: InterVarsity Press, 2004), 39.

[2] This book affirms both. *Infallibility* emphasizes the Bible's trustworthiness and divine purpose — it cannot fail to reveal God's truth. *Inerrancy* emphasizes the Bible's accuracy and freedom from factual error — it does

theological disputation. The Bible is the only general revelation of God (valid for all) and it is a closed canon (no new books will be added). Scripture takes precedence over all human tradition and authority, over all intellectual reasoning, and over all personal revelation/experience.

Unfortunately, Scripture can be misused. When Satan tempted Jesus in the desert he used Scripture out of context. The Bible's message has been twisted to support atrocities like slavery and the Holocaust, cults like Mormonism and Jehovah's Witness, and even other religions such as Islam. We therefore must also agree to some principles for interpretation.

This book is not about interpretation or textual criticism but it seems wise to briefly lay out what is commonly believed by conservative Bible-honoring scholars. The conservative-leaning evangelical Chicago Statement on Biblical Inerrancy says, "We affirm that inspiration, strictly speaking, applies only to the autographic text of Scripture, which in the providence of God can be ascertained from available manuscripts with great accuracy."

None of the original manuscripts exist, but this is probably because God did not want us worshipping fragments of paper rather than the Word who is the incarnate Son. Confidence in Scripture's preservation has been shared across denominations and centuries, as Christians believe God providentially protected His word.

In the last few centuries God has provided us with an overwhelming amount of ancient text fragments such that textual expert Bruce M. Metzger proclaimed:

---

not contain mistakes. As an historical note, earlier theologians (e.g., Augustine, Aquinas, Calvin) often used the concept of infallibility. The modern term "inerrancy" arose especially in 19th–20th century debates (e.g., the Chicago Statement on Biblical Inerrancy, 1978) to assert precision amid rising biblical criticism. Both demonstrate a high value on scripture and there is therefore no linguistic need to judge between them here.

The textual critic of the New Testament is embarrassed by the wealth of material. ... It cannot be emphasized strongly enough that the wealth of material available to the New Testament textual critic today is so much greater than that available for any ancient classical author that the necessity of resorting to emendation is reduced to the smallest dimensions.[3] He adds that variant readings are merely matters of spelling, grammar, or style, and that the New Testament is marvelously preserved. "It is safe to say that no doctrine of the Christian faith depends upon a disputed reading of the text" (152).[4]

Scholars have wisely sought and prioritized the oldest fragments, realizing that if a miscopy is made it could be transmitted into many subsequent copies. Meticulous research has been done on the Bible, and we can be supremely confident that our original sources are accurate. As another textual expert F. F. Bruce states:

The evidence for our New Testament writings is ever so much greater than the evidence for many writings of classical authors, the authenticity of which no one dreams of questioning. And if the New Testament were a collection of secular writings, their authenticity would generally be regarded as beyond all doubt. The variant readings about which any doubt remains among textual critics of the New Testament affect no material question of historic fact or of Christian faith and practice.[5]

Principles for correct biblical interpretation include understanding the historical and literary context of the book, the intended audience,

---

[3] Metzger, Bruce. The Text of the New Testament: Its Transmission, Corruption, and Restoration, 3rd ed. (New York: Oxford University Press, 1992), p. 146. He goes on to say "It is safe to say that no doctrine of the Christian faith depends upon a disputed reading of the text" p.152 ia600202.us.archive.org)

[4] Metzger, Bruce. The Text of the New Testament: Its Transmission, Corruption, and Restoration, 3rd ed. (New York: Oxford University Press, 1992), p. 146.

[5] See F. F. Bruce, The New Testament Documents: Are They Reliable? (Grand Rapids: Eerdmans, 1960), especially pp. 19–20.

and that we must make an attempt to discern the author's intended meaning. This includes knowing the genre of the work, analyzing grammar and keywords as needed, as well as looking for consistency within the passage and

...the debate is not about sovereignty but rather about providence.

across Scripture. Intertextuality, i.e., using Scripture in the light of the whole biblical text, is vital. Finally, when things are difficult or seem to conflict, we can consult Christian tradition, reason, and the Holy Spirit's personal revelation. The ultimate goal must be to let Scripture speak its truth (exegesis) rather than to read our preconceived ideas into the text (eisegesis).

A final area of complete agreement is that God is sovereign. People incorrectly believe the debate is about sovereignty, but sovereignty means having the right to rule or decide things. No one is questioning God's right to rule and do as He pleases. God is absolutely sovereign whether one is a determinist or a believer that God has given humanity libertarian free will. The question is not whether God has the right to rule or the power to rule but rather how God has decided to exercise His right and His power. In other words, as Reformed theologian Dr. John Piper points out, the debate is not about sovereignty but rather about providence[6]. The question is: how has God chosen to get His will done in this creation?

Before we can answer our main question we must better understand some terminology. We will then look at the big picture about why God created our reality. Thereafter we will look at the beliefs of the early Church, how doctrine evolved, and then consider how to interpret the many proof-text Scriptures that are relevant to the debate. Finally, this book will consider the impact upon practice within the Church, and

---

[6] Piper rightly points out that sovereignty is God's right and power to do all He wills, while providence is what God does with His sovereignty. See Piper, John. *Providence.* Wheaton, IL: Crossway, 2020, 23

lay out a call to action as we seek a united doctrine to better understand and obey God and give Him glory in our world.

Identifying the Plants: Some Definitions

Biblical belief systems often have shared vocabulary but very divergent theological definitions. If we are to compare Calvinism (determinism) and Free Will (classical/relational theology) it is important to note differences in definitions even when we are using the same words. These differences have led to many hours of unproductive discussions, circular logic, and exasperation on both sides.

Calvinist theology, following Augustine and later codified in the Reformed confessions, interprets the following words through the lens of divine determinism—God's eternal decree irresistibly brings about faith and salvation in the elect. In contrast, the Free Will or Classical Christian tradition interprets them relationally—God's grace genuinely invites, enables, and cooperates with human response. Here is a quick comparison so that the reader can try to see Scripture and reasoning from both perspectives throughout this book so as to better weigh the arguments and decide what is true.

Faith (pistis)

Calvinist View: Faith is a *gift irresistibly given* to the elect, a product of regeneration rather than its cause. According to this view, the unregenerate cannot believe until God sovereignly grants faith (cf. Ephesians 2:8; Philippians 1:29). Thus, faith is a *sign* of election, not an act of free trust.

Free Will / Classical View: Faith is a *relational response* to God's gracious revelation. It is trust freely exercised by the human heart, enabled by prevenient grace (Free Will synergy) or the remnant of God's Image (Classical). "Prevenient grace is God's active love that goes before, awakening and enabling sinners to respond without forcing them to do so." Walls and Dongell, *Why I Am Not a Calvinist*, 162). Jesus said, "And I, if I be lifted up from the earth, will draw all men to Myself" (Jn. 12:32, NAS). We do not have faith nor can we repent without prior grace—God initiates while we are still sinners (Free Will) or has protected His image in us (Classical) (Jn 6:44; Tit 2:11; Acts 16:14 "the Lord opened Lydia's heart"). Furthermore, "Faith comes from hearing, and hearing by the word of Christ" (Romans 10:17, NAS). God initiates; humanity must respond. Faith is an act of the free will and God has made the will of everyone capable of repenting.

Grace (charis)

Calvinist View: Grace is *particular and effectual*—given only to the elect and always accomplishing salvation. It cannot be resisted; its purpose is to bring about faith and perseverance (John 6:37, 44).
Free Will / Classical View: Grace is *universal and enabling*—"the grace of God has appeared, bringing salvation to all men" (Titus 2:11, NAS). Grace awakens, persuades, and empowers, but humans may resist it (Acts 7:51). God's grace is persuasive love, not coercive force.

Election (eklogē)

Calvinist View: Election is *unconditional*, an eternal decree selecting *individuals* for salvation apart from foreseen faith or merit (Rom. 9:11–18).
Free Will / Classical View: Election is *corporate and conditional*—God's plan to redeem all who are "in Christ." It is based on foreknowledge of faith (Rom. 8:29; 1 Peter 1:2). God's choice is of a people and a purpose, not the pre-selection of individuals to believe.

Assurance of Salvation (plērophoria)

Calvinist View: We can have assurance of our salvation because it is not in our hands. God elected some to salvation and He will complete His work in all who were chosen. If a person seems chosen but falls away, they were never chosen in the first place. Seeing election as being "corporate" empties it of being able to comfort the individual.

Free Will / Classical View: "In Arminian theology, assurance rests not on a secret decree but on a living relationship with Christ through faith" (Walls and Dongell, *Why I Am Not a Calvinist,* 188). Assurance comes from our union with Christ and the personal indwelling of the Spirit. In Christ we are chosen, adopted, and sealed (Eph 1:13–14). Corporate election doesn't remove personal comfort—it grounds it in Christ rather than in a hidden decree.

Sin Nature/Original Sin (NEVER in Bible)

Calvinist View: While not found in Scripture, it is taught there and sometimes Paul calls it "the flesh." Humanity inherits both Adam's guilt and his corruption. All people are born totally depraved—incapable of choosing good or responding to God apart from irresistible grace. Original sin is both forensic (imputed guilt from Adam's sin, Rom. 5:12–19) and ontological (a corrupted nature). Thus, even infants are guilty before acting, because Adam's fall is counted as theirs. Even after salvation while we may be able to resist temptation by God's grace, our sin nature means we will constantly and repeatedly sin.

Free Will / Classical View: Adam brought physical death into the world by sinning and, since he had the least amount of temptation, proved all humans would sin. Humanity inherits mortality and a bent toward sin, but not Adam's guilt. Rather than saying "Original sin"(Augustine's doctrine) or even "sin nature", the Bible refers to our fallen condition as "the flesh" ("Sarx" σάρξ) or "body of death" (Rom. 7). Humans retain the ability to respond with moral responsibility due to God's prevenient grace and/or the remnant of their marred image of God.[7] Romans 7 concludes with Christ saving us from the Body of Death, righting our nature, and allowing us to fully follow His ways.

Predestination (proorizō)

Calvinist View: Predestination is God's eternal, unconditional decree determining who will be saved and who will be damned. This divine choice is not based on foreseen faith or merit, but solely on God's sovereign will and purpose (Ephesians 1:4–5; Romans 9:11–18). God's predestination ensures His glory by demonstrating both mercy to the elect and justice/punishment toward the reprobate. Human freedom plays no determining role in this election, for God's will irresistibly brings about all that He ordains.

Free Will / Classical View: Predestination refers to God's foreknowledge and purpose to save all who freely respond to His grace. It is conditional—based on God's foreseeing human faith and response rather than arbitrary decree. Paul writes, "Those whom He foreknew, He also predestined to become conformed to the image of His Son" (Rom. 8:29, NAS). Thus, God's plan is corporate and relational: He predestines "in Christ" all who choose to believe (Eph. 1:4–5). This view maintains divine sovereignty while preserving genuine human freedom and thus responsibility, seeing predestination as God's loving intent that believers freely enter His saving purpose.

---

[7] Romans 5 was mistranslated by Augustine because he used the Latin not the Greek to create his doctrine. Paul also clearly contrasts Adam and Christ in that chapter suggesting we now can all be justified: "As through one transgression there resulted condemnation to all men, even so through one act of righteousness there resulted justification of life to all men" (Romans 5:18, NAS).

Will (thelēma)

Calvinist View: Human will is *bound by sin* at birth due to Adam's sin acting as the federal Head of humanity. It is incapable of choosing God unless irresistibly renewed by grace. Thus, all decisions ultimately flow from God's decretive will.

Free Will / Classical View: Human will is *damaged by the fall* but is capable of repentance either because there is a sufficient remnant of God's image (classic) or because it is *empowered by prevenient grace* as God draws all people to Himself. After salvation the will is restored to genuine moral responsibility and the capability to love like God. God's will seldom if ever overrides but rather it invites human cooperation: "I have set before you life and death... so choose life" (Deuteronomy 30:19, NAS).

Repentance (metanoia)

Calvinist View: Repentance is *a result of regeneration*—a grace God gives only to the elect, enabling them to turn to Him and be saved (2 Timothy 2:25).

Free Will / Classical View: Repentance is a *grace-enabled human act of turning* toward God. "God is now declaring to men that all people everywhere should repent" (Acts 17:30, NAS). While prompted by grace, it remains a voluntary moral choice. Regeneration comes after repentance.

Salvation (sōtēria)

Calvinist View: Salvation is a *monergistic act*—God alone accomplishes all parts of salvation for the elect, from calling to glorification (Rom. 8:30). The human role is passive.

Free Will / Classical View: Salvation is *synergistic*—a divine-human relationship of cooperation. God initiates, but humans must respond in faith, obedience, and perseverance. Paul writes, "Work out your

22

salvation with fear and trembling; for it is God who is at work in you" (Phil. 2:12–13, NAS).

Other Important Terms

Determinism (hard): All events, including human choices, are necessitated by prior causes and/or divine decree; alternative possibilities are not metaphysically available.

Compatibilism (soft determinism): Human choices are determined by one's strongest desires/nature so they can be called "free." God's decree infallibly ordains outcomes by ordaining desires and means. R.C. Sproul writes, "and free choice, by definition, involves choosing what we desire."[8]

Libertarian freedom: People act of their own volition. Human will is real and not merely illusory. Freedom is not just acting out desires but also must include the ability to resist desires or "to do otherwise." The will is required for moral responsibility. God's grace can be enabling and persuasive without causally determining choice. This arises from God's prevenient grace and/or the remnant of the image of God within us. **NOTE:** The reader can assume all uses of "Free Will" here mean "libertarian" (the ability to do or not do something) and synergistic (the human will to do good is marred/weakened by sin but empowered by grace so that people may choose to repent).

In Calvinist theology, divine sovereignty expresses itself through deterministic causation—God ensures that His chosen ones believe and persevere. In Free Will theology, divine sovereignty expresses itself through relational invitation—God sovereignly allows genuine human

---

[8] Sproul, R. C. *What Is Reformed Theology?: Understanding the Basics.* Grand Rapids, MI: Baker Books, 2016, Kindle Loc. 1781.

> *...(free) human will is an essential component of terms like love, faith, and hope.*

response, valuing love freely given over submission irresistibly compelled. (See Appendix 1 for definitions in a Table)

The difference, in essence, lies not in whether grace is necessary (both affirm it), but in whether grace is coercive or cooperative, pre-programmed or personal. Calvinism says all is for God's glory and that means He fully controls everything.

The Free Will/Classical view says human will is an essential component of terms like love, faith, and hope. Where compatibilism defines freedom as acting according to one's strongest desire (and they are all bad before regeneration), Scripture repeatedly addresses the sinner as capable—under grace's influence—of resisting desire, repenting, and believing (Acts 17:30; Heb 3:15). The Bible's imperatives, invitations, laments, and warnings assume more than merely descriptive freedom; they assume responsive moral power under grace. Free Will says God's highest glory is revealed not in control, but in communion and love.

Providence

As noted before, Providence is how God uses His sovereignty. The Calvinist believes everything that happens on earth is ordained by God. This view emphasizes:

- Every event is decreed by God from eternity.
- What happens unfolds from God's eternal plan
- Evil occurs as part of God's meticulous decree, not merely as something He foresees and allows.

Nothing happens unless God has actively willed it within His decree—including sin like child rape and abortion, though God remains "not morally blameworthy" in Reformed argumentation.

For Calvinists, how God can decree all things then not be blamed for something (all of sin) is the key philosophic conundrum. This is typically dealt with by saying God has two wills or levels or aspects (e.g., primary and secondary causes, means and ends, etc.) or even multiple perspectives on time consciousness. Calvinists include most Presbyterians, Lutherans, Reformed churches, Puritans, etc.

To take an example from history, in Genesis 37-50 God *ordained* Joseph's brothers to sin for a higher purpose. Note He did not permit it—He caused it--their hatred was part of God's eternal plan for salvation history. He then saved His people and blessed much of the world by having Joseph save food before the famine.

A Free Will theologian says all is permitted by God, and so some justification must still happen for why He permits it, but God does not cause/ordain any evil because "…in Him there is no darkness at all" (1 John 1:5). God partners with people in relationship to move a world in rebellion toward a world conformed to God's will: "…that which is good and acceptable and perfect" (Rom. 12:2b NAS). This view emphasizes:

- Nothing happens outside God's sovereign knowledge and allowance. He allows events to occur, even evil ones, but He redeems evil in the lives of believers.
- Human freedom and creaturely causation/will are real. Evil happens because God allows humans and demons free will.
- Divine holiness is preserved—God is never the author of sin. However, the cost is that God allows a lot of things to be outside His perfect will.

This position is often associated with the classical Arminian / Wesleyan / Catholic / Eastern / most early Christian writers' view of providence. The main mechanism to move from God's permissive will to His perfect will is prayer, as Jesus taught us to pray "thy will be done on earth as it is in Heaven." Presumably God's will is perfectly accomplished in Heaven.

So in Genesis 37-50, God *permitted* Joseph's brothers to hate him and sell him into slavery, but He did not ordain their evil desire nor cause their sin. He then sovereignly redeemed and repurposed it. God sovereignly permits evil but then He also outwits it.

Permitted vs. Ordained

Concept	Permitted by God	Ordained by God
Human freedom	Genuine and indeterministic	Real but always within God's exhaustive decree
God & evil	God allows evil but does not cause it	God decrees evil events as part of His plan (but remains morally pure)
Mode of control	Sovereign permission	Meticulous decree
Primary emphasis	God's love and holiness; cooperation with human agency	God's sovereignty and purpose in all things

A Free Will theologian can even say God is ordaining all things *in that* He ordained a world with creatures who have libertarian free will. Taken as a whole our world is absolutely what God ordained, and He is in total control even though He is not "guiding every dust particle."[9] God's purpose here is not to have perfection or glory or to display His power or His justice—though these may all occur. His purpose here is to create a training ground that His children may learn to love.

The Chief End (Primary Purpose) of Humanity

The *Westminster Shorter Catechism* is in many circles the absolute standard of Calvinist belief. It beautifully declares humanity's chief end is "to glorify God and to enjoy Him forever."[10] The second clause is undisputable truth—we will indeed delight in God eternally as His

---

[9] "God is not worn out running the galaxy. He's not taxed at all guiding every dust particle all the time." John Piper quote at: https://www.azquotes.com/quote/1319887

[10] *The Westminster Shorter Catechism (1647), Q.1, in The Westminster Confession of Faith and Catechisms* (Glasgow: Free Presbyterian Publications, 2003), 373.

children. However, the first clause can be challenged. Did God create us primarily (chiefly) to give Him glory? Answering this question correctly has huge implications, and so it must be explored even before we look at the historic roots of Augustinian-Calvinism and the rest of what the Bible says about free will and determinism.

God Created for Love and that Resulted in Glory

Before examining free will and predestination, we must begin with God's purpose in creation itself: Did He create primarily for His own glory—or out of love? Most Christians seem to take it for granted that God created to give Himself glory. When Christians want to deflect praise, they often use a shortcut slogan popularized during the Reformation and say "to God be the glory" (*soli Deo gloria* or *glory to God alone*). Christians want to live in such a way that His character, goodness, and wisdom are made known and honored, and they want to reflect the greatness of the Creator rather than to draw attention to themselves. Scripture supports this, as we find "Whether, then, you eat or drink or whatever you do, do all to the glory of God" (1 Cor. 10:31, NAS).

However, while Christians correctly wish to live for God, and this can be expressed as giving Him glory, Scripture mostly talks about how He is glorious rather than saying He created *for* glory. If God created to gain glory it would mean he lacked something in eternity, violating His nature of aseity. Aseity means God is completely self-sufficient, having absolutely no needs, no lacking, and so no external reason to create. He filled all, was all, and always was--perfectly complete all by Himself. True, all that God does is glorious, and true, God is due all glory—but was glory really the main purpose or "chief end" of creating humanity?

The Bible consistently ties God's glory to His moral beauty and self-giving love rather than to self-promotion. When God reveals His glory to Moses, He proclaims His character: "The Lord, compassionate and

27

> *God did not need creation to get more glory— He already had all glory*

gracious, slow to anger, and abounding in lovingkindness and truth" (Exod. 34:6-7). The psalmist prays, "Not to us, O Lord, not to us, but to Your name give glory, because of Your lovingkindness, because of Your truth" (Ps 115:1). Isaiah declares that those created for God's glory are the people He formed in love (Isa 43:7), and Habakkuk foresees a day when "the earth will be filled with the knowledge of the glory of the Lord as the waters cover the sea" (Hab 2:14)—that being when His goodness and mercy are universally known.

In the New Testament this connection only deepens. Jesus announces, "Now is the Son of Man glorified" (John 13:31) precisely as He goes to the cross—the supreme act of self-giving love (John 12:32; 17:22-23). Paul identifies divine glory with Christ's sacrificial humility: "He humbled Himself by becoming obedient to the point of death ... therefore God highly exalted Him" (Phil 2:5-11). We behold "the glory of the Lord" in the face of the crucified and risen Christ and are "transformed into the same image from glory to glory" (2 Cor 3:18; 4:6). John summarizes the whole revelation: "God is love... In this is love, not that we loved God, but that He loved us and sent His Son" (1 John 4:8-10). Together, these passages show God's glory shines most brightly through His self-emptying love. The biblical pattern is not glory *instead of* love, but usually glory *through* love—love is the light in which His glory is seen.

Glory was not the "chief end" or primary purpose of creating humanity—love was. God had no need for more glory—He had all glory even before creation. In John 17 Jesus says, "And now, glorify Thou Me together with Thyself, Father, with the glory which I had with Thee before the world was...And the glory which Thou hast given Me I have given to them; that they may be one, just as We are one" (verses 5 and 22, NAS). God did not need creation to get more glory—He already had all glory. Instead of us being created to give

Him glory, glory flows in the other direction. Far from demanding glory, God delights in sharing it, and Jesus gave us God's glory! God shares His glory with us, making us in His image, and one day glorifying us with His personal presence.

Scripture presents God's aim as doxological and relational: 'from him and through him and to him are all things' (Rom 11:36), yet the Father glorifies the Son precisely in self-giving love (John 13:31–35; 17:1–5, 22–24). The thesis of this chapter, then, is not 'love instead of glory,' but rather God created for love and therefore deserves even more glory. God's glory appears as the overflow of his triune love; therefore His mode of salvation must honor personal agency, persuasion, and communion rather than compulsion

There are other reasons to reject the assumption that God created mankind for the chief purpose of glorifying Himself. Glory sought for its own sake is vanity. As Jesus said, "If I glorify Myself, My glory is nothing" (John 8:54). Seeking glory is also self-defeating. If you knew a man who did something to glorify himself, would that not reduce the glory he is due? Proverbs remind us, "It is not glory to search out one's own glory" (Prov. 25:27). Real glory is obtained when you do the right thing for the right reason, and that reason cannot be self-glory. In fact, the more you sacrifice yourself (rather than aggrandize yourself) the more glory you can obtain. Glory is in fact best won when it is not sought.

What is the absolute best reason to create? God is the best possible Being and so the best reason would be to more fully express His nature. What is our best descriptor of God? "God is love" (I John 4:8). Love, then, seems to be a great possible motive for creation. In fact, it is the only motive worthy of God. Love is best described in the Bible by the Apostle Paul:

> *Love is patient, love is kind, and is not jealous; love does not brag and is not arrogant, does not act unbecomingly; it does not seek its own, is not provoked, does not take into account a wrong suffered, does not rejoice in*

unrighteousness, but rejoices with the truth; bears all things, believes all things, hopes all things, endures all things. (1 Cor. 13:4-7 NAS)

Note that this is the opposite of self-aggrandizement or self-seeking glory. Love is an extreme case of selflessness, and *therefore* it is most worthy of glory. Love does not elevate the self but rather it shares, seeks communion, and even is willing to suffer for others.

Does love as a reason for creation conflict with our understanding of God's state of complete aseity? God did not *need* to be given love in eternity as He is capable of giving and receiving love due to His Trinitarian nature. He is One God in three persons. However, love is a very curious thing. It is not real unless given away, and it is most realized when it is given to the unlovely.

That must be why God created! He did not want or need more glory, but rather He expressed His nature of love by wanting to more fully give Himself to something that was more clearly *other*. The triune God is so eternally full in love that creation becomes His overflow (Jn 17:24; 17:5, 22). Furthermore, the Father, Son, and Holy Spirit must be the easiest Beings to love. He created us and gave us free will so that He could love even beings that may be difficult to love.

Peering from eternity God's grand plan was formed. If He gave creatures His image, and allowed them free will, would any of them learn to love? Amazingly, the answer was an emphatic yes! It would not be easy; there would be much pain and sorrow along the way, and even an extreme Personal sacrifice—but that is what love did. Love was both the goal of creation and the mechanism of change. He created everything for those who would have ears to hear, those who would surrender to His call, those who would repent and sit at the Master's feet. God would have a Church, a Bride, a community of His elect sons and daughters who would be refined by the fires of earth that they might reign with Him in the glory of Heaven for eternity.

God's purpose in creation was not self-glorification but rather He wanted to create a family that could be a part of His love for eternity. Glory is the byproduct of His love. In Scripture, God's glory is disclosed by His character, and chief among His attributes is love (Exod 34:6–7; Jn 3:16; Rom 5:8).

God's ultimate purpose for creating was to form a family who could freely receive and reflect His love. Creation is the overflow of Trinitarian love—the Father, Son, and Spirit delighted in sharing themselves with creatures who are *other* but also who are made in His image. We are God's offspring (Acts 17:28), made capable of loving, and so also capable of choosing. There are at least two other solid reasons to believe God did not create for glory.

We Cannot Contribute Significantly to God's Glory Anyway

The notion that God created humanity to give Himself glory is further seen to be erroneous as we recognize how little we have to contribute. "All flesh is like grass, And all its glory like the flower of grass. The grass withers, And the flower falls off" (1 Pet. 1:24, NAS). While we do see in the Bible that we can bring God glory, we must recognize that it is the epitome of pompous self-aggrandizement to think we can make any *significant* contribution to God' s glory. Every good gift originates with Him, and every act we accomplish is fueled by His gracious gifts of breath and life. While God chooses to accept our paltry service and give us noble causes to bring Him some modicum of glory, we must recognize that gaining glory through human action was not the primary purpose of creation.

Our acts to bring Him glory only have value because they are expressions of love—not because what we bring Him has any real value in itself. It boggles the mind why God would want to impress us or value *what we bring* to Him. He loves and values us as His children, not as His worker bees. Anything we bring Him was His already. Can an ant or a mosquito bring a human glory? Does a human want to impress the ants and mosquitos? The discrepancy between us and God is magnitudes greater than that between insects and humans. Our love freely given, reflecting His love, is a far more precious thing than any works or products that give God glory – all of which He already had.

Any glory we bring to God is a result of His love and grace on our lives. The saints will one day throw down their crowns before the King of Kings and declare He is the true power behind all meritorious actions (Rev. 4:10). We cannot significantly add to His glory because He already has infinite glory. We were designed to *reflect* His glory, to "image" His glory, and the greatest way to do that is to grow into His nature of Love.

Our Flawed World Was Not Made For Glory

If God's goal were primarily to maximize His glory, He could have made a flawless, painless world displaying His perfection. Instead, He created a world where love must be freely chosen—and therefore where rejection, sin, and pain are possible. Far from maximizing God's glory, this world has given Him much pain. He feels our pain like we do, but He also experiences pain as a loving Father who cares for His children. This resonates with the Apostle Paul's definition of love, as our God is patient (long-suffering) and He endures "all things" for His beloved.

As a side note it may be worth realizing that if God ordained all things, God's patience would be a mere affectation. To ordain a slow process and then say you are suffering through it at the very least reduces the merit of the suffering. To cause yourself pain and then say you suffer from it is also disingenuous. Even the pain of Christ on the cross is diminished if we say God caused it rather than our sin caused it. A God of hard determinism cannot be patient and cannot really be said to suffer. However, love is patient, God is love, and God is frequently said to be patient and long-suffering.

A world filled with sin is less glorious than a perfect one, and so God must not have created for the primary purpose of glory. But you may reply that God gets even more glory from redemption than from perfected creation. He created a flawed world so that He could redeem it and display both His love and His justice.

Hell is for people who reject love; it is not some kind of trophy case to God's justice.

If we concede that redemption is more glorious than perpetual perfection (a debate that cannot possibly be won either way), we still do not end up having this world. If redemption is more glorious than original innocence, and God is maximizing glory, then God should have redeemed everything and everyone.

It seems nonsensical to say God wants to reveal His justice to humans and so He created some people for the sole purpose of tormenting them in Hell forever. First, that is not justice but cruelty. Second, He does not need to impress us, and third He can easily reveal His full nature in many other ways. Hell is for people who reject love; it is not some kind of trophy case to God's justice. We know from Scripture that not all will be redeemed, as Jesus himself speaks of the fires of Hell more than any other person in the Bible. This is a tragedy…but also possibly an expression of love. Being separated from God's direct and awesome presence in Hell is probably far better than to be a rebel in God's glorious light.

The fact that the world is not perfect now tells us His plan is not to get His perfect will accomplished now. This is so clear that it seems to be an assumption made by all of the writers of the Bible. They did not need to say mankind has free libertarian will because the existence of sin proves it daily.

Judaism praised the Lord God Most High but never formulated determinism. They saw God's unchanging nature as referring to His covenantal relationship to His people rather than as an ontological lens through which everything else about God must be seen. As Christianity broke from its Hebraic moorings it adopted Greek philosophy, and "immutability assumed the status of an axiomatic

God uses nothing less than the fires of freedom to forge the hearts of His children to be more like Him in their essential nature of love.

presupposition for the discussion of other doctrines."[11] Even Augustine saw he was pulling Christian doctrine away from Hebrew teachings as he accused Pelagius of "putting the Old Testament of the same level with the Old."[12]

As we will see, determinism springs from heretical groups which the early Church soundly rejected before Augustine and the fifth century. Our early Church Fathers recognized determinism's roots as pagan philosophy and decried it as heresy. Even today, Christians who believe in determinism are in complete agreement with the world's prevalent secular philosophies (atheism and materialism) and the worst cult Christianity ever spun off—Islam.

God has allowed a fallen world to develop love in His children. He is using pain and suffering to polish His image in them. If "patience" and "bearing all things" are a part of love's definition, then we need adversity to learn it. To accomplish His goal of having a loving family God had to make a world with free will because freedom is essential to learn love. Love cannot be compelled—it can be modelled, described, and encouraged. God uses nothing less than the fires of freedom to forge the hearts of His children to be more like Him in their essential nature of love.

This is why there was a forbidden fruit in the Garden of Eden. Love that cannot be refused is not love but programming. God endowed humanity with real freedom because real love requires it. Evil entered not by God's decree but by His permission, for He values relationship

---

[11]Jaroslav Pelikan, *The Emergence of the Catholic Tradition (100–600)*, vol. 1 of *The Christian Tradition: A History of the Development of Doctrine* (Chicago: University of Chicago Press, 1971), 22.

[12] Augustine in *Gest. Pelag.* 5-15; cited in Jaroslav Pelikan, *The Emergence of the Catholic Tradition (100–600)*, vol. 1 of *The Christian Tradition: A History of the Development of Doctrine* (Chicago: University of Chicago Press, 1971), 22.

more than control. He has revealed Himself more as a Person than as an ultimate Force.

Before He was shackled by Greek philosophic categories like immutability, and through that lens an absolutist understanding of omniscience, omnipresence, and omnipotence, the Bible speaks of Him as being One God in three _Persons_. He is the God of love who also happens to be absolutely powerful, not the God of power who happens to only love and save a select group of people.

God does not cause evil and then redeem it to look good. He allowed freedom, experienced the heartbreak of our rejection, and still chose to enter our brokenness to redeem what our free will marred. God created us "very good" but that very goodness meant the ability to choose right or wrong, hate or love (Gen 1:31). God was not the author of sin as part of some grand plan to self-glorify, but rather He allowed sin as part of His grand plan of redemption. While we deserved His wrath for our sin, God turned our tragedy into triumph because He bore "all things" as love does (Rom. 8:28). All glory is His, and yet He shares His glory with us. We will dwell in His glory for all eternity.

The Glory of Love Displayed on the Cross

The love that moved God to create the world is the same love that moved Him to redeem it. Calvinists of course also affirm God's nature of love, but they prioritize His power and glory so they can justify believing some people are made for eternal punishment. My argument here is not that God created for love to the exclusion of glory, but rather that He created primarily for the purpose of love and that fact contributes even more to His glory. I am also declaring God loves all people and wants a relationship with every person; He did not create a single soul for the sole purpose of being tormented in Hell.

Our freedom to love God (rather than reject Him) is worth far more than compelled salvation for the sake of glory. It is the free choice to love God that most gives Him pleasure. When my children were young for my birthday they would often draw me pictures. They didn't have money so they gave what they could. If they were lazy or in a rush it might just be some lines with a crayon. Sometimes they were quite pretty, and my second daughter even started including captions with puns because she knew I like those.

In truth, I could easily have gone out and bought nicer pictures, but it was their gifts I pinned up and displayed. The tangible gift was not the real gift--the picture itself holds no value. Rather, what warmed my heart was that my children wanted to express their love for me in whatever way they could.

There is nothing you can give God that He doesn't already have. There is no act of obedience, no sacrifice, no pile of money that He needs. What blesses our Father's heart is when you freely choose to love Him. This can take the form of many actions "for His glory", but it is not the result of the action that pleases Him so much as the heart that gives it. God protects His image in us, the human freedom to love and so to choose the other instead of the self, even beyond the Fall of Adam because in so doing He empowers us to love Him.

If this logic holds, we have already unsettled a key bulwark of determinist thought. Once creation is primarily about love and only secondarily about God's glory we must start asking some hard questions. How does prioritizing love over glory change our theological understanding? How does it change our practices? How does this omnipotent God offer His love to all people? These questions will be somewhat dealt with here, but for a more complete understanding of how to live in this light please see my book *Love Above Glory: God's Purpose for Creation and You!*.

The pinnacle of history is the death of Jesus on the cross, paying the complete debt of sin. In that supreme act of love He also accomplished the supreme act of glory (at least that we can fathom this side of Heaven). After His betrayal by Judas, knowing He faced the cross, Jesus declared, "Now is the Son of Man glorified" (John 13:31). He was referring not to spectacle but to sacrifice. At Calvary, the radiant heart of God was laid bare: self-emptying, forgiving, redeeming love. The cross is both the highest expression of divine glory and the clearest revelation of divine love.

Humanity's purpose is not to feed God's ego but to share His essence—to become like Him in love.

Humanity's purpose is not to feed God's ego but to share His essence—to become like Him in love. When we do, His glory naturally fills the universe, "as the waters cover the sea" (Hab. 2:14). God did not create to gain glory but to share life and love. Glory is what happens when love overflows.

Creation exists because divine love refused to remain contained within the Trinity. Put in human terms, the Father desired children; the Son desired brothers and sisters; the Spirit desired friends to comfort, guide, and serve beside. To glorify God, therefore, is to love as He loves—freely, sacrificially, joyfully. When His creatures reflect that love, His glory shines most brightly. Creation began in love, redemption was accomplished by love, and the Church exists to reflect that love forever.

Chapter 2: Roots of Reform: Evidence from History

❧❧❧

"For from Him and through Him and to Him are all things. To Him be the glory forever." Romans 11:36 (NAS)

"God will not force Himself upon anyone against his will." Billy Graham (1918-2018), *The Endless Love of God*, BillyGraham.org

Calvinism -- later memorialized by the TULIP acronym—did not sprout ex nihilo in the sixteenth century. Its seeds were planted earlier, germinating in the fifth century writings of Augustine of Hippo (AD 354–430) but then mostly laying dormant until the Reformation. Both Luther, a monk of the Augustinian order, and Calvin mistakenly believed they were returning theology to its ancient Christian roots when in fact they were in crucial ways just reviving an Augustinian error.

Calvin knew his theological forebearer well, writing in his Preface to the *Treatise on the Eternal Predestination of God*, "Augustine is so wholly within me, that if I wished to write a confession of my faith, I could do so... out of his writings." Most Calvinists in academia today laud this connection as they proclaim theology must return to its "pure fountain" in Saint Augustine. R.C. Sproul notes dozens of times in his *What is Reformed Theology* that Calvinists look to Augustine as their theological forebearer. The popular Reformed theologian Benjamin Warfield wrote, "The Reformation, inwardly considered, was just the ultimate triumph of Augustine's doctrine of grace."[13]

However, as we will see in this chapter, prior to Augustine the mainstream church taught synergism and genuine human freedom. Augustine's fifth-century writings seeded a determinist strand that was later systematized by Calvin. This chapter surveys pre-Augustinian sources, Augustine's pivot, and how Reformation reception reshaped Western soteriology for good and bad.

The Early Church Consensus Against Determinism

Like many flowers, the beauty of Calvinism depends on the eye of the beholder. Calvinism has been praised as the purest expression of divine sovereignty requiring supreme faith and derided as a later arising weed that chokes the field of divine love. To understand it fairly, we must examine its roots—how it grew from Augustine's philosophical soil, why Calvin used it to reject Roman Catholic teaching in the sixteenth century, and what theological climate allowed it to flourish in the United States despite it being rejected by 96% of the world's self-professing Christians today.[14]

---

[13] Benjamin Warfield, Calvin and Augustine, Philadelphia, PA: Presbyterian and Reformed Publishing, 1956, 332

[14] There is no perfect way to measure this. Total membership of Reformed/Presbyterian/Reformed-heritage churches is about 70–80 million worldwide, so under 3%. A 2011 Pew Forum report shows Presbyterian/Reformed churches make up about 7% of Protestants globally, or roughly 56 million people. Protestants are about 37% of Christians (Pew Research Center) so Reformed/Presbyterians are at about 7% × 37% = ~2.6% of all Christians. If you include related Reformed branches—Congregationalist, United churches, etc.—the total is about 75 million (still under 1% of the world's population). Many more *lean* Calvinist,

Prior to Augustine of Hippo, the Christian consensus held that human beings possess genuine freedom to accept or resist grace[15]. Determinism was treated as pagan (Stoic/Neoplatonic) or heretical (Gnostic/Manichaean) and was rebutted on biblical, theological, and moral grounds. A survey of 84 pre-Augustinian authors finds no Church Father who taught unconditional individual predestination, irresistible grace, or the severe determinism that would later be canonized in Augustinian-Calvinism[16].

Determinism is rarely even hinted at in Judaism, and Second-Temple Jewish voices frame sin and judgment in terms of personal responsibility, not Adamic fatalism. Adam was not seen as a "Federal head" (terminology that came much later) who sinned and so by some mysterious logic bequeathed sin to all humanity. Instead, he was viewed as an archetype. Adam had the least possible temptation and yet sinned, and so too will all of humanity commit sin.

The Pre-Augustinian Christian Consensus

The early Church clearly continued the Jewish understanding, as the first century book of 2nd Baruch says, "For his works have not taught you, nor has the artful work of his creation which has always existed

---

and these make up 30% of Protestants in the USA. Still, an extremely small percentage of Christians worldwide.

[15] I acknowledge that "Absence of evidence ≠ evidence of absence." However, while there may be some slight diversity in accents, there is a clear and prevalent direction. Before Augustine, Christian Fathers of the faith consistently taught accountable freedom and resist fatalism while no one articulates unconditional, individual, double-track predestination with irresistible grace. The only sources even suggesting this are unscholarly Calvinists who did not understand the definition of terms in Chapter one and so read their own ideas/definitions back into early Christian writings.

[16] Wilson, Ken. *The Foundation of Augustinian-Calvinism.* Independently Published, 2019. ISBN 978-1082800351.

persuaded you. Adam is, therefore, not the cause, except only for himself, but each of us has become his own Adam" (54:18-19).

Another first century work is 2 Esdras that similarly states Adam brought upon the earth a curse, but that it is our own works that cause our death. "O thou Adam, what hast thou done? For though it was thou that sinned, thou art not fallen alone, but we all that come of thee. For what profit is it unto us, if there be promised us an immortal time, whereas we have done the works that bring death?" (2 Esdras 7:48-49).[17]

Pre-Augustinian Christian writers repeatedly affirm free will and deny determinism. In fact, when the issue is discussed, it is almost always to condemn heretics who wanted to drag deterministic pagan beliefs into Christianity. Early Christians rejected predeterminism often using the following Scriptures:

> "*I call heaven and earth to witness against you today, that I have set before you life and death, the blessing and the curse. So choose life in order that you may live, you and your descendants*" (Deut 30:19, NAS).

> "*Jerusalem, Jerusalem, who kills the prophets and stones those who are sent to her! How often I wanted to gather your children together, the way a hen gathers her chicks under her wings, and you were unwilling*" (Matt 23:37, NAS).

> "*This is good and acceptable in the sight of God our Savior, who desires all men to be saved and to come to the knowledge of the truth*" (1 Tim 2:4, NAS).

Justin Martyr is among the earliest Christian apologists to discuss Adam and Eve. Writing around AD 160, he clearly says humans were

---

[17] Note that there is no claim here suggesting these are to be considered Scripture—these sources are simply showing Judaism continued to reject determinism into the first century AD.

"made like God" in sinlessness until we became sinners and brought death upon ourselves due to our own acts of sin:

> ...*the Holy Spirit rebukes men, who were made, like God, free from suffering and immortal, if they kept His precepts, and were deemed worthy of being called by Him His sons. But they became like Adam and Eve and prepared death for themselves,[18]*

Note that he does not see anyone born with original sin—no one is guilty until they sin—but he also acknowledges that all will sin. This was the common profession of the early Church. Martyr also wrote:

> *We have learned from the prophets, and we hold it to be true, that punishments, and chastisements, and good rewards, are rendered according to the merit of each man's actions. Since if it be not so, but all things happen by fate, neither is anything at all in our own power....And again, unless the human race have the power of avoiding evil and choosing good by free choice, they are not accountable for their actions, of whatever kind they be. But that it is by free choice they both walk uprightly and stumble, we thus demonstrate....For not like other things, as trees and quadrupeds, which cannot act by choice, did God make man (First Apology, 43).*

Irenaeus (AD 125-202), the disciple of Polycarp, who was in turn the disciple of the Apostle John, also battled the heretical cults of his day. Condemning Marcion (who rejected the Old Testament and much of the New, as well as split the world into spiritual which was good and physical that was deemed bad) he wrote:

> *Matthew 23:37 set forth the ancient law of human liberty, because God made man a free [agent] from the beginning, possessing his own power, even as he does his own soul, to obey the behests (ad utendum sententia) of God voluntarily, and not by compulsion of God. For there is no coercion with God, but a good will [towards us] is present with Him continually. And therefore does He give good counsel to all. And in man, as well as in angels, He has placed the power of choice (for angels are rational beings),*

---

[18] Justin Martyr, *Dialogue with Trypho*, 124

so that those who had yielded obedience might justly possess what is good, given indeed by God, but preserved by themselves. (Against Heresies, IV.37.1).

Irenaeus championed free will in his refutation of Gnostic determinism, attributing our being created in the image of God (*imago Dei*) as being our free will. "But because man is possessed of free will from the beginning, and God is possessed of free will, in whose likeness man was created." (*Against Heresies* IV.37.4). He also stressed God's justice is impugned without genuine free choice to sin or not sin. He denied anything can happen outside of God's sovereignty[19] but understood God's will to include letting human will be retained.

Clement of Alexandria (c. AD 150-215) wrote around AD 190 about how humans have residual free choice after Adam[20] and that it is divine foreknowledge that leads to divine election (*Stromata* 1.18; 6.14). He said God calls all humanity to repent, but the "called" are those who respond and so were seen by God and elected from eternity. He denounced as unjust a god who would call some to be elect and others to be damned, saying that is the god of Marcion the Gnostic and not the God of the Bible. He also made it clear that free will is essential for salvation, that it is empowered by God's grace, and it results in us doing good works which in turn changes our natural inclinations:

But since some are unbelieving, and some are disputatious, all do not attain to the perfection of the good. For neither is it possible to attain it without

[19] Irenaeus of Lyons, *Against Heresies* (Latin: *Adversus Haereses*), Book II, Chapter 5, Section 4. In: *Irenaeus: Against Heresies*, translated by Dominic J. Unger, revised by John J. Dillon. ACW (Ancient Christian Writers) / Newman Press, 2012.

[20] Clement of Alexandria, *Stromata* ("Miscellanies"), Book I, Chapter 1; Book IV, Chapter 24; Book V, Chapter 14. In: *Clement of Alexandria: Stromata*, edited and translated by Thomas Taylor, in *Ancient Christian Writers* (Vol. 9), Paulist Press, 1962 (reprint).

the exercise of free choice; nor does the whole depend on our own purpose; as, for example, what is defined to happen. "For by grace we are saved:" not, indeed, without good works; but we must, by being formed for what is good, acquire an inclination for it. (Stromata 5.1)

Clement's main opponents were followers of the Gnostic Marcion. They believed faith was an irresistible gift of God to the "elect" only, but Clement said such a view robs humans of choice and thus responsibility. Clement believed all humans are in need of divine grace, and so God provides grace to all, drawing all humanity to Himself (*Stromata* 5.1; John 12:32).

Tertullian (AD 160-240) believed, despite having a corrupted nature, the divine image still empowers humans enough to be capable of accepting God's gift of salvation. He refuted Gnostic discriminatory deterministic salvation (*Adversus Valentinianos*, 29) and explained how God can permit Good and Evil while still being sovereign due to His foreknowledge (*De Cultu Feminarum*, 2.10). Writing around AD 205 he said,

I find, then, that man was by God constituted free, master of his own will and power; indicating the presence of God's image and likeness in him by nothing so well as by this constitution of his nature. (Against Marcion II.5; cf. *De Anima* 21).

He furthermore opposed infant Baptism, saying babies were still innocent and that baptism should be a mature personal choice (*De baptism* 18).

Origen of Alexandria (ca. AD 185-254), who was a bit more of a controversial figure but nevertheless hugely influential on early Christian thought, wrote an entire chapter on free will. He was also better linked to Jewish thought as he may have been the first Greek theologian to learn Hebrew in order to fairly interpret the Word of

God[21]. He said, "It is a clearly defined doctrine of the Church that every rational soul is possessed of free will and volition...we are not subject to necessity" (*De Principiis* III.1.2). He strongly asserted God only invites rather than compels because God wants "willing lovers" (*Hom. Jer.*20.2). He refuted misconceptions about Romans 10 and showed how God only acts indirectly upon Pharaoh's heart, simply supporting Pharaoh's own hardening. He condemns the belief that God saves or destroys whoever He wants (*Princ.* 3.1.7), saying it is humanity that accepts or rejects God's free gift.

Perhaps the clearest thinker of his time about the process of salvation, Origen explains a synergistic (cooperative) view. He writes that initial faith is human faith because it is our choice to repent. However, saving faith requires God's supporting power, which God graciously gives to all who repent (*Commentary on Romans*, 4.5.1). He also firmly situates election as a doctrine based upon divine foreknowledge as he writes:

> For the Creator makes vessels of honor and vessels of dishonor, not from the beginning according to His foreknowledge, since He does not pre-condemn or pre-justify according to it; but [He makes] those into vessels of honor who purged themselves, and those into vessels of dishonor who allowed themselves to remain unpurged (Peri Archōn 3.1.20).

Origen saw God's foreknowledge as not a cause but rather as an observation (*Contra Celsum*, 2.20) and so refuted misinterpretations of Romans 9:16 which says: "So then it does not depend on the man who wills or the man who runs, but on God who has mercy" (NAS). Origen insisted God's mercy works together with our will—that salvation is synergistic, not unilateral. It is not that a person's willing or running is of no avail, but that the beginning and completion of every good work are from God. For Origen, the will and the effort of man are required,

---

[21] Jaroslav Pelikan, *The Emergence of the Catholic Tradition (100–600)*, vol. 1 of *The Christian Tradition: A History of the Development of Doctrine* (Chicago: University of Chicago Press, 1971), 21

yet they would accomplish nothing if the mercy of God were not present to help. The mercy of God does not destroy the freedom of the will because He shows mercy to those who turn to Him so that they may be able to will and to run aright (*Commentary on Romans* VI.9).

Origen goes on to explain that Paul's statement elevates grace but denies human boasting--not freedom. Humans must "will and run," but these actions are insufficient without grace. Grace enables and perfects the human will; it does not replace or overpower it. God's mercy gives strength to those who choose to turn toward Him, consistent with Origen's broader teaching that rational souls are free and responsible.

In contrast to the deterministic reading Augustine would later adopt, Origen argues Paul's examples of Pharaoh and Jacob/Esau (Rom 9:10–18) show God's foreknowledge and educational justice, not arbitrary election. God hardens or has mercy according to His knowledge of each soul's response (*Commentary on Romans* VI.9). God does not indiscriminately harden those whom He has not foreknown will despise His call, since those who are hardened are assumed already to have rejected it:

> *Let us begin, then, with those words which were spoken to Pharaoh, who is said to have been hardened by God, in order that he might not let the people go; and, along with his case, the language of the apostle also will be considered, where he says, Therefore He has mercy on whom He will, and whom He will He hardens. For it is on these passages chiefly that the* **heretics rely, asserting that salvation is not in our own power, but that souls are of such a nature as must by all means be either lost or saved;** *and that in no way can a soul which is of an evil nature become good, or one which is of a virtuous nature be made bad. And hence they maintain that Pharaoh, too, being of a ruined nature, was on that account hardened by God...And how shall the justice of God be defended, if He Himself is the cause of the destruction of those whom, owing to their unbelief (through their being hardened), He has*

afterwards condemned by the authority of a judge? (*On First Principles* III.1.8, bold mine) [22]

Origen affirmed foreknowledge precedes predestination, and God's choices are just because they respond to freely chosen dispositions in souls. Ultimately Origen taught, "It is our own doing whether we become wheat or tares, vessels of honor or dishonor" (*De Principiis* III.1.21).

There are many other examples of the Christian consensus on free will before Augustine. Quotations can be cited from Cyprian, Novatian, Lactantius, Hilary of Poitiers, and the Cappadocians (especially Gregory of Nazianzus) that stress humans can choose to sin or by God's grace repent, that people are innocent until they choose sin, and that a sovereign God graciously offers salvation to all rather than to a select few.

Basil of Caesraea (ca. AD 330-379) refutes Stoic notions of deterministic "Providence" and Chaldean astrological fatalism by saying that while humans in themselves are too weak, God empowers human faith so that real good can be accomplished. He stated any belief that humans are inevitably evil destroys Christian hope (*Hom. Hex*.6.7). His strongest condemnation of determinism was aimed at "...the detestable Manichaean Heresy" (*Hom. Hex.* 2.4) of which Augustine was a part for more than a decade.

Even as we approach the contemporaries of Augustine we find the exact same theology as it was taught by Jesus and passed down by His Apostles. Methodius (d. AD 312) confirmed all humans retain genuine free will even after the fall (*Symp* 8.16; PG 18:168d), and Cyril of Jerusalem (ca. AD 348-386) taught humans enter the world sinless and

---

[22] Origen. *On First Principles*. Book III. In *Nicene and Post-Nicene Fathers, First Series*, vol. 4, ed. Philip Schaff, trans. by Rev. John E. Swete. Grand Rapids: Eerdmans, 1989.

that it is foreknowledge that determines divine election[23]. Eusebius of Caesarea wrote (c. AD 320), "A power of choosing good and evil has been given by the Creator to rational souls" (*Preparation for the Gospel* VI.11).

Theodore of Mospsuestia (ca. AD 350-428) defended Christianity against the Manichaean notion of "inherited guilt," echoing Origen by writing, "Man's freedom takes the first step, which is afterwards made effective by God…[with] the will of each man as being absolutely free and unbiased and able to choose either good or evil"[24].

John Chrysostom (c. 337-407) the great "golden mouth" evangelist and ascetic who had to be abducted and forced to become Archbishop of Constantinople penned one of the clearest explanations of man's will interacting synergistically with God's in his commentary on Romans 9. It is so similar to Origen and consonant with all other early Christians as to conclusively evidence that this was the consensus of the early Church. First, it is foreknowledge that God uses to know who will repent and be His. Commenting on Esau and Jacob he says:

> *Because He does not wait, as man does, to see from the issue of their acts the good and him who is not so, but even before these He knows which is the wicked and which not such.*

[23] Cyril of Jerusalem. *Catechetical Lectures* (Greek: Κατηχήσεις), 1.3. In *Nicene and Post-Nicene Fathers*, Second Series, Vol. 7, edited by Philip Schaff and Henry Wace. New York: Christian Literature Publishing Co., 1894; reprint, Grand Rapids: Eerdmans, 1989

[24] Theodore of Mopsuestia. *Commentary on the Gospel of John (In Joannem Evangelium Commentarius)*, on John 5:19. Fragment preserved in *Theodore of Mopsuestia: The Commentary on the Gospel of John*, fragments translated in Rowan A. Greer, *Theodore of Mopsuestia: Exegete and Theologian*. Westminster Press, 1961, 52–53.

Second, Romans 9 is not about individuals being elected to salvation but rather is juxtaposing salvation by works (the Jews) and salvation by choosing to have faith (the gentiles who were grafted in):

I, however, have a good reason to give you why the Gentiles were justified and you were cast out. And what is the reason? It is that they are of faith, you of the works of the Law.

Finally, God acts due to free will rather than imposing salvation or condemnation by external decree. Free will is then empowered by God to make it saving faith:

Because when he says, it is not of him that wills, nor of him that runs, he does not deprive us of free-will, but shows that all is not one's own, for that it requires grace from above. For it is binding on us to will, and also to run: but to confide not in our own labors, but in the love of God toward man.[25]

In his commentary on John he reinforces this perspective:

And to this end He draws no one by force or compulsion: but by persuasion and benefits He draws all that will, and wins them to Himself. Wherefore when He came, some received Him, and others received Him not. For He will have no unwilling, no forced domestic, but all of their own will and choice, and grateful to Him for their service.[26]

---

[25] John Chrysostom, *Homilies on the Epistle of St. Paul to the Romans*, Homily 16 (on Romans 9), in *Nicene and Post-Nicene Fathers*, First Series, vol. 11, ed. Philip Schaff, trans. J. B. Morris (Peabody, MA: Hendrickson, 1994), 517–524.

[26] John Chrysostom, *Homily 10 on the Gospel of John*, in *Nicene and Post-Nicene Fathers, First Series*, vol. 11, ed. Philip Schaff and Henry Wace, trans. by Marcus Dods (Grand Rapids: Eerdmans, 1979), 289.

Synthesis of Chrysostom's View:

Theme	Description	Key Source
Grace precedes and empowers	God initiates every good work and provides the means for salvation.	Romans Hom. 18
Freedom is preserved	Grace does not cancel free will; it enables genuine moral choice.	John Hom. 25
Virtue must be voluntary	If God forced righteousness, it would cease to be virtue.	Hebrews Hom. 7
Synergism, not determinism	Salvation involves cooperation: "It is ours to choose, His to assist."	Romans Hom. 18

Ambrose of Milan (d. AD 397) baptized Augustine of Hippo on Easter in AD 387. He taught the traditional view regarding sin rather than Augustine's version wherein people are guilty at birth (*De fide* 5.5, 8, 60; *Exc. Satyri* 2.6; cf. 1.4). While he taught slavery to sin was a condition "inherited" because of Adam, it was not a literal sin that produced damnation (*De Abrah* 2.79). He also agreed predestination was based on foreknowledge, that God compels no one but rather waits patiently for repentance, and that God gives faith by grace in response to a person's initial faith (*Paen.* 1.48; 1.5; *Ep.* 41.6).

Ultimately, in the manuscripts passed down to us through time, not a single Church Father writing from AD 95-430 considered Adam's fall to have erased human free choice to respond to grace, despite a nearly ubiquitous belief in human depravity[27]. Early Church Historian Dr. Ken Wilson wrote:

> *Of the eighty-four pre-Augustinian authors studied from 95-430 CE, over fifty authors addressed the topic [of predestination]. All of these early Christian authors championed traditional free choice against pagan and*

---

[27] For a more extensive list of quotations see https://soteriology101.com/2014/12/16/did-the-early-church-fathers-teach-calvinistic-doctrine/?utm_source=chatgpt.com

heretical Divine Unilateral Predetermination of Individuals' Eternal Destinies. (The Foundations of Augustinian-Calvinism, 35).

Nearly all ancient Christianity historians concur with Wilson's analysis. Even Calvinism defenders Peterson and Williams admit, "Indeed, one could easily argue that it was Augustine, not Pelagius, who was out of step with the tradition of the church" and "Augustine's monergistic emphasis upon salvation by grace alone represented a significant departure from the traditional teaching of the church." [28] Presbyterian minister and professor Rev. Charles Finney (1792-1875), the main figure in the second Great Awakening in America, wrote about original sin and other Calvinist doctrines:

> *If men are without excuse for sin, as the whole law and gospel assume and teach, it cannot possibly be that their nature is sinful, for a sinful nature would be the best of all excuses for sin. This doctrine is a stumbling-block both to the church and the world, infinitely dishonourable to God, and an abomination alike to God and the human intellect, and should be banished from every pulpit, and from every formula of doctrine, and from the world. It is a relic of heathen philosophy, and was foisted in among the doctrines of Christianity by Augustine, as every one may know who will take the trouble to examine for himself.[29]*

Across Greek and Latin traditions, grace was seen as necessary and enabling, yet resistible, preserving accountability and the justice of divine judgment. Our early Christian forefathers polemicized against Gnostic and later Manichaean determinisms, and against the Stoic notion of an inescapable chain of causes (a precursor to atheistic determinism today). Early Christian defenders judged such views as

---

[28] Peterson and Williams, *Why I Am Not an Arminian*, 35 and 37

[29] Charles Finney Systematic Theology Lecture XXIV (in some editions, in discussions of *Moral Depravity / Original Sin*); see:
https://www.ccel.org/ccel/f/finney/theology/cache/theology.pdf, p251

morally corrosive, undermining repentance and prayer, and theologically unworthy of the God who sincerely calls all to salvation.

These are harsh accusations. Is there a Calvinist/Augustinian response to the claim that the early Church believed in free will? Calvinist defender James White launched four podcasts in response to Wilson's book, and none of them deal sufficiently with this crucial issue of history. In fact, here is his main (supposed) refutation (follow the link in the notes for the full podcast):

> But the reality is we have only a small portion of the extant literature. And so, one of the first things that caught me, when I first started looking through this, was how many times [Wilson claims] "It was the universal view..." The only fair way of actually saying that is: In the extant literature that we have, that specifically addresses this issue, it seems that the predominant view prior to would be this, and then Augustine changed it.[30]

What? First, someone needs to explain to White what the word "extant" means. Second, is he really trying to say that just because **all** of the extant writing during the first 400 years of Christianity support free will that doesn't mean there was a Christian consensus? It stretches credulity to believe every scrap of pro-deterministic literature by early Christians was somehow lost. This is the epitome of argument by absence, and no logical person should ever consider such irrationality. Since the historic roots seem polluted, the only way forward for an Augustinian-Calvinist is to make a complete break with the past and disregard historic theology altogether. That is in fact what some propose.

---

[30] https://www.aomin.org/aoblog/reformed-apologetics/zechariah-149-then-ken-wilsons-book-against-calvinism/ 32:50 mark, from White vs. Wilson part 2.

Should We Believe Historic Theology?

Some Calvinists argue that early Christian consensus does not determine truth—only the Bible determines truth[31]. This statement can only be made in ignorance of the fact that it was early Christian consensus that determined the Bible's closed canon. If we claim to have the full and inerrant Bible we must believe God was powerful enough to speak to His people and guide their decision in determining what was His Word and what was fiction. We must believe the people the Holy Spirit led to compile His Word also knew how to interpret it.

Besides being the reason the Bible was collected and revered, are the early Christians credible as true believers? Most likely yes, but certainly they are far more credible than Augustine. These Christian theologians were periodically persecuted in the Roman empire until Constantine issued the Edict of Milan in AD 313. Justin Martyr event lent his name to mean "one who dies for the true faith of Jesus Christ."

During Augustine's lifetime Christianity was the official religion of the empire, and it moved from just being tolerated to actually being reenforced by the state. Pure religion does not need coercion and can stand despite persecution. It seems far more likely the early church was comprised of Spirit-filled believers than the later Church, because they chose Christ despite persecution.

Furthermore, many of the early Church Fathers can trace their faith to Jesus through His disciples. Surely this proximity and spiritual lineage deserves respect. Finally, most of them spoke and wrote in the

---

[31] See Kruger, Michael J. "What Is Sola Scriptura Protecting Us Against? More Than You Think." Canon Fodder: Michael J. Kruger's Blog, October 31, 2017. https://michaeljkruger.com/what-is-sola-scriptura-protecting-us-against-more-than-you-think/ and White, James R. "Solo Scriptura? Tradition 0?" Alpha & Omega Ministries (Reformed Apologetics Blog), September 28, 2005. https://www.aomin.org/aoblog/reformed-apologetics/solo-scriptura-tradition-0/ and Understanding Sola Scriptura." Ligonier Ministries. Last modified December 1, 2009. https://learn.ligonier.org/articles/sola-scriptura-protestant-position-bible-new-reformation-trust/

Greek of the New Testament, whereas Augustine by his own admission never even learned the language well (Augustine, *Confessions*, I.13.). We can easily see how this oversight led to misinterpretations and unfounded doctrines. One such linguistic misunderstanding about original sin will be explained at length a little later.

Yes, ultimately it is the Bible that determines truth, but if there are two interpretations of the Bible we would be much wiser to side with the many early Christian defenders than with Augustine. We would also be much wiser to preserve God's goodness and our moral responsibility rather than relinquish these just to highlight God's power.

As a final note, we know it was Augustine who moved the Church regarding Original Sin and other deterministic ideas because the Eastern Orthodox Church, which of course could read Greek, largely resisted Augustinian novel developments on inherited guilt and irresistible grace. It is therefore paramount that we understand where Augustine gleaned his deterministic beliefs.

Augustinian Seed: Pagan Philosophy & Christian Theology

For two decades after conversion, Augustine defended free choice and synergism. Beginning c. 412, amid the Pelagian controversy, he recast grace and will: fallen humans cannot choose God unless irresistibly moved; God elects some, passes over others. This shift leaned on Latin exegesis (e.g., *'in quo'* at Rom 5:12) and on categories familiar from his earlier Stoic/Manichaean milieu. Whether one deems it a necessary correction or a rupture, it was incontrovertibly a departure from the pre-Augustinian mainstream.

Before Augustine's conversion to Christianity, he was a man steeped in philosophy and heretical beliefs. He spent nearly a decade as a devout follower of Manichaeism, a dualistic and deterministic religion founded by Mani (strongly denounced by Basil of Caesarea above). Manichaeism taught human actions were bound by spiritual forces of light and darkness beyond their control. This deterministic framework denied genuine human freedom in moral choices and believed salvation was only possible for the elect--those "chosen" by the divine light.

After more than a decade of dedication to Manichaeism, Augustine renounced it in favor of Neoplatonism, another philosophy steeped in deterministic assumptions. Neoplatonists such as Plotinus held that all things flow necessarily from the One (the divine source), creating a cascade of causes and effects that shaped the universe in fixed, hierarchical ways. In this worldview, the lower could never change its position except by the influence of the higher, leaving no room for libertarian free will[32].

In AD 386 Augustine converted to Christianity, and for the first 20 years of his Christian ministry he defended free will, human moral responsibility, and the idea that God's grace worked synergistically with human choice. He rose in the ranks of ministry, and due to his strong written renunciation of the beliefs of Mani, the Church made an exception to its rule to never appoint a bishop if that person ever followed the Manichaean heresy.

Around AD 412, during the Pelagian controversy, Augustine radically altered his theology[33]. He began to argue human beings were completely incapable of choosing God without irresistible grace, and he taught God predestined some to eternal life and passed over others, allowing them to fall into damnation. Denying libertarian free will, Augustine asserted all human choices were determined by either divine grace or sinful nature[34].

---

[32] Augustine, *Confessions*, Books 5–7 (on his Manichean and Neoplatonic phase).

[33] Augustine, *On the Spirit and the Letter and Against the Pelagians* (on his later deterministic theology).

[34] See Augustine, *De Libero Arbitrio; Enchiridion* 100; *City of God* XX.7; Ep. 93; *Predestination of the Saints* 8.

According to Wilson and many other sources, this sharp turn in theology was not driven by biblical discovery but rather constituted a reversion to Augustine's earlier philosophical convictions. "Augustine's deterministic theology was a re-baptizing of Stoic fatalism and Manichean elitism in Christian terminology" (Wilson, *Foundations*, 109–110). Augustine's entire intellectual formation occurred within pagan and heretical deterministic frameworks, and so as a Christian bishop he fell back to reliance upon Stoic and Neoplatonic categories when interpreting Scripture.

Augustine's background and lack of learning Greek caused him to misread determinism into biblical texts, even where it was foreign to the intent of the original writers. "When Augustine reinterpreted Scripture through the lens of Stoic determinism, he created a theological system that fundamentally departed from the early Church's understanding of free will and divine justice" (Wilson, *Foundations*, 128).

One extremely important linguistic misunderstanding led to Augustine's doctrine of Original sin. Rather than seeing Adam as an archetype, Augustine initiated the belief that Adam acts as a Federal Head (although that wording came much later). Augustine (and later Calvin) claimed that in Adam all humans became sinful and so humans are sinful at birth. Augustine said the mechanism of sin's transmission is our parent's having pleasure during sex, reasoning that Jesus' parents didn't have sex, and eventually supporting the fable that Mary was perpetually a virgin. Thus was also born centuries of strange sexual beliefs and opinions in the Catholic Church.

Augustine's mistake happened as he read in Latin the portion of Romans 5:12 that says, *"in quo omnes peccaverunt"* which means "in whom all sinned." From that he developed the novel idea that people actually sin in Adam. This is an incorrect translation. Luckily, English translations have been getting it right all the way back to the King James. The verse actually says: "Therefore, just as through one man sin entered into the world, and death through sin, and so death spread to all men, because all sinned" (Rom. 5:12, NAS). Adam was the first to sin and so he brought physical death into the world, but his act does not make subsequent people sinful. We make ourselves sinful when we choose to sin—you cannot be sinful and have never sinned.

Augustine was also influenced by the Christians in North Africa practicing infant baptism. Augustine reasoned that baptism is for the forgiveness of sin, and so instead of denouncing that flawed practice as Tertullian did[35], he reasoned infants must be sinful, and he taught unbaptized babies go to Hell (Augustine, *Enchiridion* 93; *On Merit and the Forgiveness of Sins and the Baptism of Infants* 1.16; *Letter* 166.7). Augustine later tried to justify his position with a grievous mistake or possibly a bald-faced lie by writing, "The Church has always held that baptism is given for the remission of sins, not only of those actually committed, but also of original sin" (Book I. 9–10).

The idea that babies are sinful and deserve eternal punishment in Hell seems not only unjust but outrageous. Anyone who has had a miscarriage or a child die in infancy should know their child is with its loving Creator. Infants cannot sin as they do not have enough maturity to commit a willful transgression, nor really even the ability to control their minds or bodies in any way that is offensive. Rest assured, these small bundles of life and joy will someday sin if they are allowed to grow—but they are not deserving of hell for the simple fact that they were born/created. Even Augustine, who invented the doctrine, admits he cannot find any justification for God to send babies to Hell.

---

[35] *On Baptism (De Baptismo)*, ch. 18. In *Ante-Nicene Fathers*, Vol. 3, edited by Alexander Roberts and James Donaldson. Buffalo, NY: Christian Literature Publishing Co., 1885. Tertullian warns against baptizing infants prematurely: "Let them come when they are grown up; when they can understand; when they are instructed whither it is that they come... Let them become Christians when they have become able to know Christ." (ch. 18)

"I cannot find a satisfactory and worthy explanation—because I can't find one, not because there isn't one" (s.294.7[36]).

Augustine's Questionable Theological Innovations

Augustine did irreparable harm to many other Christian doctrines as well as showed a tendency to innovate excessively by mixing in his previous philosophical and heretical convictions. While no one wants a discussion to devolve into *ad hominen* attacks, it is reasonable to report Augustine's many theological innovations to explain why we should scrutinize a man whom so many admire. Indeed, when given the facts, even those steeped in Reformed theology and taught to revere Augustine may wish to question his interpretive methods and theological prowess.

First, he supported the myth of Mary's perpetual virginity (despite the books of James and Jude being written by her sons) (*Sermon* 186.1; cf. *On Holy Virginity* 4). He supported the use of force against theological opponents (*Letter* 93.5; *Letter* 185.6; *City of God* 22.6), which we will see Calvin believed and put into action. Augustine even altered Cicero to create a Christian theological justification for war (*City of God* 19.7). He helped justify compulsory state churches by saying there is a visible and an invisible church (*On Baptism Against the Donatists* 3.19; *City of God* 20.9), taught that babies who are unbaptized go to hell (*On the Merits and Forgiveness of Sins, and on the Baptism of Infants* 1.9–10), and as we'll see in Chapter Seven he confused and warped the early Church consensus about the intermediate state to lay the foundation of the much-abused doctrine of Purgatory (*Enchiridion* 69; *City of God* 21.13–16).

Augustine also invented fairly incredible theological positions that persist to today. He systematized the idea that the millennial Kingdom is just symbolic, supporting "amillennialism" because that was much

---

[36] Translation by Edmund Hill, Augustine's Works (Sermon 294), p. 184

more conducive to a state church (*City of God* 20.7; 20.9; *Tractates on the Gospel of John* 9.7). He also was one of the first "cessationists," declaring the Spirit's miraculous gifts ceased after the New Testament period (*Homilies on the First Epistle of John* 6.10; as opposed to *City of God* 22.8). This was most likely also to justify a state church. After all, an established church cannot have individuals hearing directly from God and thus being empowered to rebuke its abuses of power.[37]

Finally, Augustine's sexual misconduct should disqualify him to be an elder in the Church, and certainly does not reflect a "good tree" from which comes "good fruit" (Mat. 7:17). His exploits are well-documented, and he himself confesses and repents of his sin in *Confessions*. He lived with a concubine for many years and had a child with her (*Confessions* 4.2; 6.15), only to summarily dismissed her and their son off to Africa so he could marry someone to elevate his social status. He thus got engaged to a young girl (probably 12-years-old) (*Confessions* 6.13), and even after his conversion to Christianity took another concubine to bed while waiting for his fiancé to come of age (*Confessions* 6.25). He later dismissed his betrothed and never married, and to his credit he later lamented such sinfulness (*Confessions* 6.15–6.26).

Augustine remained, however, what most would call today a misogynist with some strange beliefs about sex. He believed sex is always sinful (even in marriage) and that men are better help mates for men than are women.[38] He also wrote, "Thus a good Christian is found to love in one and the same woman the creature of God, whom he desires to be transformed and renewed; but to hate the corruptible and mortal conjugal connection and sexual intercourse: i.e. to love in her what is characteristic of a human being, to hate what belongs to her as a wife."[39]

---

[37] Augustine, *Sixth Homily on 1 John*, 10

[38] De Genesi ad Litteram, 9.5-8

[39] Augustine, *On the Sermon on the Mount*, 1.41

Being consistent with his belief that God causes all things, and wanting to justify what he saw as God's actions, in his *City of God* Augustine declares that the women who were raped in 410 during the sack of Rome were caused to be raped by God for their own good. God ordained their rape because they were too proud of being virgins, or if not that, to prevent them from becoming arrogant. Here is what he wrote:

> *As, therefore, some men were removed by death, that no wickedness might change their disposition, so these women were outraged [raped] lest prosperity should corrupt their modesty.*

> *Neither those women then, who were already puffed up by the circumstance that they were still virgins, nor those who might have been so puffed up had they not been exposed to the violence of the enemy, lost their chastity, but rather gained humility; the former were saved from pride already cherished, the latter from pride that would shortly have grown upon them.*
> (Augustine, *City of God* 1.28, NPNF translation, Schaff, 1887)

Augustine never learned Greek well and by his own admission valued flowery Latin speech above plain language. His concocting and supporting so many flagrant theological errors should at least give his admirers pause and certainly justifies our looking more critically at his theological writings on determinism and original sin.

In summary, Harvard historian Harry Wolfson wrote that Augustine's "doctrine of grace is only a Christianization of the Stoic doctrine of fate."[40] This was echoed by Wilson who wrote:

> *The great Augustine underwent numerous conversions in his personal journey—Stoicism, Manichaeism, Neoplatonism, Christianity with works meriting grace, Christianity with unmerited grace, and then*

---

[40] Harry Wolfson, *Religious Philosophy: A group of Essays* (Cambridge, MA: Belknap Press of Harvard UniversityPress, 1961), 176

Christianized Manichaean radicalized grace (*Foundations*, loc 2.113 Kindle).

Augustine's intentions may have been pastoral—to magnify grace and combat human pride—but the resulting theology made God's will the only truly active will in the universe, thereby making God responsible for all good…and for all evil.

Sadly, Augustine claimed to be in line with other early Christian writers, thereby leading astray the sixteenth century Reformers who discovered in his doctrines a way to fight a corrupted Catholic Church. History conclusively attests that the seed of Calvinism was sown by Augustine who (intentionally or otherwise) grafted ancient heresy and pagan philosophy onto biblical revelation resulting in a deterministic God and all five points of TULIP that will be discussed in the next chapter.

Medieval Growth: From Augustine to the Scholastics

Whereas both Catholicism and Eastern Orthodox Christians successfully eschewed Augustine's anti-historic determinism, the Catholic Church found truth and beauty in some of Augustine's other thoughts and so made him a "Father of the Church" and a "Saint." For Catholics, this involves two verified miracles occurring because people prayed to him after his death (U.S. Conference of Catholic Bishops). The Eastern Orthodox Church rejected Augustine and nearly all of his doctrines, recognizing much of his theology was influenced by heretics and his lack of being able to read Greek.

After Augustine's death in AD 430, his ideas took root slowly in the west. The early medieval Church still emphasized synergy—cooperation between grace and free will for salvation. The Second Council of Orange (AD 529) affirmed a kind of original sin and the necessity of grace but explicitly rejected double predestination, stating:

We not only do not believe that any are foreordained to evil by the power of God, but even state with utter abhorrence that if there are those who wish to believe so, they are anathema (Canons of Orange, Canon 25).

Yet Augustine's writings remained fertile soil for later reformers dissatisfied with Rome's sacramental system and works-based teachings. By the 14th century, theologians such as Gregory of Rimini and Thomas Bradwardine began reviving Augustine's views on divine sovereignty, arguing that human merit could play no role in salvation[41]. These thinkers, though still within the Catholic Church, were watering an Augustinian root that would soon bloom beyond the garden walls of Rome.

Reformation Replanting: Luther, Calvin, & Revolt vs Rome

When the Augustinian monk Martin Luther nailed his 95 Theses to the Wittenberg door in 1517, he sought reform, not revolution. But his theological ax—aimed at indulgences—struck a deeper trunk: the question of human freedom. In response to the extreme greed of the Catholic Church with its emphasis on good works and payments to get relatives out of Purgatory, Luther decided to wholesale reject works-based salvation.

Being very familiar with the writings of Augustine, he took it a step further and rejected all human freedom. In his 1525 treatise *The Bondage of the Will* (against Erasmus) he argued fallen humans possess no capacity to choose God apart from grace, making the novel claim that faith itself should be considered a work.

Luther wanted a pure Church with biblical doctrine, and he thought in Augustine's writings he had discovered how his contemporary Church had deviated from historic Christianity. In *The Bondage of the Will* he refers to Augustine 13 times. Luther followed Augustine's

---

[41] Gregory of Rimini, *Lectura super primum et secundum Sententiarum*; Bradwardine, *De causa Dei* 1.34–35

teachings almost verbatim, declaring the will "bound as a beast of burden."

The predestination doctrine—with the elect being chosen before time—had an added bonus. Martin Luther used it to fortify his followers against the charge that to leave Mother Church meant excommunication and an awaiting Hell. The Catholic Church insisted people had to be in communion with itself to be saved (*Unam Sanctam*, 1302). Luther comforted his protesting (hence the term Protestant) followers by saying God decided who was and who was not elect before time began, so they did not need to worry about Catholic claims (*The Bondage of the Will* 1525, WA 18:600–787). He specifically said that while you can never know if someone else is elect, you can at least believe yourself to be one of the chosen few, even if disenfranchised from the Catholic Church (*Lectures on Romans* 1515–1516, LW 25:373–377; *Table Talk* No. 3745).

John Calvin's Theological Entrenchment

While Luther led the Reformation in a rather bombastic style (someone had to do it fearlessly!), John Calvin was the scholar who refined and systematized Augustine's thought with precision and logic. He was probably drawn to Augustine because they both shared an affinity for Stoicism, with Calvin writing his first book *De Clementia* about the Stoic philosopher Seneca. Calvin also had a meticulous personality and so must have been naturally attracted to a God who micromanaged every detail of existence. He theologically locked in Augustine's doctrines declaring, "By predestination we mean the eternal decree of God, by which He determined with Himself whatever He wished to happen with regard to every man" (*Institutes*, III.21.5).

Calvin's theology was so profoundly shaped by Augustine of Hippo that many historians call Calvin "the most Augustinian of the Reformers." Calvin openly acknowledged this dependence, referring to Augustine 265 times in his *Institutes of the Christian Religion*. In that work he frequently cites Augustine as "wholly ours" (*Institutes*, IV.17.24), indicating that he viewed Augustine as the primary forerunner of Reformation thought.

Clear evidence of Calvin's dependence upon Augustine are found in his views of grace, predestination, human depravity, infant baptism, church and state relationship, and divine sovereignty. Scholars widely affirm this connection. Eminently Reformed theologian B. B. Warfield wrote, "The system of doctrine taught by Calvin is just the Augustinianism common to the whole body of the Reformers" (*Calvin and Augustine*, 1909, 22). Similarly, historian Philip Schaff observed that "Calvin reproduced Augustine's theology with greater consistency and logical rigor" (*History of the Christian Church*, Vol. 8, §92).

Calvin's views on total depravity and irresistible grace mirror Augustine's anti-Pelagian writings, especially *On the Spirit and the Letter* and *On the Predestination of the Saints*. Alister McGrath summarizes this dependence: "Calvin's theology may be regarded as a systematic restatement of Augustine's soteriology" (*Reformation Thought: An Introduction*, 2012, 149).

In short, Calvin's theology was not an independent creation but rather a continuation and refinement of Augustine's doctrines. Most likely this was accomplished with the correct intention of returning the Church to its ancient biblical moorings, but he was deceived into thinking Augustine's later theology was an expression of the ancient Church's beliefs. His Reformed system stands as, "It was Augustine who gave us the Reformation. For the Reformation, revived Augustinianism, was just the ultimate triumph of Augustine's doctrine of grace" (Warfield, *Calvin and Augustine*, 33).

Calvin was a good enough scholar and had access to sufficient early Church materials to know something was amiss, and he struggled to reconcile their writings with what he thought they believed through Augustine. Calvin noticed the early Church defended Free Will, but he decided to interpret that through the Augustinian lens. He wrote, "As to the fathers, if their authority weighs with us, they have the term [*free will]* constantly in their mouths; but at the same time they show what kind of freedom man possesses. For Augustine everywhere speaks against it, explaining that free will is enslaved by sin"[42] and "The Latin Fathers have always maintained that man is possessed of free will, as if man stood as yet upright, and had not fallen from his original integrity." [43] Thus Calvin noticed the early writers believed in free will and not in Augustine's original sin (inherited through sexual activity of the parents), but he decided to reinterpret the entire Christian consensus of 400 years of theology through the lens of determinism because he was deceived into believing Augustine's beliefs were in concert with early Christianity.

Calvin saw himself as using Augustinian doctrine to prune the excesses of medieval Catholicism—removing human merit, penance, and priestly mediation. He promoted the Reformation's true battle cry of the five *"solas"*: grace alone, faith alone, Scripture alone, Christ alone, for God's glory alone. But in pulling out Rome's roots of synergism in salvation, he also uprooted the flower of human freedom.

To the Reformers, Rome's theology had become a tangled thicket—overgrown with indulgences, purgatory, and sacramentalism. They rightly insisted salvation was not earned but given. Yet in reacting so strongly against works-based righteousness, they overcorrected. Where Catholicism emphasized *cooperating* with grace through the sacraments, Calvinism emphasized *incapacity* of the will until regeneration. Saving grace became not an invitation but a compulsion.

---

[42] John Calvin, *Institutes of the Christian Religion*, trans. Henry Beveridge (Edinburgh: Calvin Translation Society, 1845), Vol. 1, Book II, Chap. II, §4, p. 308; also August. Lib. 1 cont. Julian. (Institutes II.2.8)

[43] (*Institutes of the Christian Religion*, trans. Henry Beveridge, Vol. 1 [Edinburgh: Calvin Translation Society, 1845], II.ii.9, p. 313)

Ironically, and unintentionally, both systems obscure God's love. Catholicism does so by institutionalizing it and controlling it by ritual whereas Calvinism obscures the universal scope of God's love

God does not pursue His own glory at the expense of His creatures.

as seen in Scripture by restricting saving grace to an elect chosen before time without any reference to their future activities. Both sought to glorify God, yet in Calvin's system, God's glory became the root motive for everything—to include the damnation of souls. The secondary purpose of glory chocked God's primary purpose of love.

Early Calvinists are frequently seen quoting, "The Lord has made everything for its own purpose, even the wicked for the day of evil" (Proverbs 16:4, NAS). This proverb was not just interpreted as meaning God glorifies Himself both in mercy and in judgment (as He certainly does), but also meaning God made wickedness and evil for His glory. Certainly God can use wickedness to bring Himself glory, but Scripture never says God *does* evil or that He *ordains/predestines* evil—he doesn't even tempt people! (James 1:13). "...God is light, and in Him there is no darkness at all" (1 Jn. 1:5b, NAS).

Would a good God create billions of people for the sole purpose of tormenting them in Hell forever...to prove He is just? God does not pursue His own glory at the expense of His creatures. To create a human being for the purpose of torment in Hell forever is not good, not just, not loving, and certainly not the God of the Bible. Instead, He consistently declares His love for all and His desire to save all and He shares His infinite glory with humanity. His loving nature is the true reason He deserves all glory.

Calvin's Geneva: Marrying Church and State

Calvin adopted most of Augustine's teachings, to include infant baptism and especially to include the doctrines that supported a church having earthly power. In his hometown of Geneva, a council of

Christians was put in charge of civic affairs. Calvin supported and at times directly influences the execution of other Protestants and dissenters for what were considered heretical beliefs, though the legal responsibility always rested with the Genevan civil authorities. Calvin's theological and political influence in Geneva's consistory and council made his approval decisive in several cases, the most famous being the killing of Michael Servetus.

Michael Servetus (1511–1553), a Spanish physician and theologian, denied the Trinity and infant baptism—both considered essential doctrines by Calvinists and Catholics alike. He had previously been condemned by the Catholic Inquisition in France. Fleeing arrest, he unwisely passed through Geneva, where he was recognized and arrested.

Calvin had corresponded with Servetus for years, trying (unsuccessfully) to persuade him to recant. When Servetus appeared in Geneva, Calvin testified against him and supplied writings proving his "heresy". The Genevan Council condemned Servetus for blasphemy and heresy and executed him by burning at the stake on October 27, 1553. Calvin approved the sentence, though he urged a less cruel method (beheading). He later defended the execution by writing:

> *Whoever shall now contend that it is unjust to put heretics and blasphemers to death will knowingly and willingly incur their very guilt. This is not laid down on human authority; it is God who speaks and prescribes a perpetual rule for his Church. It is not in vain that he banishes all those human affections which soften our hearts; that he commands paternal love and all the benevolent feelings between brothers, relations, and friends to cease; in a word, that he almost deprives men of their nature in order that nothing may hinder their holy zeal. Why is so implacable a severity exacted but that we may know that God is defrauded of his honor, unless the piety that is due to him be preferred to all human duties, and that when his*

glory is to be asserted, humanity must be almost obliterated from our memories?[44]

It is important to put this incident and quotation in context. As historian Bruce Gordon explains, "In the sixteenth century there was virtually no conception of religious toleration. Heresy was not a matter of private opinion but a threat to the body politic.[45]" Still, we see a rather overbearing man who claims it is sin not to kill people who believe differently and who seems consumed with zeal so as to repudiate natural human affection.[46] At the very least the episode shows how Reformation determinism and magisterial politics often converged into coercive religion—an inheritance later free-will Protestants would challenge.

While Michael Servetus is the most famous, there were other radical Protestants or moral offenders who faced severe punishment under Calvin's Geneva. Jacques Gruet (1547) was executed for blasphemy and conspiracy against the ministers (Naphy 1994, 118–121). Ameaux, a member of Geneva's upper class, was publicly humiliated in 1546 for calling Calvin a false teacher (Parker 1975, 158–159). Jérôme Bolsec, a former Carmelite, opposed Calvin's doctrine of predestination and in 1551 was imprisoned and banished from his hometown (Bouwsma 1988, 69–70). Overall, there were about forty executions for religious or moral offenses during Calvin's long tenure, which is probably comparable to other surrounding city-states such as Zurich and Bern (Naphy 1994, 122; Benedict 2002, 302–305). Today, Christianity is

---

[44] Philip Schaff, *History of the Christian Church*, vol. 8, §144, "Calvin and Servetus," accessed 31 Oct 2025, https://ccel.org/ccel/schaff/hcc8/hcc8.iv.xvi.xxii.html

[45] Calvin, Yale University Press, 2009, p. 200.

[46] This kind of harsh punishment for dissent is reminiscent of our own age's biggest Christian heresy: Islam. The Islamic God aligns nearly perfectly with determinism. Even the word "Islam" means "submission." In many Islamic countries it is a death sentence to try to convert or to be converted out of Islam. Both belief systems seem to be saying "might makes right" rather than "there is a right and God exemplifies it."

waning not only in these cities, but in the whole country of Switzerland and all of Europe where determinism took hold (Pew Research Center 2018).

Calvin's theology did not distinguish between church and civic enforcement as later Reformed thinkers would. He believed the magistrate had a divine mandate to uphold true religion and suppress blasphemy. In his *Institutes* (Book IV, ch. 20, sec. 9) he wrote, "The duty of the magistrate extends to both tables of the law... he must not only be careful that men breathe, eat, drink, and are maintained in outward peace, but also that idolatry, sacrilege against God's name, blasphemies, and other offenses against religion be suppressed by public authority." Nearly no one in today's USA would desire this level of scrutiny, control, and repression of individualism. However, this was a common assumption of 16th-century Catholics, Lutherans, and Calvinists. As we will see later, history had to await the Free Will Protestants to advocate freedom of religion and freedom of speech.

Martin Luther (1483–1546) and John Calvin (1509–1564) shared belief in election and salvation by grace through faith but diverged in their theological principles and ecclesial visions. Luther maintained only teachings contrary to Scripture should be rejected, allowing historic traditions—such as vestments, liturgical forms, and even episcopal governance—to remain if they served the gospel.[47] Calvin, by contrast, advanced the Regulative Principle of Worship, insisting that nothing should be practiced in the Church unless expressly warranted by Scripture.[48] His followers in Geneva smashed statues, icons, and stained glass in sanctuaries, viewing such imagery as idolatrous remnants of Rome.[49]

---

[47] Justo L. González, The Story of Christianity, Vol. 2, The Reformation to the Present Day (New York: HarperOne, 2010), 27–31.

[48] Alister E. McGrath, Reformation Thought: An Introduction, 4th ed. (Malden, MA: Wiley-Blackwell, 2012), 170–73.

[49] Ibid., 175.

Their political theologies also differed. Luther argued the Church should instruct the conscience of rulers, but that the state alone wielded "the sword", an idea expressed in his 1523 treatise *Temporal Authority: To What Extent It Should Be Obeyed.*[50] Calvin envisioned a theocratic model in which civil magistrates were servants of the Church's moral authority, as exemplified in the Genevan Consistory and his discussion of civil government in *Institutes of the Christian Religion* (Book IV, chapter 20).[51] (See Appendix 2 for a Chart on the historic Development of Calvinism)

The Reformation Divides...and Still Conquers

Ironically, the deepest fissure among Reformers arose over communion—the "sacrament" meant to symbolize Christian unity. The medieval Catholic Church elevated the Eucharist into a priestly rite, teaching transubstantiation: that the bread and wine became the literal body and blood of Christ, even though Jesus Himself called the cup "the fruit of the vine" after identifying it symbolically (Matthew 26:29). The mistake about the bread and wine becoming the actual Jesus somehow finds its roots in accusations of cannibalism made by those who persecuted the early Church, and it is vital to note that the Church Fathers defended themselves without ever even claiming or elaborating "a doctrine of the real presence" [52]

The Church also denied the cup to the laity and weaponized communion by declaring that anyone excluded from its ceremony was bound for Hell (anathema). This instrument of control, called an *interdict*, was used repeatedly against entire kingdoms, with popes

---

[50] Martin Luther, *Temporal Authority: To What Extent It Should Be Obeyed* (1523), in Luther's Works, Vol. 45 (Philadelphia: Fortress Press, 1962), 75–129.

[51] John Calvin, Institutes of the Christian Religion, trans. Henry Beveridge (Peabody, MA: Hendrickson, 2008), IV.20.

[52] Pelikan, *The Emergence of the Catholic Tradition, 28.*

declaring that if a ruler was out of communion, his whole realm was spiritually damned.[53]

Luther opposed transubstantiation yet retained belief in a real presence through consubstantiation, affirming that Christ's body and blood were truly present "in, with, and under" the elements.[54] Calvin rejected both metaphysical explanations, teaching instead a "real spiritual presence" in which believers partake of Christ through faith by the Holy Spirit rather than through the physical substance of bread and wine.[55] Their disagreement, dramatized at the Marburg Colloquy of 1529, ensured the Protestant movement would remain divided.[56]

Europe soon entered a century of upheaval as wars of religion swept the continent. The Protestant Reformation fractured Western Christendom, producing both theological renewal and political turmoil. Catholic monarchies—especially Spain and the Habsburg Empire—defended the old faith, while many northern European princes, particularly within the German states, embraced Protestantism for both religious and political independence. The Catholic Church responded with the Inquisition and the Counter-Reformation, led by

---

[53] *Fourth Lateran Council*, Canon 3, in *Decrees of the Ecumenical Councils*, ed. Norman Tanner (London: Sheed & Ward, 1990), 1:233–35; Roger of Wendover, *Flores Historiarum*, ed. Henry G. Hewlett (London: Rolls Series, 1886), 3:50–51; Walter Ullmann, *The Growth of Papal Government in the Middle Ages* (London: Methuen, 1970), 379–81.

[54] Martin Luther, *The Babylonian Captivity of the Church* (1520), in *Luther's Works*, vol. 36, ed. Jaroslav Pelikan (Philadelphia: Fortress, 1959), 35–36.

[55] John Calvin, *Institutes of the Christian Religion*, 4.17.10–12, trans. Henry Beveridge (Peabody, MA: Hendrickson, 2008), 1409–12.

[56] Roland H. Bainton, *Here I Stand: A Life of Martin Luther* (New York: Abingdon, 1950), 204–06.

the Council of Trent (1545–1563), which sought to address internal abuses while reaffirming traditional doctrine.[57]

The Reformation succeeded in breaking away from a corrupt ecclesiastical system and even provoked moral reform within Catholicism. Yet by embracing Augustinian determinism and dividing over communion, it failed to achieve its ultimate aim: a return to the original Christian faith. A true reformation should "re-form" the Church to its earliest pattern—the New Testament community shaped directly by Jesus and His Apostles. The Reformation will not be complete until Christianity returns to its original core beliefs and practices, free from fatalistic philosophies, heretical innovations, and ambitions for political control.

Rise of the Free Will Reformers

Thankfully, God was not finished with the Reformation. A new generation of believers sought to recover historic Christian beliefs from before Augustine. Their critique not only distinguished them from Calvinism but also inspired many within the Reformed world to rethink their theology and refine modern Protestant thought.

In the generation following Luther and Calvin, the Protestant world became a mosaic of theological camps divided over the nature of grace and human freedom. Luther and Calvin, both shaped by Augustinian theology, emphasized the bondage of the will and divine election. Many of their successors recoiled from doctrines that seemed to make God the author of sin and humanity mere puppets.

Luther's colleague Philipp Melanchthon softened his mentor's determinism. Later, the Calvinist-trained Jacobus Arminius reinterpreted predestination through God's foreknowledge. In England, Thomas Cranmer and John Wesley, reading the early Church

---

[57] Hubert Jedin, *A History of the Council of Trent*, trans. Ernest Graf (London: Thomas Nelson, 1957), 1:13–15.

Fathers, taught a Christianity that championed genuine human freedom. Protestantism thus became a dynamic and diverse movement wrestling not only with the mystery of divine sovereignty and human choice but also with other contested doctrines.[58]

The first major defender of free will was Jacobus Arminius (1560–1609), a Dutch Reformed pastor and professor who initially subscribed to Calvin's theology but came to question its logic in light of Scripture and early Christian teaching. Arminius affirmed humanity's fallen nature and the necessity of grace but argued that grace was prevenient—awakening and enabling faith without coercing it. He taught that God's election was conditional upon foreseen faith, Christ's atonement was universal in scope, and grace, though powerful, could be resisted. His followers, the Remonstrants, summarized their views in five articles (1610), appealing to Scripture and conscience against what they saw as fatalistic theology.[59]

The conflict culminated at the Synod of Dort (1618–1619), convened by the Dutch Reformed Church to settle the controversy. The Synod rejected the Remonstrant articles and articulated five counterpoints defending absolute predestination, limited atonement, and irresistible grace—principles later summarized in English by the acrostic TULIP:

Total Depravity – Humanity is utterly unable to choose God or do good.

Unconditional Election – God elects whom He wills, apart from foreseen faith.

Limited Atonement – Christ died only for the elect; others perish to display divine justice.

---

[58] Alister E. McGrath, *Reformation Thought: An Introduction*, 5th ed. (Oxford: Wiley-Blackwell, 2021), 161–67.

[59] Jacobus Arminius, *Declaration of Sentiments* (1608), in *The Works of James Arminius*, trans. James Nichols (London: Longman, 1825), 1:589–92.

Irresistible Grace – The elect cannot resist God's saving call.

Perseverance of the Saints – The elect will necessarily persevere; once saved, always saved.

Although the acronym itself was coined centuries later, it neatly summarizes Calvinism's theological system. TULIP became the emblem of Augustine's deterministic theology transplanted into Protestant soil.

The Reformation's second century thus witnessed a theological retrenchment: what had begun as a movement to restore biblical faith divided into rival visions of God's sovereignty and human freedom. The tension between divine grace and human choice—between Geneva and Leiden—became the enduring axis of Protestant theology.

Not all Reformers, however, followed Geneva's determinist path. A broad range of Protestant thinkers upheld the Reformation's biblical authority while rejecting or revising Calvin's doctrines of predestination and irresistible grace. Their return to the early Church Fathers inspired a recovery of original Christian doctrine.

The Anabaptists, emerging in the 1520s under leaders such as Conrad Grebel, Balthasar Hubmaier, and Menno Simons, emphasized discipleship, voluntary faith, and believer's baptism—all grounded in genuine freedom of conscience. They were derogatorily called "Anabaptist" meaning "baptize again" since they saw no Scriptural reason nor validity in infant baptism, insisting baptism was a mature choice. They also insisted faith cannot be coerced and true conversion requires personal surrender rather than divine compulsion. This radical defense of spiritual liberty laid early foundations for later Protestant advocacy of religious freedom.[60]

In England, John Wesley (1703–1791) expanded the Arminian vision within the Anglican tradition. Deeply influenced by the pre-Augustinian Fathers and Anglican writers such as Jeremy Taylor and

---

[60] Justo L. González, *The Story of Christianity*, vol. 2: *The Reformation to the Present Day* (New York: HarperOne, 2010), 47–50.

William Law (since Arminius's works were scarce in English), Wesley developed a theology of "responsible grace"—God's prevenient grace restores the human capacity to respond freely to His call. This view returns soteriology to the early Church's synergistic view (human and God cooperate in salvation) but also incorporates the Reformers' strong rejection that anything good can come from fallen nature. It takes God's grace to energize human will so that it can hear God's call, repent, and surrender to God's offer of salvation. Rejecting the Calvinist notion of a predetermined elect, he proclaimed "all may be saved." His followers, the Methodists, spread this hopeful view of grace across Britain and America, emphasizing holiness, sanctification, and evangelism.[61]

Rather than accepting this return to the early Church's teaching, many Protestants resisted and retreated deeper into Calvinism while others developed Compatibilism and other ways of seeing how Calvin's ideas could be believed without blaming God for evil.

In conclusion, this chapter showed Calvinism taught Augustine's deterministic ideas which were not the teaching of the early Church. The only reasonable way to reject this chapter's revelation of the roots of determinism is to be able to show conclusively that the early Church got it wrong—that the Bible teaches something they did not see. If there is any doubt on the matter the natural default should be to side with the early church, as it was taught by the disciples of Apostles, it was purified by persecution, and it fluently spoke the language of the New Testament. The early Church's fairly universal stance against determinism places the burden of proof squarely upon those who claim Scripture teaches what the earliest believers did not.

The next chapter is therefore the most important one in this book—what does scripture say about soteriology? Is there

---

[61] John Wesley, *Sermons on Several Occasions* (London: 1746), "Free Grace"; Randy L. Maddox, *Responsible Grace: John Wesley's Practical Theology* (Nashville: Kingswood Press, 1994), 23–31.

overwhelming evidence for Calvinism or are there good exegetical explanations for the verses that look pro-TULIP? Finally, we will look at many verses that clearly teach against the doctrines of TULIP that are not possible to be reconciled and so Calvinists must declare them mysteries.

PETER A. KERR

Chapter 3: Fertile or Fallow?
Evidence from Scripture

"All Scripture is inspired by God and profitable for teaching, for reproof, for correction, for training in righteousness; that the man of God may be adequate, equipped for every good work" 2 Tim. 3:16-17, NAS.

"Any view of divine sovereignty that implies arbitrariness on the part of the divine will, is not only contrary to scripture, but is revolting to reason, and blasphemous." Rev. Charles Finney, Presbyterian minister, *Lectures on Systematic Theology* (Oberlin, 1846), Lecture 76, "Divine Sovereignty"

All Scripture must be read as a coherent narrative revealing the character of God. Proof-texts detached from their covenantal and literary contexts easily mislead. The aim of this chapter is not to pit isolated verses against each other but to show that, when read canonically, the Bible's portrayal of election and grace harmonizes divine initiative with genuine human response.

Below are the primary proof texts often cited by Calvinists to support the doctrines summarized by TULIP. Each is interpreted here from the Free Will or Synergistic perspective—the position historically held by roughly 96% of all professing Christians worldwide today[62].

---

[62] See end note 9 for a discussion on how this is calculated

This includes the vast majority of believers within Wesleyan and Arminian traditions (such as Methodists, Nazarenes, and Assemblies of God), as well as Molinists, Roman Catholics, Eastern Orthodox, and others who remain in continuity with the classical, pre-Augustinian theology of the early Patristic Church.

This chapter argues that when read in literary, historical, and canonical context, the proof texts used to support Calvinist determinism instead affirm God's universal grace, relational election, and genuine human responsibility. While Calvinism emphasizes unilateral divine determinism, free-will interpreters emphasize divine foreknowledge and universal grace. Sovereignty need not cancel freedom, but rather God's omniscient governance allows truly free creatures to participate in His purposes.

If something seems particularly confusing here the reader may need to return to Chapter One to review the different definitions of key Scriptural words. Readers are also encouraged to have a Bible handy to be able to see these verses in context as misinterpretations most commonly arise from using verses without considering how they fit into the main thrust of the writer's arguments.

NOTE: *Unlike God and His Word, I (the author) am fallible. I have attempted to list the most prominent texts that support a Calvinist framework, as well as clearly delineate both the Calvinist interpretation as well as the free will response. If I misrepresent anything here or missed important Scriptures please email me (see the last pages of this book for my address) and I will consider incorporating your ideas in the next edition.*

Identifying the soil: Explaining Calvinist Proof Texts

Romans 9:15-16 "For He says to Moses, 'I will have mercy on whom I have mercy, and I will have compassion on whom I have compassion.' So then it does not depend on the man who wills or the man who runs, but on God who has mercy" (NAS). [As well as all of Romans 9]

Calvinist Interpretation: Calvinist interpreters traditionally understand this passage to mean God sovereignly determines whom He will save and whom He will harden—entirely apart from any human response. Human volition plays no role in the reception of mercy; it depends solely on God's unilateral decree. From this view, Romans 9 serves as a grand assertion of divine determinism, demonstrating that all events, including salvation and condemnation, unfold according to God's immutable will (Calvin, *Institutes*, III.xxiii.2; Piper 1993, 57–59).

Free-Will Response: Romans 9 is arguably one of the most misinterpreted chapters in the New Testament and so will be discussed here at length. Jaroslav in his tracing of doctrine explains that how we interpret this pericope reveals if we revere the Old Testament or if we have detached from a Jewish understanding to forge ahead with a Reformed view[63].

Romans 9–11 forms a single argument explaining Israel's unbelief in light of God's covenant faithfulness. A careful reading of the context shows Paul is not addressing *individual predestination to salvation* but rather God's sovereign freedom in directing *nations and groups* within redemptive history[64]. His concern is covenantal and historical, not metaphysical or personally deterministic. Paul is explaining why ethnic

---

[63] Jaroslav Pelikan, *The Emergence of the Catholic Tradition (100–600)*, vol. 1 of *The Christian Tradition: A History of the Development of Doctrine* (Chicago: University of Chicago Press, 1971), 23 (and then throughout his volumes).

[64] See N. T. Wright, *Paul and the Faithfulness of God* (2013), and Ben Witherington III, *Paul's Letter to the Romans* (2004).

Israel—though chosen as a nation—largely rejected the Messiah, while Gentiles were now being grafted into the covenant promises. Even the eminent Reformed theologian John Stott frames Romans 9–11 primarily as addressing the problem of Israel's place in redemptive history, seeing election in a national/covenantal context rather than simply as a mechanistic pre-selection of individuals[65].

The "mercy" of which Paul speaks is God's decision to extend His covenant compassion beyond Israel to the Gentiles (Romans 9:23–24). This passage concerns how God orders salvation history, not who is individually saved or damned. When Paul writes that salvation "does not depend on the man who wills or the man who runs," he is rejecting the idea that ethnic privilege, legal observance, or human achievement can secure covenant inclusion. He is not denying the existence of free will but refuting human boasting and pride in works-based righteousness.

Paul clarifies this point: "There is no distinction between Jew and Greek, for the same Lord is Lord of all, abounding in riches for all who call on Him" (Romans 10:12). The message of Romans 9–11 as a whole is that God's gracious initiative drives redemption history, yet human faith remains the condition for participating in His mercy (Romans 9:30–32; 10:9–10).

John Chrysostom (c. 349–407), himself a native Greek speaker and so best able to interpret the passage linguistically, explicitly rejected any deterministic reading of Romans 9:

> *He does not say that it is impossible for one who wills to be saved, but that it is not of him alone. For we need both things—that we should choose, and that God should extend His hand. Therefore, when he says, 'It is not of him that wills,' he is not depriving us of free will, but*

---

[65] Stott, John R. W. *The Message of Romans: God's Good News for the World.* The Bible Speaks Today series. Downers Grove, IL: InterVarsity Press, 1994 (or 2001 revised edition).

> *showing that the greater part belongs to God.* (*Homilies on Romans* 16.2)

Chrysostom interprets Paul's words as a warning against self-reliance, not a denial of human agency. "All depends indeed on God, but not so as to deprive our free will... God draws, but He draws the willing" (*Homily on Romans*).

No potter forms a vessel solely to destroy it

Similarly, Origen of Alexandria (c. 184–253) reads Romans 9 through the lens of divine foreknowledge, not fatalism:

> *God's mercy is given to those whom He knows will turn to Him... Pharaoh's hardening was not caused by God's will but by Pharaoh's own obstinacy, which God foreknew and used to manifest His power.* (*Commentary on Romans* 7.13–16)

For both Origen and Chrysostom, divine sovereignty and human freedom coexist harmoniously. God initiates grace, but man must freely cooperate with it. Paul's examples—Isaac and Ishmael, Jacob and Esau, Pharaoh—illustrate that God's redemptive purposes are not bound to lineage or merit but to His gracious plan. These cases from Israel's past never imply individuals were eternally predestined to salvation or damnation. Pharaoh's hardening, for instance, demonstrates divine patience: Pharaoh hardened his own heart multiple times before God confirmed that condition with judicial hardening (Exodus 7–9[66]). God *used* Pharaoh's rebellion but did not *cause* it.

Paul's central claim in Romans 9 is that faith—not ancestry or law-keeping—defines who belongs to God's people: "They are not all Israel who are descended from Israel" (Romans 9:6). The potter-and-clay metaphor (Romans 9:20–21) underscores God's sovereign right to shape His redemptive story, not His supposed pleasure in creating some for destruction. No potter forms a vessel solely to destroy it;

---

[66] Pharaoh's hardening is judicial, not creative; God confirms the condition Pharaoh freely chose (Exod 8:15, 32; 9:34)

rather, he fashions each for a purpose but may discard what becomes defiled (Jeremiah 18:1–10).

When the entire argument is taken together, Romans 9 reveals not God's *narrowing* of election to a few, but His *broadening* of mercy to include the Gentiles. God is free to save whomever He wills; none can question His right to extend compassion to those once considered outsiders. "He has mercy on whom He wills" (Romans 9:18) does not mean He condemns the rest for being born—it means He is sovereignly gracious toward all who believe. **The conclusion of the chapter (Romans 9:30–33) confirms this: Paul contrasts "righteousness by faith" with "righteousness by law," he does not even mention some sort of argument between divine decree and human helplessness that Calvinists read into the text.**

Thus Romans 9 does not teach individual predestination to salvation or damnation. It defends God's freedom to redefine His covenant community through faith in Christ—inviting both Jew and Gentile alike into His mercy. Paul's argument is corporate and historical. God's freedom in mercy opens the covenant to Gentiles; His justice hardens only the self-hardened. The passage proclaims God's inclusive plan, not a decree of exclusion.[67]

Romans 9:13 "Just as it is written, Jacob I loved, but Esau I hated". (NAS)

Calvinist Interpretation: God hated Esau and loved Jacob before they were even created, even when it does not make sense to us. God chose Jacob (his name means "heel grabber" or "deceiver" in Hebrew) over his older brother who was the rightful receiver of his father's inheritance.

---

[67] For a more detailed analysis of all three chapters see Ben Witherington III, *Paul's Letter to the Romans: A Socio-Rhetorical Commentary* (for Romans 9–11).

Free-Will Response: First, any Jewish reader would know that Jacob is the progenitor of Israel and that he honored his father and sought the inheritance (if in an unethical way). Culturally Esau is the progenitor of the Edomites who frequently teamed up with Israel's enemies. Paul's audience would understand Esau's rejection of his father's blessing for a bowl of stew and hairy animalistic nature conclusively makes him the bad character not the good one in the story.

Second, Paul's readers would know he is quoting Malachi 1:2–3, where God says: "I have loved Jacob; but I have hated Esau, and I have made his mountains a desolation and appointed his inheritance for the jackals of the wilderness." In its original context, this refers not to the individual brothers Jacob and Esau, but to their descendants— Israel and Edom—long after their deaths. God's "love" for Jacob means He chose Israel as the covenant nation. His "hatred" for Esau means He *did not* choose Edom for that same redemptive purpose. Even Reformed theologian Thomas Schreiner writes, "Neither as they occur in Genesis nor as they are used by Paul do these words [e.g., 'Jacob I loved, but Esau I hated'] refer to the eternal destinies either of the two persons or of the individual members of the nations sprung from them; the reference is rather to the mutual relations of the two nations in history."[68] It is a statement of divine election for service, not of eternal salvation or emotional animosity.

In Hebrew idiom, *love* and *hate* often function as comparative hyperbole—strong, polar words used to express preference, priority, or covenantal favor, not literal affection or animus. Examples include:

Genesis 29:30–31 — Jacob "loved Rachel more than Leah," yet the text then says, "When the LORD saw that Leah was *hated* (Heb. *śānēʾ*), He opened her womb." Leah wasn't literally despised; she was *less loved* or *unpreferred.*

---

[68] Schreiner, Thomas R., *Does Romans 9 Teach Individual Election unto Salvation? Some Exegetical and Theological Reflections*, JETS 36/1 (1993): 25-40.

Deuteronomy 21:15–17 — A man has two wives, one "loved" and one "hated." Again, this means *favored* versus *unfavored*, not emotional hatred.

Luke 14:26 — Jesus says, "If anyone comes to Me and does not *hate* his father and mother... he cannot be My disciple." Christ is not commanding literal hatred of our parents but emphasizing supreme loyalty—to love Him *more than* family.

In each case, "hate" is a figure of speech for "love less." This Hebraic style uses extremes to sharpen contrast and make the choice unmistakable.

When Paul cites Malachi in Romans 9:13, his goal is to illustrate God's sovereign freedom to choose the line through which the Messiah would come, not to define individual salvation. Jacob and Esau serve as representative heads of nations (Israel and Edom). God's "love" of Jacob means choosing him for covenantal blessing; His "hate" of Esau means passing him over for that role. The focus is on vocation, not damnation. Paul's Jewish audience would have recognized this rhetorical contrast immediately, understanding that the idiom expressed divine preference for a covenant purpose, not eternal rejection of a soul. Paul's citation of Malachi 1:2–3 reinforces divine freedom in history, not fatalistic selection of souls.

Ephesians 1:4–5 "He chose us in Him before the foundation of the world... He predestined us to adoption as sons."

Calvinist reading: God unconditionally predestined certain individuals for salvation before the foundation of the world.

Free-will response: Paul's focus is not on *who* was chosen but on *how* the covenant people are constituted. God's election is corporate— "in Christ" the Church was chosen[69]. (Greek: *eklexato hēmas en autō*— plural, so "He chose **us** in Him"). God predestines the *class* of those

---

[69] See William Klein, *The New Chosen People* (2016).

"in Christ" to be holy and adopted, not specific individuals. Everywhere "elect" is used in the Bible it is plural and refers to the Church of believers and never to a specially-chosen individual. This is God's eternal plan that all who freely unite with Christ are destined for glorification. This is clarified in verse 13 that says we are only sealed after we believe ("having believed, you were sealed"). This also means regeneration, the infilling of the Spirit, happens *after* not before repentance (See also Rom. 5:1; Luke 13:3; 2 Peter 2:3; Acts 16:31; Rom. 3:24-25; John 3:6-7; Titus 3:5-7 etc.).

John 6:44 "No one can come to Me unless the Father who sent Me draws him."

Calvinist reading: No one can come to Christ unless irresistibly drawn by the Father. God ordained from eternity who will be His.

Free-will response: We completely affirm this sentence in its most plain meaning. It never says "irresistible" but rather says it is God who acts first by calling us to repentance and empowering our ability to repent through prevenient grace. Prevenient grace is the Spirit's universal work awakening the human will to respond, without compelling it. The Greek *helkō* ("draw") can mean "attract" or even the softer "woo," and is the same word used in John 12:32 that says, "I will draw all men to Myself.[70] " God draws universally through grace and revelation, empowering the will to choose to repent. This draw is not irresistible because God cannot force the will and still say we have a will. Put in other terms, repentance must be a choice or else it is not repentance.

To repent is not simply to say you are sorry you got caught and you hope not to be punished—it involves a deep acknowledgment of fault, a desire that you had not done the thing you now find onerous, and a willful dedication to resist temptation in that area in the future.

---

[70] See Leon Morris, *The Gospel According to John* (NICNT); BDAG 3 ed., 472

Salvation involves loving God more than anything else, and love cannot be forced. Compelled love is not love. The human will may respond or resist God's calling. "You men who are stiff-necked and uncircumcised in heart and ears are always resisting the Holy Spirit; you are doing just as your fathers did" (Acts 7:51, NAS).

John 10:26-28 "You do not believe because you are not of My sheep."

Calvinist reading: Only the predestined "sheep" can hear and believe; others cannot.

Free-will response: Jesus speaks to those hardened by unbelief, not excluded by decree. The "sheep" are those who respond to His voice (v.27). Being a sheep results *from* hearing and believing, not the reverse. "But as many as received Him, to them He gave the right to become children of God, *even* to those who believe in His name," (John 1:12, NAS).

Acts 13:48 "As many as were appointed to eternal life believed."

Calvinist reading: You must be appointed to have eternal life, so that appointment is called "election" and happens before time. Belief comes after appointment.

Free-will response: The participle *tetagmenoi* translated here "were appointed to" can mean "disposed" or "set toward" eternal life, describing receptive hearts rather than divine decree (F. F. Bruce, *The Acts of the Apostles*, 269). Many lexicons (e.g., BDAG) and early commentators (Theophylact, Erasmus) favor "inclined" rather than "ordained" or "appointed." Furthermore, a good judge does not "appoint" without good cause, and that cause was God's foreknowledge that they would repent.

Romans 8:29-30 "For whom He foreknew, He also predestined to become conformed to the image of His Son, that He might be the first-born among many brethren; and whom He predestined, these He also called; and whom He called, these He also justified; and whom He justified, these He also glorified. (Rom. 8:30 NAS)

Calvinist reading: This is the "golden chain" of causation. It goes from irresistible call to justification to glorification and implies fixed, unbreakable election.

Free-will response: This "chain" starts with Gods' foreknowledge. The Greek word here is *"proegnō"* which means a *relational* foreknowledge[71]—God's prior knowing of those who repent, accept His grace, and will love Him (see also 1 Pet 1:2). Thus yes, those He knew from the beginning, who are the reason He created (why create if no one will repent?), are called (and empowered by grace to repent), justified, and glorified. God's predestining purpose is to conform believers to Christ's image, not to exclude some people who have no chance to repent. The gospel is repeatedly offered to <u>all humanity</u> as in Acts 17:30, "Therefore having overlooked the times of ignorance, God is now declaring to men that all everywhere should repent" (NAS).

Proverbs 16:4 "The LORD has made everything for its purpose, even the wicked for the day of trouble."

Calvinist reading: God made the wicked as well as the good, and all are created/ordained by Him for His glory.

Free-will response: This refers to God's ordering of moral consequence, not creation *of* wickedness. God uses evil choices for His justice but does not decree/ordain them. In James 1:13 we see God emphatically does not even TEMPT people. If He doesn't do that, then He certainly doesn't do evil or make people evil without any trace

---

[71] Douglas Moo, *The Epistle to the Romans*, NICNT (2018), on *proegnō*.

of His good image in them and thus

A sovereign God can even decide also the possibility of choosing good
to limit the expression of His instead. He allows evil but redeems
sovereignty in this world to get the it to His glory. The cross was the
loving family He wants in the next. ultimate expression of evil and the

ultimate expression of loving redemption. If nothing goes wrong because all is as God ordains it then the entire idea of "redemption" is a farce. However, God is so great He can turn our sin into His glory and use the wickedness He allows and even people who do evil to work for good for those who are called and who love him (see Rom. 8:28).

Isaiah 46:10 "My purpose will be established, and I will accomplish all My good pleasure."

Calvinist reading: God declares He gets exactly what He wants accomplished. This suggests He ordains all things.

Free-will response: It is true that God gets exactly what He wants—but what He wants is humans with Free Will so they can learn to love. A sovereign God can even decide to limit the expression of His sovereignty in this world to get the loving family He wants in the next. God's sovereignty is not expressed here by coercive determinism but rather His redemptive plan includes genuine human choice, as seen in Isaiah's broader theme of Israel's calling and response (Isa 48:18). God frequently gives humans the choice to obey or not to obey.

The Calvinist God is less glorious not more so than the God believed by the early Church. He would be uncapable of giving up His micro-management of the world and He must be made blind to His foreknowledge at the point of "election." Furthermore, Calvinism frequently shirks all challenges as to "why" by saying because it was "God's good pleasure." How do Calvinists know exactly what God's good pleasure is? A coerced will cannot love and so is of lesser value. My child would far more desire a real puppy with limited free will than a perfect robot puppy that only did as it was told. God's good pleasure is to give humans free choice that we may learn how to love and thus give Him even more glory and pleasure.

Romans 11:7 "What then? That which Israel is seeking for, it has not obtained, but those who were chosen obtained it, and the rest were hardened"

Calvinist reading: "The elect obtained it, but the rest were hardened" means God destined both the chosen to salvation and those chosen to perdition. No one can resist God's action "hardening" a heart.

Free-will response: All of Israel was not saved because many thought they were saved by ethnicity or works rather than by faith. This is consistently Paul's point in Romans. Those who were chosen obtained salvation—they were the ones God saw in eternity who would repent. The hardening that is mentioned is judicial—God gives people over to their own unbelief (Rom 1:24). It is conditional (they hardened their hearts first). It is not arbitrary or related to being "unelected" before time. Rom 11:23 proves this as it reads, "If they do not continue in unbelief, they will be grafted in again."

2 Timothy 1:9 "Who has saved us… not according to our works, but according to His own purpose and grace which was granted us in Christ Jesus from all eternity."

Calvinist reading: God gives us grace and works His purpose that was decided from all eternity. People are not saved by works or self-generated faith but only by God's election.

Free-will response: Grace was eternally purposed *in Christ*, not individually dispensed before existence. God foreordained the gracious *means* of salvation, not the fixed identity of recipients. Election is a doctrine that pertains to the whole Church as a community—all those who repent and surrender to God's prevenient (universal) grace are part of the elect. Paul is declaring that we are not saved by our own works but by God's grace, and it was God's purpose from eternity to send Christ Jesus to save us.

Philippians 2:13 "for It is God who works in you both to will and to work for His good pleasure."

Calvinist reading: God causes our will and does all the work for the sake of His good pleasure.

Free-will response: Paul speaks to believers cooperating with grace, not being puppets. God energizes willing hearts. The exhortation "...work out your salvation with fear and trembling;" (Phil. 2:12 NAS) immediately preceding this verse clearly presupposes voluntary participation. Using this verse out of context seems to risk misrepresentation.

1 Peter 2:8 "They stumble because they are disobedient to the word, and to this doom they were also appointed."

Calvinist reading: People are appointed to salvation, or as the verse states, to be doomed.

Free-will response: The appointment concerns consequence, not cause. Those who reject Christ are *appointed* to stumble because of their disobedience—not disobedient because appointed.

Genesis 50:20 "You meant evil against me, but God meant it for good."

Calvinist reading: Even when we experience evil we can be confident that God caused it for good.

Free-will response: God's foreknowledge allowed Him to *use* evil for good, not *cause* it. Divine providence can redeem human evil without negating moral agency—what C. S. Lewis called a chessmaster using the free moves of others.[72]

Matthew 11:27 "No one knows the Father except the Son, and anyone to whom the Son chooses to reveal Him."

Calvinist reading: God chooses some to salvation—people do not choose God. Only the power of Christ can overcome original sin and reveal God to the sinful hearts of men.

Free-will response: Jesus reveals the Father to those who humbly receive Him. Once again it is context that matters. The following verses say, "Come to Me, all who are weary and heavy-laden, and I will give you rest. Take My yoke upon you, and learn from Me, for I am gentle and humble in heart; and you shall find rest for your souls" (Matt. 11:28-29, NAS). Obviously this is an invitation – an appeal -- to freely choose Christ. If we do, Jesus will reveal Him. The choice is moral and reciprocal: divine initiative meets human receptivity.

Revelation 13:8 "And all who dwell on the earth will worship him, everyone whose name has not been written from the foundation of the world in the book of life of the Lamb who has been slain. (Rev. 13:8 NAS)

Calvinist reading: If your name is written in the book of life it cannot be erased. God chooses who will be saved from the foundation of the world.

Free-will response: Greek syntax allows the clause "from the foundation of the world" to modify "the Lamb slain," not "written.[73]"

---

[72] In *The Problem of Pain*, Lewis uses a chess-board analogy: "In a game of chess you can make certain arbitrary concessions … But if you conceded everything that at any moment happened to suit him … then you could not have a game at all."

[73] Aune, *Revelation 6–16*, WBC 52B, 1998, p. 738.

Thus, it refers to Christ's eternal redemptive plan, not pre-temporal election of individuals. Furthermore, we know you can get "blotted out" or "erased" from the Book of Life as Rev. 3:5 says, "He who overcomes shall thus be clothed in white garments; and I will not erase his name from the book of life, and I will confess his name before My Father, and before His angels" (NAS). This is just one of many warnings that Christians must persevere (rather than making perseverance a granted gift).

John 6:37 "All that the Father gives Me will come to Me, and the one who comes to Me I will certainly not cast out."

Calvinist use: The Father has already chosen a specific group of people ("all that the Father gives Me") who will infallibly come to Christ—proof of unconditional election and irresistible grace.

Free-will reply: The giving here refers to believers—those who respond in faith. God "gives" to Christ *those who believe* (v. 40: "everyone who believes in Him will have eternal life"). The Father "gives" believers because they willingly receive the Son (see also John 17:6-8).

John 17:2, 6, 9 "You gave Him authority over all flesh, that to all whom You have given Him, He may give eternal life... I have manifested Your name to the men whom You gave Me out of the world."

Calvinist use: "Given" means there is a fixed number of elect people entrusted by the Father to the Son. These were chosen before time.

Free-will reply: The "given" are those who responded to God's call as just prior to this we read "They have kept Your word... they have believed" (vv. 6–8). God "gives" to the Son all who freely believe His word (cf. John 6:37, 40). The giving is relational, not deterministic.

John 15:16 "You did not choose Me but I chose you, and appointed you that you would go and bear fruit."

Calvinist use: Humans cannot choose God—God chooses us. This is a statement showing unconditional election.

Free-will reply: The context is the apostles' commissioning, not eternal predestination. Jesus chose them *for service* and fruitfulness, not for exclusive salvation. Just prior in John 15:8 we are told the disciples give God glory and prove they are His disciples by bearing much fruit. Fruit is works not salvation.

John 3:3-8 "Unless one is born again he cannot see the kingdom of God... The wind blows where it wishes... so is everyone who is born of the Spirit."

Calvinist use: This teaches monergism—God sovereignly regenerates without human cooperation. He chooses to select whom He will just like the wind blows where it will.

Free-will reply: The text describes the *necessity* of regeneration, not the *mode*. Later verses (3:14–18) clearly place the condition on belief—"whoever believes in Him shall not perish." The Spirit's work is mysterious and powerful, but not irresistible. We are born of the Spirit when God's grace allows us to choose repentance and so we are born again.

John 8:47 "He who is of God hears the words of God; for this reason you do not hear them, because you are not of God."

Calvinist use: This shows only the elect can understand God's words. Those "of God" are the elect, and those who are not elect cannot hear and have the gift of faith.

Free-will reply: "Of God" means those who align themselves with God's truth and moral will. Jesus rebukes His listener's resistance, not their destiny. Seeing predestination here is eisegesis—reading into Scripture a former conviction. The listeners are "not of God" because of hardened unbelief. Just prior in John 5:40 we see, "You are unwilling to come to Me". Human will resists God and so they cannot hear Him.

John 1:12-13 "But as many as received Him, to them He gave the right to become children of God... who were born, not of blood nor of the will of the flesh nor of the will of man, but of God."

Calvinist use: Emphasizes that new birth is solely God's work, not human decision.

Free-will reply: The verse distinguishes *natural* will or heritage from *spiritual* rebirth, not from free response. The "receiving" in verse 12 precedes regeneration—human faith is the condition for divine adoption. Because people repented, God's power was applied and they were born of God.

Ps. 51:5 "Behold, I was brought forth in iniquity, And in sin my mother conceived me."

Calvinist use: We are born with original sin—already deserving of Hell from the womb.

Free-will reply: Neither the Jews nor the early Christians interpreted this passage as meaning babies go to Hell or that humans are born with sin rather than being born with a nature that will sin. First, making doctrine out of a single Psalm is foolhardy and poor exegesis. This is how the Church justified persecuting Galileo due to Psalm 93:1 which states, "the world is firmly established, it cannot be moved". Psalm 51 is filled with hyperbole as David expresses his anguish. David was not physically harmed yet he writes a few verses later "Make me to hear joy and gladness, Let the bones which Thou hast broken rejoice" (Ps. 51:8, NAS). It seems the Holy Spirit knew this verse would be violently plucked from its intended meaning, as we see in verse 13 a statement that sounds like people will not come to salvation unless David teaches them: "*Then* I will teach transgressors Thy ways, And sinners will be converted to Thee" (Ps. 51:13, NAS).

That should suffice, but if people want another reason for David's phrasing, it could be referring to how birth makes a mother unclean in Jewish law—we are all born through blood and thus unclean.

Summary on Calvinism

To summarize, thinkers like John Calvin, Jonathan Edwards, and John Piper (first, second and third John!) emphasize our salvation cannot depend on fickle human will. That's a deep truth, but also essentially a straw-man argument because Free Will theologians like Wesley agree divine grace must always precede and empower human response. Calvinists also appeal to passages like Romans 9, Ephesians 1, and John 6 to show God's will ultimately prevails in history, which again was never in dispute.

The most logical way to interpret Scripture is to do so in context of the immediate passages as well as of the larger picture it paints of God's character. **God is loving (1 John 4:8), God does not play favorites (Acts 10:34–35; Romans 2:11), God wants all to be saved (1 Timothy 2:3–4), God takes no pleasure in the death of the wicked (Ezekiel 33:11), God loves children (Matthew 19:14), and God is patient, not wanting any to perish (2 Peter 3:9).** These very clear and plain declarations should color our interpretation of more difficult or nebulous passages rather than being overlooked in favor of a systematized doctrine invented in the fifth century.

At the very least, the above demonstrates the most prominent Bible verses Calvinists use to justify TULIP, though internally coherent, rely on decontextualized readings that do not reflect the broader biblical witness. There are good responses to every verse that is interpreted as evidencing Calvinism. While the Calvinist system possesses an admirable internal logic that can be consistently applied and so it appeals to simplistic interpretations, it often pulls Scripture out of context and even warps definitions to fit a preconceived system.

The system's coherence also comes at a steep cost that no theologian should wish to pay. It tends to define sovereignty in philosophical rather than biblical terms (as exhaustive control rather than as perfect kingship). The result is that divine love, human accountability, and the sincerity of God's invitations in Scripture must be explained as mysteries or refuted by the "two parallel truths" of Compatibilism that we'll examine in Chapter 4.

Bible Verses Refuting TULIP and Supporting Free Will

The following verses evidence Free Will theology, and I only selected the top ten verses to oppose each of the points of TULIP because there are simply far too many to list here. It is freely (pun intended) admitted that this is a tad biased since there is no Calvinist refutation of these verses, but I am not predisposed (another pun intended!) nor qualified to write a refutation I do not believe.

In my experience, the vast majority of these verses just elicit from Calvinists some kind of comment about "it is a mystery" or a diatribe about God having two wills that are unified in Him but opposite when we consider them (more about that in Chapter 4). In fact, even though the entire New Testament is strewn with admonishments to "seek, and you will find" (Matthew 7:7), to "knock, and it will be opened to you" (Luke 11:9), and with the promise that "the Spirit of truth will guide you into all the truth" (John 16:13), Calvinists insist upon many mysteries and unknowns. As we will see later, Calvin himself everywhere declares it "immoral" and "unlawful" to question God's design described by TULIP. The more a theology must admit it has no explanations of Bible verses and rational facts, the more that theology needs a real reformation.

Before the ten verses, for each point of TULIP I added a brief case that in my mind is irrefutable and by itself conclusive on the matter. To give some context up front for people more familiar with Calvinist doctrine, here is what is being evidenced by the following verses:

Moving TULIP Back to Pre-Augustinian Consensus

Total Depravity → Human inability to follow God is healed by prevenient grace as God draws all people to Himself and/or as we retain some of the image of God. People are "dead in their sin" because they are separated from God who is Life, not because they cannot choose. They still can and do make choices, and it is a choice to repent and believe. God is the one who initiates salvation by loving all and giving His grace to all. Some people then make a choice to believe and surrender to God's call. All will sin but no one is condemned or guilty of another man's sin (Adam's) at birth—one becomes sinful when one sins.

Unconditional Election → God's election is corporate and relational. The "elect" is another way to say "Church" before there really was one (in the council of eternity or even in ca. AD 45-90 when the Bible is written). The word "elect" is always plural in the Bible and refers to those God foreknew would surrender to Him (after being empowered by prevenient grace). Salvation is initiated and empowered by God but also requires human surrender (which is more glorifying to God than God overcoming the will). Peering through eternity God indeed knew some people would be transformed by His love, making the elect (His Church) the reason for creation.

Limited Atonement → Christ's atonement is universal in scope, conditional in application. God loves the whole world, Jesus died once and for all, and the invitation to salvation is for all who will repent and believe. However, salvation is not universal because some will reject God by deciding to not repent and not believe. They are therefore morally responsible for their disobedience rather than simply predetermined to disbelieve and go to Hell.

Irresistible Grace → Grace persuades, never coerces. Satan and the demons are about coercion and possession—a God of love invites, encourages, leads, and woos the heart. Salvation is about loving God more than anything else—to include oneself. Since it involves love, saving grace cannot be coercive but must always be a choice.

Perseverance → Salvation is relational and participatory, not automatic. If we are unfaithful He remains faithful because it is a covenant not a contract. No external force can tear us away from God's love. However, we are repeatedly admonished to stay the course and not shipwreck our faith, and Hebrews 6 suggests while we do not lose our salvation we can (as an act of our own will) throw it away/give back the gift of salvation.

T — Total Depravity (or "Total Inability")

Conclusive Argument: Gen. 1:26–27 (NAS) "Then God said, 'Let Us make man in Our image, according to Our likeness'... So God created man in His own image, in the image of God He created him; male and female He created them" and later, "Whoever sheds man's blood, by man his blood shall be shed, for in the image of God He made man" (**Gen. 9:6**, NAS).

This is particularly striking because it occurs after the Fall and after the Flood, yet God still affirms that humankind *is* made in His image. The imago Dei was not destroyed by sin, only marred. If humanity were "totally depraved," bearing no vestige of divine image or moral capacity, God's appeal to that image as the basis for justice and dignity would be incoherent. This continuity of the divine image implies:

- Humanity retains moral awareness and responsibility.
- The conscience and will, though weakened, remain responsive to God's call.
- The human person is capable of repentance, love, and genuine moral choice.

Furthermore, **Romans 2:14–15** says: "For when Gentiles who do not have the Law do instinctively the things of the Law, these, not having the Law, are a law to themselves, in that they show the work of the Law written in their hearts, their conscience bearing witness and their thoughts alternately accusing or else defending them" (NAS). Paul explicitly teaches even "unregenerate" Gentiles—those without

Scripture, covenant, or saving faith—can still "do instinctively the things of the Law." If there were no ability to obey then God's commands to repent and believe would mock our helplessness rather than be a true invitation from a heart of love.

Genesis 4:7 "If you do well, will not your countenance be lifted up? And if you do not do well, sin is crouching at the door; and its desire is for you, but you must master it."
Interpretation: God directly appeals to Cain's moral agency. Even after the Fall, humans are capable of responding to God's exhortation to do right, showing moral responsibility remains intact.

Deuteronomy 30:19 "I call heaven and earth to witness against you today, that I have set before you life and death, the blessing and the curse. So choose life in order that you may live, you and your descendants."
Interpretation: God commands human choice. This makes no sense if humanity is incapable of choosing the good. The imperative "choose life" assumes the power to respond.

Joshua 24:15 "Choose for yourselves today whom you will serve… but as for me and my house, we will serve the Lord."
Interpretation: Joshua invites a real decision. The people are capable of turning either way—proof that divine appeal engages free moral agency.

Isaiah 1:18 "Come now, and let us reason together," says the Lord, "Though your sins are as scarlet, they will be as white as snow."
Interpretation: God invites sinners to rational dialogue and repentance, not coercion. This assumes people retain the capacity to hear and respond.

John 1:9 "There was the true Light which, coming into the world, enlightens every person."
Interpretation: Christ enlightens *every person*. Universal prevenient light means all are drawn to truth and can respond to grace.

John 12:32 "And I, if I am lifted up from the earth, will draw all people to Myself."
Interpretation: The cross draws all people, not just the elect. The drawing is persuasive, not irresistible. If it were irresistible we would see everyone saved, and that is not congruent with biblical teaching.

Acts 17:30 "God is now declaring to men that all people everywhere should repent."
Interpretation: God calls *all* to repent. His universal call would be irrational if some humans lacked the ability to respond.

Titus 2:11 "For the grace of God has appeared, bringing salvation to all people."
Interpretation: Grace is universally extended. God's enabling grace awakens the will; it is not reserved only for the elect.

Revelation 3:20 "Behold, I stand at the door and knock; if anyone hears My voice and opens the door, I will come in to him."
Interpretation: The invitation is conditional—"if anyone." Christ knocks; humanity must open. God's approach respects human will. It should be noted this is listed last because it was certainly written to believers and so can be dismissed if you say only believers can open the door or if you say this is not about salvation but simply about God's self-revelation.

U – Unconditional Election

Conclusive Argument: 1□ Timothy 2:3-4 (NAS) "This is good and acceptable in the sight of God our Savior, who desires all people to be saved and to come to the knowledge of the truth."

God desires "all people" to be saved—not just a select, predetermined few. If election were truly "unconditional" (in the strongest sense: God elects some without regard for any human response) then this universal "desire" would appear to be mere rhetoric, since many would still perish according to unconditional-election logic. Instead, the verse affirms human response ("to come to the knowledge of the truth") is part of God's design. That implies election is not entirely without condition or outside the arena of human response. This verse supports a view of election that is conditioned on faith or response (or at least accountable human hearing/knowledge), rather than a purely unconditional, sovereign choice with no human enabling or condition. The initiative is God's because He "desires all people to be saved" but humans must "come". R.C. Sproul and others try to discount this by saying this is God's declared will which differs from His secret will, but all that really does is make God seem like a two-faced hypocrite rather than a loving Heavenly Father (as explained in Chapter 4).

Ephesians 1:4 "He chose us in Him before the foundation of the world, that we would be holy and blameless before Him."
Interpretation: Election is corporate and "in Christ." God predetermined that those who believe in Christ would become holy, not that certain individuals would believe.

1 Peter 1:1–2 "To those who are chosen according to the foreknowledge of God the Father, by the sanctifying work of the Spirit."
Interpretation: Election is rooted in foreknowledge—God's

omniscient awareness of those who would freely believe, not arbitrary selection.

Romans 8:29 "For those whom He foreknew, He also predestined to become conformed to the image of His Son."
Interpretation: God's predestination flows from foreknowledge; it does not cause faith but affirms those who freely respond to His call. Most of the time predestination is used it has the context of God's foreknowledge. It is disingenuous to discount God's foreknowledge in any discussion of predestination.

Matthew 22:14 "For many are called, but few are chosen."
Interpretation: The "chosen" are those who respond rightly to the universal call. God's calling and human acceptance precede being chosen. Why would God call people He predestined to ignore His calling? Why call if people are just chosen and need not respond? In summary, why would God "call" at all if He already forced some to respond and others to reject Him.

In context this is extremely clear as this verse summarizes the parable of the king inviting all people to a wedding feast. "Then he said to his slaves, 'The wedding is ready, but those who were invited were not worthy. Go therefore to the main highways, and as many as you find *there*, invite to the wedding feast." (Matt. 22:8-9, NAS). The initial invitation was to Israel, but they were not worthy because they did not rely on faith to be saved. The servants then invite "both evil and good" (Matt. 22:10, NAS), conclusively refuting both limited atonement or unconditional election. All were invited but guests had to accept the invitation and even dress appropriately in Christ's righteousness to stay at the wedding.

Acts 10:34–35 "I most certainly understand now that God is not one to show partiality, but in every nation the one who fears Him and does what is right is welcome to Him."

Interpretation: Election is impartial, moral, and conditional upon faith. God welcomes all who fear and respond to Him.

2 Peter 1:10 "Be all the more diligent to make certain about His calling and choosing you."
Interpretation: Election can be confirmed—or lost—through perseverance, showing it is relational, not fixed by decree. Augustine claimed "perseverance" is a gift not given to all, but it makes much more sense to see it as something we are repeatedly admonished to choose.

Scripture consistently exhorts believers to remain steadfast in faith: "If indeed you continue in the faith firmly established and steadfast, and not moved away from the hope of the gospel" (Colossians 1:23); "For we have become partakers of Christ, if we hold fast the beginning of our assurance firm until the end" (Hebrews 3:14); "The one who endures to the end, he shall be saved" (Matthew 24:13); "Work out your salvation with fear and trembling" (Philippians 2:12); and "Keep yourselves in the love of God" (Jude 21). These repeated appeals to human perseverance affirm that salvation is a dynamic relationship of faithfulness, not a fixed status decreed apart from our response.

John 3:15-18 "that whoever believes may in Him have eternal life. For God so loved the world, that He gave His only begotten Son, that whoever believes in Him should not perish, but have eternal life. For God did not send the Son into the world to judge the world, but that the world should be saved through Him. He who believes in Him is not judged; he who does not believe has been judged already, because he has not believed in the name of the only begotten Son of God" (NAS).
Interpretation: Faith/belief is the condition of salvation, not an effect of secret election. The "whoever" eliminates exclusivity. People are not chosen to salvation, they are all invited to believe and if they

do they are part of the elect Church for whom God created our present reality. Even Reformed scholar D.A. Carson admits the word "world" refers to every person as he writes, "In John, the term *kosmos* regularly designates the whole of humanity in its fallenness—the object of God's redemptive love, not merely a select group. John 3:16 declares that God's salvific will extends to all people without distinction, emphasizing the universality of divine love rather than its limitation to the elect."[74]

1 Timothy 2:4 "[God] desires all people to be saved and to come to the knowledge of the truth."
Interpretation: God's will for universal salvation contradicts a pre-selection of a few. This verse alone should prove conclusive in rejecting TULIP to an objective reader. If God desires something, will He not make a way for it to happen? Can God desire all to be saved and simultaneously desire some to be lost in Hell to show His justice? While God wants all to be saved, and has made a way for all to be saved, and will even glorify His name with those who are not saved, salvation involves choice because it is loving God more than anything else.[75] It cannot be forced and still be love.

Romans 11:20–22 "They were broken off for their unbelief, but you stand by your faith... if you do not continue in His kindness, you also will be cut off."
Interpretation: Inclusion and exclusion depend on belief or unbelief, not preordained destiny.

---

[74] D. A. Carson, *The Gospel According to John*, Pillar New Testament Commentary (Grand Rapids: Eerdmans, 1991), 205.
[75] See Luke 18:18–23 about the rich young ruler who was told to sell all, and Luke 14:26

2 Thessalonians 2:13 "God has chosen you from the beginning for salvation through sanctification by the Spirit and faith in the truth."

> *To sincerely preach that "Christ died for you" requires that it actually be true.*

Interpretation: Election operates *through faith* and sanctification, not apart from them. God's choice cooperates with human response.

L — Limited Atonement

Conclusive Argument: 1 John 2:2 (NAS) "And He Himself is the propitiation for our sins; and not for ours only, but also for those of the whole world."

This verse explicitly distinguishes between "our sins" (believers) and "the sins of the whole world." The scope is universal, not selective. John could have said "for our sins only," but he deliberately expands it: "not for ours only, but also for those of the whole world." The Greek phrase *holou tou kosmou* leaves no exegetical room for "only the elect." It mirrors John 3:16, where "God so loved the world" refers to all humanity. The word "propitiation" (hilasmos) means a satisfaction or covering of sin. If Christ is the *propitiation* for the sins of the whole world, then His atoning work is sufficient for all, even if it becomes efficient only for those who believe. The universal offer of salvation depends on a universal atonement. To sincerely preach that "Christ died for you" requires that it actually be true.

Limited Atonement undermines the gospel offer's sincerity (cf. 1 Tim. 4:10—Christ is "the Savior of all men, especially of believers"). The early church uniformly rejected Limited Atonement, as Irenaeus wrote, "He came to save all through Himself—all, I say, who through Him are born again unto God—infants, and children, and boys, and youths, and old men" (*Against Heresies* 2.22.4).

John's intent is pastoral and inclusive. Writing to believers, he broadens their assurance: Christ's work is not restricted to their group or region—it embraces the entire human race. As Dr. Jerry Walls wrote, "The picture of God found in Calvinism cannot be reconciled with the God revealed in Jesus Christ, whose compassion and desire for the lost know no limits" Walls and Dongell, *Why I Am Not a Calvinist*, 147).

John 3:16–21 "For God so loved the world, that He gave His only begotten Son, that whoever believes in Him should not perish, but have eternal life. For God did not send the Son into the world to judge the world, but that the world should be saved through Him. He who believes in Him is not judged; he who does not believe has been judged already, because he has not believed in the name of the only begotten Son of God. And this is the judgment, that the light is come into the world, and men loved the darkness rather than the light; for their deeds were evil. For everyone who does evil hates the light, and does not come to the light, lest his deeds should be exposed. But he who practices the truth comes to the light, that his deeds may be manifested as having been wrought in God" (NAS).

Interpretation: As noted above in the "U" section, the object of God's love and Christ's mission is *the world*—not a select group within it. "World" (Greek *kosmos*) consistently refers to humanity in general in John's writings.

1 Timothy 2:3–6 "This is good and acceptable in the sight of God our Savior, who wants all people to be saved and to come to the knowledge of the truth. For there is one God, and one mediator also between God and mankind, the man Christ Jesus, who gave Himself as a ransom for all."

Interpretation: As also noted above, God's saving will extends to *all people*; Christ's ransom is explicitly *for all*. Paul uses the same Greek term (*pas*) for "all" in both verses—showing the scope of redemption is universal, not selective.

Hebrews 2:9 "But we do see Him who was made for a little while lower than the angels, namely, Jesus, because of His suffering death crowned with glory and honor, so that by the grace of God He might taste death for everyone."
Interpretation: Jesus "tasted death for *everyone*." The Greek *hyper pantos* means "on behalf of all." No limitation is implied.

2 Peter 3:9 "The Lord is not slow about His promise, as some count slowness, but is patient toward you, not wishing for any to perish but for all to come to repentance."
Interpretation: God's will is universal salvation, not selective redemption. His patience proves He desires repentance from *all*, not only from the elect.

1 Timothy 4:10 "For it is for this we labor and strive, because we have set our hope on the living God, who is the Savior of all mankind, especially of believers."
Interpretation: God is called "Savior of all mankind," with believers being the ones who receive that salvation in actuality. The distinction—"especially of believers"—shows universal provision, conditional application.[76]

Titus 2:11 "For the grace of God has appeared, bringing salvation to all people."
Interpretation: Grace has appeared *to all*—not merely to the elect. Calvinists sometimes say "all kinds of people," but nothing in the

---

[76] The Reform response seems fairly weak here, as Piper says: "Christ's death so clearly demonstrates God's just abhorrence of sin that he is free to treat the world with mercy without compromising his righteousness. In this sense Christ is the saviour of all men." In what sense? A Savior actually gives salvation. Piper, John, *The Justification of God: An Exegetical and Theological Study of Romans 9:1-23* (Grand Rapids: Baker, 1983), 101.

context restricts the meaning. Paul is emphasizing the universal scope of Christ's redemptive revelation.

2 Corinthians 5:14–15, 19 "For the love of Christ controls us, having concluded this, that one died for all, therefore all died; and He died for all, so that those who live would no longer live for themselves, but for Him who died and rose on their behalf... namely, that God was in Christ reconciling the world to Himself, not counting their wrongdoings against them."
Interpretation: "One died for all" (v.14) and "reconciling the world" (v.19) are both universal in scope. Paul teaches that Christ's death *extends to all humanity*, though reconciliation is realized only through faith.

Romans 5:18 "So then, as through one transgression there resulted condemnation to all mankind, so also through one act of righteousness there resulted justification of life to all mankind."
Interpretation: Paul parallels the universality of Adam's fall with the universality of Christ's redemptive act. The offer of justification is coextensive with the reach of sin—available to all.

John 12:32 "And I, if I am lifted up from the earth, will draw all people to Myself."
Interpretation: Jesus' crucifixion is the means by which He draws *all* to Himself. The Greek *pantas* is unqualified—He draws universally, not selectively. Chrysostom interpreted this as meaning "not by compulsion, but by persuasion and love."

I — Irresistible Grace

Conclusive Argument: Acts 7:51 (NAS): "You men who are stiff-necked and uncircumcised in heart and ears are always resisting the Holy Spirit; you are doing just as your fathers did."

This verse, spoken by Stephen moments before his martyrdom, directly contradicts the notion that God's saving grace is irresistible. Grace can be resisted. The Greek term *antipiptō* here for "resisting" literally means "to fall against" or "to oppose." These are not regenerate people yet to be converted—they are people under the convicting influence of the Spirit, resisting His call. If grace were irresistible, this charge would be meaningless.

The Holy Spirit is actively striving with sinners throughout Scripture (Gen. 6:3; John 16:8). His convicting work is real, but God allows genuine freedom—people may *resist* or *yield*. Speaking of salvation, love that cannot be resisted is not love but coercion. The God who "desires all men to be saved" (1 Tim. 2:4) woos but does not force—that is why not all are saved. The early Fathers saw salvation as a synergy—God initiates, empowers, and enables, but man must cooperate. As John Chrysostom said: "All depends indeed on God, but not so as to deprive our free will... God draws, but He draws the willing." (*Homilies on Romans* 18)

Matthew 23:37 "Jerusalem, Jerusalem... How often I wanted to gather your children together... and you were unwilling."
Interpretation: Jesus desired their repentance, but they resisted. Grace can be resisted; God does not force belief.

Acts 7:51 "You men who are stiff-necked... you always resist the Holy Spirit."
Interpretation: Direct biblical statement that people can resist the Spirit's drawing, contradicting irresistible grace.

Luke 7:30 "But the Pharisees and the lawyers rejected God's purpose for themselves, not having been baptized by John."
Interpretation: God's gracious plan for them was rejected. His will can be thwarted by human stubbornness.

John 5:40 "You are unwilling to come to Me so that you may have life."
Interpretation: Unwillingness, not inability, is the barrier. Grace invites; man may refuse.

Hebrews 10:29 "How much severer punishment... for one who has insulted the Spirit of grace?"
Interpretation: Grace can be "insulted" and rejected—proof of resistibility.

2 Corinthians 6:1 "We urge you not to receive the grace of God in vain."
Interpretation: Grace can be received "in vain." This is impossible under irresistible grace.

Galatians 5:4 "You have been severed from Christ... you have fallen from grace."
Interpretation: Believers can depart from grace, showing it is not irresistible or irrevocable.

Hebrews 3:15 "Today if you hear His voice, do not harden your hearts."
Interpretation: The Spirit's voice can be resisted by hardening—human choice remains operative.

Revelation 22:17 "The Spirit and the bride say, 'Come!'... whoever wishes, let him take the water of life without cost."
Interpretation: The Spirit calls universally; response depends on the will—"whoever wishes."

Romans 10:21 "All the day long I have stretched out My hands to a disobedient and obstinate people."

Interpretation: God persistently extends grace to those who reject Him. His invitation is sincere but resistible.

P — Perseverance (of the Saints)

Conclusive Argument: Hebrews 6:4–6 (NAS): "For in the case of those who have once been enlightened and have tasted of the heavenly gift and have been made partakers of the Holy Spirit, and have tasted the good word of God and the powers of the age to come, and then have fallen away, it is impossible to renew them again to repentance, since they again crucify to themselves the Son of God and put Him to open shame."

There can be no doubt the people described here are genuine believers. Even Calvinists must affirm they have the Heavenly gift and Holy Spirit. The Greek term here *parapiptō* means to *fall alongside, abandon, or apostatize*. It conveys deliberate turning away from a once-embraced faith. The writer does not say these people *appeared* to be believers; he says they were and yet fell away. This does not mean salvation is fragile or easily lost; rather, it means believers retain moral freedom. Salvation is a covenantal relationship—God remains faithful, but humans may sever their fellowship through persistent unbelief (see many verses below).

The Calvinist view treats perseverance as automatic rather than relational, whereas Scripture teaches faithful endurance—a continuing response of trust empowered by grace (cf. Col. 1:23; Heb. 3:14). God preserves those who persevere, but He never nullifies the reality of free will. In *What Is Reformed Theology?: Understanding the Basics*[77] R.C Sproul attempts but fails to explain the passage. He admits the passage *sounds like* it describes regenerate believers and the possibility of apostasy, yet he insists it is merely a rhetorical *argumentum ad absurdum*—this is just a

---

[77] Sproul, R. C. *What Is Reformed Theology?: Understanding the Basics*. Grand Rapids, MI: Baker Books, 2016.

hypothetical. No reasonable system of interpretation can exist if we allow people to dismiss anything they do not like as just being hypothetical.

Ezekiel 18:24 "When a righteous man turns away from his righteousness, commits iniquity… will he live? All his righteous deeds shall not be remembered."
Interpretation: A person once righteous can turn and perish. Perseverance is not guaranteed.

John 15:6 "If anyone does not remain in Me, he is thrown away as a branch and dries up."
Interpretation: Remaining in Christ is conditional. Salvation requires continuing faith.

Romans 11:20–22 "You stand by your faith… otherwise you also will be cut off."
Interpretation: Continuance depends on faith. Falling from belief results in being cut off.

1 Corinthians 9:27 "I discipline my body… so that, after I have preached to others, I myself will not be disqualified."
Interpretation: Even Paul considered apostasy possible; perseverance requires diligence.

Galatians 5:4 "You have been severed from Christ… you have fallen from grace."
Interpretation: Believers can truly "fall from grace," contradicting "once saved, always saved."

Hebrews 10:26–29 "If we go on sinning willfully after receiving the knowledge of the truth, there no longer remains a sacrifice for sins."
Interpretation: Persistent rejection after conversion leads to

judgment. Salvation is conditional on continued faith. See above on Hebrews 6.

2 Peter 2:20–21 "If after they have escaped the defilements of the world… they are again entangled… the last state has become worse for them."
Interpretation: Post-conversion relapse is possible and spiritually disastrous.

Revelation 3:5 "I will not erase his name from the book of life."
Interpretation: The assurance "I will not erase" implies that names *can* be erased—security is conditional.
1 Timothy 1:19 "Some have suffered shipwreck in regard to their faith."
Interpretation: Faith can be destroyed by moral failure. Perseverance requires active faithfulness.

Summary of All Five Points

Point	Calvinist Claim	Biblical Refutation
Total Depravity	Humans are totally unable to respond	God's prevenient grace enables all to respond; moral choice remains (Gen 4:7; Rev 3:20)
Unconditional Election	God selects individuals apart from faith	Election is "in Christ," grounded in foreknowledge and human faith (Eph 1:4; 1 Pet 1:2)
Limited Atonement	Christ died only for the elect	Christ died for all (John 3:16; 1 John 2:2; Heb 2:9)
Irresistible Grace	Grace cannot be resisted	Humans can resist, reject, or fall from grace (Acts 7:51; Gal 5:4)
Perseverance of the Saints	The elect can never fall away	Believers must continue in faith to remain saved (John 15:6; Heb 6:4–6)

When interpreted within their canonical and linguistic contexts, the Calvinist "proof" texts never challenge God's initiative, humanity's responsibility, and the universality of grace. Scripture portrays a God who loves the world, invites all to repent, and empowers genuine response through His Spirit. "True sovereignty is not threatened by freedom; it is expressed most gloriously in creating genuinely free creatures who can love in return" (Walls and Dongell, *Why I Am Not a Calvinist*, 132). It also teaches no external power can separate us from God's love, but it does not teach we ourselves cannot choose to walk the slippery slope of sin away from our Savior. The Bible's story—from Cain to Christ—testifies to a family invited into love.

Chapter 4: Cross-pollination: Evidence from Reason

"Every plant which My heavenly Father did not plant shall be uprooted." Matthew 15:13 (NAS)

"God has, you say, a two-fold Will, One to Preserve, and one to Kill..." Rev. Charles Wesley (1807-1888), prolific hymnwriter in the poem *"Address to the Calvinists"*

Anyone who has tried to discuss Free Will with a Calvinist theologian has experienced incredible confusion as they are assaulted by new terms and new definitions of old terms that congeal into a morass of misunderstanding. Calvinism's persuasive force does not derive directly from Scripture but from an ingenious philosophical scaffolding that overlays Scripture with speculative categories: the "revealed vs. hidden will" of God, "decretive vs. permissive will," "secondary causes," "compatibilist freedom," "effectual calling," and the "limited intent of atonement."

These distinctions form a determinist intellectual apparatus—a system designed to defend divine causation of all events while still claiming to preserve human responsibility. Ever since Augustine the Church has made Christianity increasingly closer to a complex philosophical system instead of being what it started out as: a faith that even common fishermen could grasp and spread.

One of the fundamental rules of good exegesis is to read a passage and try to understand its plainest meaning—what the passage meant to both the writer and the receiver of the Word. Augustinian-Calvinism breaks this rule in a nearly imperceptible way: it redefines words away from a plain meaning and empties them of free will.

For example, most people understand when they are told to have faith they must choose to believe God's Word and character despite the circumstances. Calvinism empties "choice" and claims faith is a gift of God—something imposed from without.

There is absolutely no way a common fisherman or field worker in Jesus' day believed no one had free will and that God was getting exactly what He wanted down to "the motes of dust that fly in the air."[1] They were not philosophers—common sense says we make libertarian free choices all the time (the ability to do or to not do things) and the evil in the world suggests something is wrong rather than that God is minutely controlling all events.

Calvin's systematization of Augustinian beliefs laudably had the goal of elevating God's majesty, magnifying God's grace over human works, and comforting his parishioners who were terrified by the Catholic Church's claim that they were on the path to Hell.

However, his system significantly overshot its target, creating fear of reprobation rather than assurance of salvation. Bringing God's power to the forefront of theology, and deciding He must use it all the time, in effect conceptualized a God where "might makes right" since even things that are patently evil like child rape must be somehow caused by Him. "At the root of extreme Calvinism is a radical form of volunteerism, which affirms that something is right simply because God willed it, rather than God willing it because it is right in accordance with His own unchangeable nature."[78] Wesley's proclamation of love that flows into prevenient grace and universal invitation recovers the early Church's belief and renders a far more heart-warming understanding.

If God chose His elect before time, not based on foreknowledge, then upon what did He base the decision? We cannot even speculate about what this "factor" may be that gives God "good pleasure". If the decision were baseless, it is irrational and unfair. If this factor has a basis, shouldn't it also take into account God's foreknowledge of the objects of His election? Ultimately, "The Calvinist system is logically consistent only at the cost of moral absurdity; it preserves divine power but sacrifices divine goodness" (Walls and Dongell, *Why I Am Not a Calvinist*, 197).

In this chapter we will look at the many logical reasons to reject TULIP and to dismantle this intellectual superstructure. While there is some redundancy with points made elsewhere, here the case of reason will be stated as succinctly, clearly, and biblically as possible.

Because we are looking at reason, it may be helpful to understand it operates on three levels, with each level bleeding into (or pollinating) the others:

(1) **Biblical coherence** – whether the system matches Scripture;

(2) **Logical coherence** – whether its concepts can even be reconciled internally;

(3) **Moral coherence** – whether its portrait of God accords with divine goodness.

The Problem of Two Wills: Revealed vs Hidden Will

Calvinist Claim: God has both a *revealed will* (what He commands) and a *hidden will* (what He decrees). Thus, He may command all to

---

[78] Geisler, Norman L. *Chosen But Free: A Balanced View of God's Sovereignty and Free Will*. Rev. ed. Minneapolis: Bethany House Publishers, 2001, 244.

repent (His revealed will) while secretly decreeing that only the elect will repent (His hidden will).

Refutation: God's will is not duplicitous, nor can there be two conflicting wills inside God's overarching will. Scripture consistently portrays God as truthful and single-minded, never double-tongued or self-contradictory:

"God is not a man, that He should lie" (Num 23:19).

"With Him there is no variation or shifting shadow" (Jas 1:17).

"He cannot deny Himself" (2 Tim 2:13).

A being who secretly decrees what He publicly forbids would be morally incoherent and untrustworthy. Furthermore, God's will is moral and consistent. In the Bible we see: "Your word is truth" (John 17:17) and "The law of the Lord is perfect" (Ps 19:7). God's commands express His moral character, not a theatrical pretense. He truly "desires all people to be saved" (1 Tim 2:4; 2 Pet 3:9). There is no biblical warrant for positing a contradictory "secret" volition that ordains most to damnation[79].

It is also patently wrong to think anyone knows God's "secret will". Is God not good at keeping secrets? How can we say God's "secret will" proves anyone's points? If it is truly "secret" and not known comprehensively then there is no persuasive force in any direction. Therefore, the entire idea needs to be dismissed as a flawed mechanism that cannot possibly assist anyone in interpreting the Bible.

If God "secretly wills" what He "publicly forbids," He becomes the author of hypocrisy. A parent who secretly wills a child's disobedience while telling them "no" and then punishing them would be morally

---

[79] A Calvinists may balk at my claiming God's two wills express moral inconsistency rather than their intended different relations to creation. However, when the decretive will directly contradicts the moral will, the distinction collapses into duplicity, because Scripture identifies God's will with His goodness (Ps 145:17; 1 John 1:5).

perverse. Scripture presents God as a faithful Father, not a manipulative deity (Matt 7:11)[80].

The "Decretive" Will and the "Permissive" Will

Calvinist Claim: Everything that happens—including sin—is part of God's "decretive will." God "permits" evil but does so "sovereignly," meaning He causes even the permission.

If God causes the permission, the permission is causation.

Refutation: Scripture never attributes causation of evil to God. It does the opposite by declaring: "Let no one say when he is tempted, 'I am being tempted by God'" (Jas 1:13) and "Your eyes are too pure to approve evil" (Hab 1:13). God allows freedom; He does not script evil and then punish creatures for obeying His decree.

The Reformed tradition's conceptualization of "permission" here is incoherent. If God causes the permission, the permission is causation. If a programmer "permits" a robot to err by coding it to err, he is the cause of the error. Reformed theologians appeal to the distinction between primary and secondary causes to defend God's moral innocence, arguing God ordains events without being their efficient cause (see *Institutes* I.xviii.1; Acts 2:23). Yet this distinction folds if the secondary cause is itself predetermined.

If God foreordains every human act, then the "secondary" cause has no true contingency and thus no independent moral agency. As Alvin Plantinga explains, "If God causes a person to do what is wrong,

---

[80] This in no way denies that God can and does work providentially through human choices to include sinful ones—what is being rejected is the metaphysical necessity of sin in His plan. Of course some differentiation exists in God's will, but Reformed formulations stretch it into a logical contradiction rather than a mystery of perspective (divine vs. human view). C. S. Lewis and other Free Will thinkers affirm God's foreknowledge and providence without needing to resort to declaring God has dual (incongruent) wills (*Mere Christianity*, bk. 4).

then that person is not free with respect to that action and cannot be held morally responsible" (*God, Freedom, and Evil*, 1974, 31). Richard Swinburne similarly argues, "For an action to be morally significant a man must have had a genuine choice between good and evil" (*Providence and the Problem of Evil*, 1998, 98–99). Determinism empties the primary/secondary cause distinction of its moral force: if every choice is fixed from eternity, secondary causes cannot bear genuine responsibility.

The Problem Within Dort's claim of a "Sincere Offer"

The Canons of Dort insist that the gospel must be "declared and published to all nations and persons promiscuously and without distinction" (II.5). God, they say, "seriously and most genuinely shows in His Word what is pleasing to Him, namely, that those who are called should come to Him" (III/IV.8). This is the Reformed doctrine of the sincere or well-meant offer: God truly calls every hearer to repentance and faith in Christ.

Yet Dort also declares Christ's atonement was intentionally limited—that He bore the sins of the elect alone and that God grants saving faith only to those same elect (II.8, III/IV.10–11). Here lies the unresolved tension. If God has eternally decreed that only certain individuals can believe and if Christ did not bear the sins of the non-elect, then what exactly is being "offered" to them?

Reformed theologians attempt to reconcile this by appealing to God's "two wills" (discussed above): His revealed will, which commands all to repent, and His secret will, which saves only some. They argue the atonement is sufficient for all but efficient for the elect. Yet sufficiency without divine intention does not make the offer truly available. To call all people to receive forgiveness that God never purposed or provided for them risks portraying God as offering what He withholds.

Thus, the "sincere offer" reveals a deep logical and moral strain within the TULIP system. A decree-limited atonement cannot ground a genuinely universal invitation. The Free Will (synergistic) view resolves this paradox simply: Christ died for all, prevenient grace enables all, and God's invitation is as sincere in heaven as it sounds on earth—"whoever believes in Him shall not perish, but have eternal life" (John 3:16).

Calvinism's Incoherent Compatibilism

Calvinism has tried to respond to its critics since the sixteenth century while struggling to maintain its primary dedication to Augustine's framework of determinism. Many within its fold (rightly) want to protect God's character and defend God from the claim that He is the author of evil and that if only His will is done then only He is responsible for sin. A fulsome movement within Calvinism is what can be called "New Calvinism" or "Compatibilism."

The basic premise of Compatibilism is that two seemingly conflicting truths are taught in the Bible. These propositions may best be expressed by D. A. Carson:

(1) God is absolutely sovereign, but his sovereignty never functions in a way that human responsibility is curtailed, minimized, or mitigated.

(2) Human beings are morally responsible creatures—they significantly choose, rebel, obey, believe, defy, make decisions, and so forth, and they are rightly held accountable for such actions; but this characteristic never functions so as to make God absolutely contingent[81].

Taken together, these two propositions describe a pervasive biblical tension: God's meticulous sovereignty does not cancel human

---

[81] D. A. Carson, *Divine Sovereignty and Human Responsibility: Biblical Perspectives in Tension* (Eugene, OR: Wipf & Stock, 2002 [orig. 1981]), 212.

freedom, and human responsibility does not limit divine control. As Frame puts it, "Scripture does not teach freedom in abstraction, but freedom as a divine gift operating within God's plan." [82]

Compatibilists stress both divine sovereignty and human responsibility are fully taught in Scripture and are therefore mutually compatible. It claims the Bible never attempts to reconcile the tension philosophically, but rather the Bible consistently affirms both realities as true. Carson observes, "The sovereignty-responsibility tension is not a problem to be solved, but a framework to be explored."[83]

In their opinion, the biblical tension between divine sovereignty and human responsibility is not an error to be corrected nor a contradiction to be dismissed, but a mystery to be reverently embraced and carefully explored. As Carson affirms, "The more biblically faithful we are, the more tension we shall feel."[84] The Reformed tradition "at its best" recognizes this, not by diminishing one truth for the sake of the other, but by affirming both as the unified teaching of God's Word.

Compatibilists also try to give people the appearance of free will when in fact they are just maintaining their TULIP convictions. Compatibilists attempt a disingenuous misdirection by redefining the very meaning of *freedom*. Jonathan Edwards argued that freedom is "the power to act according to one's desires"—even though those desires are fully determined by God (Edwards 1754, 25–27[85]; Piper 1986, 38–40[86]).

---

[82] John M. Frame, *No Other God: A Response to Open Theism* (Phillipsburg, NJ: P&R Publishing, 2001), 45–46.

[83] Carson, *Divine Sovereignty and Human Responsibility*, 204.

[84] Carson, *Divine Sovereignty and Human Responsibility*, 212.

[85] Edwards, Jonathan. *Freedom of the Will*. 1754. Reprint, New Haven: Yale University Press, 1957.

[86] Piper, John. *Desiring God: Meditations of a Christian Hedonist*. Portland, OR: Multnomah Press, 1986.

But if desires are predetermined to be anti-God, the agent cannot do otherwise. This makes moral responsibility incoherent. J. P. Moreland and William Lane Craig observe that such compatibilism "rescues determinism linguistically but not logically" (*Philosophical Foundations for a Christian Worldview,* 2003, 167–70). Saying "You are free, even though you could not have done otherwise" is a contradiction in terms. **It in effect turns moral freedom into a hollow tautology: one is "free" simply because one does what one is predetermined to "want"—and that is all evil.**

Compatibilists genuinely believe the will acts voluntarily, not mechanically, but their argument still lacks libertarian contingency— the ability to do otherwise. Scripture presupposes such contingency in divine invitations. We can recognize their claim but reject that somehow we have "free will" just because we follow our desires. Human will can decide not to follow desires. **If God fixes our desires and they in turn irresistibly coerce our will, we are right back at God in effect coercing evil.** All choices are of course bounded by the divine will—I can't be tempted beyond what I can bear (1 Cor. 10:13) and many temptations will never even be encountered.

All counter-factual "could-have-done-otherwise" conditions collapse if we see God as ordaining events rather than permitting events. Calvinism makes Scripture's numerous invitations and warnings simply performative rather than genuine offers. Compatibilism undercuts the sincerity of divine invitation and diminishes the moral efficacy and maturation of repentance.

Genuine freedom has always meant the ability to do or not do something (Kane 2005, 64–68[87]). Without actual alternative possibilities, moral responsibility transmorphs into divine puppetry. Compatibilism thus fails to reconcile sovereignty and responsibility; it merely redefines freedom until the contradiction disappears

---

[87] Kane, Robert. *A Contemporary Introduction to Free Will.* Oxford: Oxford University Press, 2005.

linguistically rather than logically (Moreland and Craig 2003, 167–70[88]). God is still just as responsible for evil if He created people whose only desires hate Him and thus they are irresistibly compelled to sin.

To have justice and moral accountability humans must have moral culpability—they must be guilty of choosing evil, not simply guilty of choosing "what they want" when God made them to only want evil. Human will is so free it can and does choose to do what it does not really want. Otherwise it would not be "will"--it would be instinct.

Economists faced the problem of humans not maximizing self-gain because this tendency threw off their predictions. Like the Compatibilist, they decided altruism must be self-gratifying—that people make a calculus and decide to not just maximize money but happiness, and the emotional component of patting oneself on the back is worth not maximizing wealth. This has become a kind of fudge-factor so that they can claim their models work despite evidence to the contrary.

My military experience testifies against both Compatibilists and economists. While serving in the U.S. Air Force I saw many people make absolutely selfless decisions. The ultimate example is when a soldier jumps on a grenade to save his comrades. This could not possibly garner sufficient warm fuzzy feelings to selfishly justify the action. Selfless acts are not from desire but from a higher recognition of the good—from the remains of our imago Dei. People can make choices that are not about what they want—they can actually sacrifice what they want the most for a worthy cause. This self-sacrifice is called love. Love is doing what is best for others and not for the self. Both the Calvinist and the economist are denying self-sacrifice and so de facto denying love.

---

[88] Moreland, J. P., and William Lane Craig. *Philosophical Foundations for a Christian Worldview*. Downers Grove, IL: InterVarsity Press, 2003.

Thus, the Calvinist idea of free will is really "non-free free will"—it is not free to say no but only to say yes to its base nature. Under this paradigm what is really

Compatibilists are removing the question of whose will is in charge from being one of fact to being one of faith

being denied is love—selfless, pure, love. But what if the remnant of the image of God within every person allows a glimmer of love? Of all things God would protect and empower it would be the part of His image that is love, and indeed we see the most brutal people still demonstrate love—even Hitler truly loved his German shepherds.

When it comes to sin, that remnant glimmer takes the form of repentance. Faith is a human choice—it is a self-denial and a God affirmation. Faith is not a work as Luther claimed—throughout the Bible God contrasts faith and works, He doesn't lump them together. Saving faith is reaching out to the Father, admitting failure, crying for help. It seems far more reasonable that God protects the ability to repent than it does that He judges humans for a sin Adam committed and that He makes everyone to hate Him with no recourse to change.

Compatibilism is best seen as obfuscation and side-stepping the issue at hand. These sincere believers rightly attempt to preserve God's goodness within a Calvinistic framework, but in reality they built an entire edifice and expect people to argue through it room by room instead of simply noting its foundation is flawed.

In many ways it seems Compatibilists are removing the question of whose will is in charge from being one of fact to being one of faith. We are simply to think the two propositions are both true because they are "both taught" in Scripture, when in fact they cannot both be true. We are then fed the misdirection about desires. Never are we given a way to reconcile the clear incompatibility – we are simply supposed to accept logical incoherence "by faith" and even think it is a beautiful theological landscape to explore.[89] **Ultimately this is not faith but fideism—belief against reason.** Biblical faith is trust in a God who invites reason ("Come, let us reason together," Isa 1:18), not in a deity whose will nullifies logic.

One cannot simultaneously say God causes all things and still absolve Him of being the Creator of evil. No matter how many intellectual gyrations one makes, either God is actively causing war and rape and theft, or else God is *allowing* other wills to freely act (human and evil spirits). Some Compatibilists such as R.C. Sproul speak of "permission" but it is hard to see how this isn't veiled causation within the Calvinist claim of all-embracing determinism. "A theology that makes God the author of sin, even indirectly, cannot be true to the God who is light and in whom there is no darkness at all" (Walls and Dongell, *Why I Am Not a Calvinist*, 198). Even Calvin cites Augustine and denounces any kind of "permission" in God saying God does not permit, but rules.[90] "They say God permits; but He does so by His counsel and decree" (*Institutes* xviii.1).

One final scripture here should overthrow any argument that God decrees all things to include evil. While to this point I have expressed moral befuddlement that anyone can think God causes child rape, a similar supremely evil act against children happened in the Old

---

[89] This sounds very much like witnessing to a Muslim. Despite catching them in numerous inconsistencies, showing how their sacred text the Koran is repeatedly mistaken (to include misunderstanding the Christian Trinity by replacing the Spirit with Mary) they simply reply that it is to be taken as a matter of faith. No amount of logic or clear thinking can prevail—Allah is always right and we must just trust that. Our God is not Allah—He is the One True God—and His Word is definitely internally consistent, historic not metaphoric, and rational rather than incompatible with reason.

[90] See the complete discussion on determinism at: Calvin, John. *Institutes of the Christian Religion*, Book III, Chapter 23. In *The Institutes of the Christian Religion of John Calvin*, trans. Henry Beveridge. Bible Study Tools.

Testament and God soundly denied having anything to do with it. Jeremiah 32:35 states:

> *And they built the high places of Baal that are in the valley of Ben-hinnom to cause their sons and their daughters to pass through the fire to Molech, which I had not commanded them nor had it entered My mind that they should do this abomination, to cause Judah to sin.* (NAS)

Notice this sin didn't even enter God's mind—it is wholly the conceptualization and implementation of evil people, possibly due to the influence of demonic spirits. Our great God's name and character are far more tarnished by attributing evil to Him by believing determinism than by saying He has temporarily restricted His will to allow humans free will.

Our great God's name and character are far more tarnished by attributing evil to Him by believing determinism than by saying He has temporarily restricted His will to allow humans free will.

The Limitations of Omnipotence

Even an omnipotent God must make certain trade-offs. He allows some things He dislikes in the short term to achieve higher purposes in the long term. Divine power operates in harmony with divine wisdom and love—not apart from them. God's omniscience ensures His decisions are perfect, but omnipotence does not mean He performs the logically impossible. He cannot grant two opposing miracles at once, He cannot have opposite wills, and He cannot make someone love Him.

Imagine that twenty percent of people pray for rain while the other eighty percent pray for sunshine. God cannot both send and withhold rain in the same place and time. Likewise, He cannot simultaneously prevent all pain and yet allow pain to mature our souls. These are not deficiencies in His power but demonstrations of His perfect rationality—mutually exclusive outcomes cannot coexist[91].

God also refrains from the nonsensical. He cannot create a "triangular square" or make two plus two equal five. Human language can construct absurdities, but nonsense cannot be made real. These are not "things" at all but contradictions in terms. God's omnipotence never extends to self-contradiction or moral absurdity. In the same way, He does not *force love*, for coerced love is a contradiction—it ceases to be love the moment it is compelled.

He also cannot both cause all things and then be said to *permit* some things (evil). "In a normal case of permission, the person granting permission does not determine the choices of the one who is granted permission…The notion of permission loses all significant meaning in a Calvinist framework" (*Why I am not a Calvinist*, 131; 132).

Many divine choices involve complexities far beyond human comprehension. For instance, God can either determine every human decision or allow humans to choose freely, but not both. The instant He overrides the will, the person ceases to be truly human or morally responsible. If I seize your hand and make you strike someone, the moral responsibility lies with me, not you. The more God directly controls human will, the less we remain moral agents capable of growth and accountability.

Calvinist founding documents attempt to say in effect, "God can give people free will to do evil while determining everything," but this is conceptually incoherent. Simply prefixing a paradox with "God can" does not render it possible. The more God determines, the less space remains for genuine human freedom. **God *does* give people free will and *remain in full control*.** When taken to the extreme this leads to

---

[91] Discussion of the mass of the Higgs boson and quantum mechanics will need to await a future book, but I will maintain there is logic in the universe's composition and that superstates support the power of will (and observation) rather than a deterministic universe.

the Free Will theology known as Molinism, which is very interesting but far too much to discuss here.

Human freedom is essential for moral and spiritual development. We learn far more from choices we make ourselves than from those made for us. God's ultimate aim is not merely to eliminate pain or death but to teach us how to love—freely, selflessly, and fully. Forced virtue is no virtue at all.

Consider a parent teaching a child to love. You can model kindness and provide opportunities, but you cannot coerce genuine affection. You might hand your son five dollars and command him to buy a gift for his sister, but it means far more if he voluntarily chooses to do so. The harder the choice, the deeper the love it reveals.

Similarly, the greater our freedom, the greater our capacity to love. When I return home and a machine like Alexa or Siri greets me warmly, it's pleasant but empty—it was programmed. When my dog runs to greet me, there is some affection. When my wife or children choose to greet me, prioritizing me over what is on TV or their phones, I feel truly loved. Real love requires real choice.

God's purpose, then, is not to insulate us from every sorrow but to shape us into His image. We glorify Him most when we become like Him in character—when our wills are freely aligned with His. To imitate God is not mere mimicry or rote obedience; it is to cooperate with the Spirit in the transformation of the heart, where obedience flows naturally from love. We do not become gods but rather Christ lives His life in us.

Jesus overturned tables in righteous anger because He was guided by perfect love and mission. We, too, act as the Spirit prompts us, not to imitate the action but to share the heart behind it. Our sanctification is the gradual training of our will to desire what God desires.

Therefore, God does not coddle us in this brief earthly life. He uses it as a training ground for eternity, shaping us into the radiant beings He intends us to be. We were not made for this temporal world but for everlasting fellowship and joyful service in His kingdom. This life is only a shadow of what is coming—a crucible in which faith is refined, love is tested, and hope learns to look heavenward toward the coming of our King.

The Problem of "All for His Glory" Including Evil

Calvinist Claim: God ordains all—including sin and damnation—to manifest His glory.

Refutation: Scripture never depicts God glorifying Himself through sin. When Moses asked to see God's glory, God replied, "I will make all My goodness pass before you" (Exod 33:18–19). "The Lord is righteous in all His ways" (Ps 145:17). Glory is revealed through goodness, not through scripting evil.

Evil glorifies God only when redeemed, not when it is decreed. Joseph told his brothers, "You meant evil against me, but God meant it for good" (Gen 50:20). God overrules evil and redeems evil; He does not originate it. God can tell demons to be about their business, but even then He is merely allowing them to act out their nature, not causing that nature nor demanding them to do evil (see Luke 8:31–32; Job 1:12; 2:6; 1 Kings 22:21-23; Rev 20:2-3). If God ordains sin to display glory, then sin becomes necessary to His nature. This directly contradicts 1 John 1:5 that says, "in Him there is no darkness at all" (1 John 1:5).

Finally, in response to the belief that all is for God's glory (including evil), Chapter One showed there is good reason to believe God created for love. Glory is diminished when specifically sought. God receives more glory when He is understood as good and seeking to love all. Evil is a human or demonic product, it is from our will not His. He transforms our guilt into His glory by loving us on the cross.

The Problem of Secret Election and Limited Atonement

Calvinist Claim: God made a "secret" decree that Christ would die only for the elect and that only those predestined are enabled to believe. God elected people due to something only He knows and not due to anything humans do. His revealed will is to save all but He only acted to save the elect.

Refutation: God's will of salvation is universal as described by "He desires all people to be saved" (1 Tim 2:4) and "He gave Himself as a ransom for all" (1 Tim 2:6) and "He is patient...not wishing for any to perish" (2 Pet 3:9). Christ's atonement is unlimited because "He Himself is the propitiation...for the sins of the whole world" (1 John 2:2) and "He tasted death for everyone" (Heb 2:9). Even Reformed commentator John Stott concedes that Paul's and John's usage of "world" and "all" "cannot easily be limited to the elect" (*The Cross of Christ*, 1986, 232). A universal command to repent paired with a secret decree that prevents most from repenting would make God duplicitous (Acts 17:30).

The Problem of Divine Justice and Impartiality

Calvinist Claim: Because all deserve hell, God is free to save only some.

Refutation: Scripture says God's justice is impartial, just as any earthly judge must be impartial in order to be considered "good." Job 34:10 declares, "Far be it from God to do wickedness" and Acts 10:34 says, "God shows no partiality." The very definition of "justice" implies moral consistency, not arbitrary favoritism. When the Bible mentions a "hardening of heart" it is always after the person first rejected God in some way. Humans initialize the hardening, and God punishes them with further hardening which results in God getting what He wants. Hardening is a judicial act following unbelief (Rom 11:23), not an eternal decree. If God decrees sin, then punishes it, He punishes His own will—collapsing justice into self-contradiction.

The whole mechanism of election seems strange. Either there is no reason some are chosen and others rejected or there is a reason that we just cannot fathom. Seeing as the first is arbitrary, irrational, and even unjust, we'll assume the second and call this reason "UQ" for "Unknown Quality". God sees our UQ and it is so important that he elects us on the basis of it—without even consulting His foreknowledge? This must certainly be an important factor that we cannot even fathom.

One would think our sin/disobedience should be more negative than our UQ can be positive, yet He saves even the worst of sinners. Thus UQ must be HUGELY important (more than all sin), yet somehow absolutely undetectable and unmentioned in the Bible. Rather than believe in this mysterious UQ, it is far easier to see how Spirit-empowered repentance and obedience are reasons God saves. God blesses and empowers those who are open to receiving His love and forgiveness and who want what He wants instead of what their fickle human hearts desire. This is not works nor merit-based salvation—this is a loving God acting in relationship to sinful humans.

Any belief that God chooses some elitist group based on an unknown quality needs to refute all of the scriptures below that evidence otherwise (the bold emphasis is mine):

Old Testament

- **Deuteronomy 10:17** — "For the LORD your God... **does not show partiality** nor take a bribe."
- **Deuteronomy 1:17** — "You shall **not show partiality** in judgment; hear the small and the great alike..."
- **Leviticus 19:15** — "You shall **not be partial** to the poor nor defer to the great; but you are to judge your neighbor fairly."
- **2 Chronicles 19:7** — "Now let the fear of the LORD be upon you... **there is no injustice or partiality** with the LORD our God."
- **Job 34:19** — God "**shows no partiality** to princes nor regards the rich above the poor..."
- **Proverbs 24:23** — "To show **partiality** in judgment is not good."

- **Proverbs 28:21** — "To show **partiality** is not good…"
- **Malachi 2:9** — "You are not keeping My ways but are **showing partiality** in the instruction." (God condemns it.)

New Testament

- **Acts 10:34–35** — "God is **not one to show partiality**, but in every nation the one who fears Him and does what is right is welcome to Him."
- **Romans 2:11** — "For there is **no partiality with God**."
- **Galatians 2:6** — "God **shows no partiality**."
- **Ephesians 6:9** — Masters are to stop threatening, "knowing that both their Master and yours is in heaven, and there is **no partiality** with Him."
- **Colossians 3:25** — "He who does wrong will receive the consequences… and there is **no partiality**."
- **1 Peter 1:17** — "If you address as Father the One who **impartially judges** according to each one's work…"
- **James 2:1, 9** — "Do not hold your faith… with an attitude of **personal favoritism**… if you **show partiality**, you are committing sin."
- **James 3:17** — The wisdom from above is "without **hypocrisy**" (also translated "**impartial**," ESV).

The Problem of Moral Accountability and Divine Integrity

God is the Logos, which can mean "word" but includes ideas of order and reason. When the Apostle John calls Christ the Logos (John 1:1–3), he identifies divine reason as the very structure of creation. To deny reason in theology is, therefore, to deny Christ's rational image reflected in humanity (Col 1:16–17).

The Word spoke into the nothingness and created our reality—complete with the immutable laws of physics. As Justin Martyr wrote, "Reason directs those who are truly pious and philosophical to honour

135

and love only what is true" (*First Apology* 2). Faith in Scripture is not irrational; it is faith in the Logos, the divine Reason Himself.

There is only one truth, and to say "there is no truth" is itself a truth claim and so internally inconsistent. We can therefore glean some insight into if something is good by seeing if it is rational. Everything that is evil has a whiff of irrationality about it. Most people can see through Calvinism with just a few simple propositions:

1) If all is decreed, sin and unbelief are decreed.

2) If sin is decreed, judgment becomes theater, not justice.

3) If God secretly wills evil, good and evil collapse in Him.

4) If all acts are necessary, God Himself lacks freedom.

Determinism thus destroys both moral accountability and divine integrity.

Concept	Calvinist Definition	Biblical Logic
Freedom	Acting according to predetermined desires	Genuine capacity to obey or resist (Josh 24:15; John 5:40)
God's Will	Hidden/Decretive vs. Revealed/Prescriptive	One unified moral will (1 Tim 2:4; 2 Pet 3:9)
Glory	Manifested through decreed evil	Manifested through redeeming goodness (Exod 33:18–19)

Human freedom is required for moral responsibility. This must be real libertarian freedom, the "freedom to do otherwise" not the "human freedom" R.C. Sproul allows which only amounts to being able to freely choose evil but being incapable of choosing the Good[92]. Logically, why would God create such creatures? It is far more

---

[92] For a long discussion of how totally depraved—how "radically corrupted"—humans are, read the section on Total Depravity in Sproul, R. C. *What Is Reformed Theology?: Understanding the Basics.* Grand Rapids, MI: Baker Books, 2016. Note also that he says humans cannot exercise "royal freedom" (which he mistakenly says "Scripture calls" it; loc. 1,785, Kindle) meaning presumably humans cannot please God in any way. This seems extreme—even a very disobedient child occasionally does something nice, and parents are predisposed due to love to see the best in their offspring.

reasonable for God to create a world where everyone perfectly followed Him rather than one where everyone is absolutely hating Him. In truth, God did neither—He created a world and humanity, pronounced them "good," and allowed humans to do evil. He then went the extra mile and died to redeem humanity, and His call goes out for people to accept His sacrifice that paid for all sin.

The Problem of Infralapsarian vs Supralapsarian

One of Calvinism's most persistent tensions lies in the long-running debate between *infralapsarianism* and *supralapsarianism*. Calvin himself admitted this "mystery," yet his followers have never resolved it because the deterministic framework of TULIP is internally inconsistent. The issue is not merely theoretical—it exposes the moral and logical incoherence of a theology that tries to reconcile divine goodness with exhaustive determinism.

The term *lapsarian* comes from the Latin *lapsus* ("fall") and refers to the logical order of God's decrees in relation to humanity's fall into sin. The question is simple: *Did God decree the election of some to salvation and others to damnation before or after the Fall?*

Two traditional answers emerged:

- **Supralapsarianism:** God first decreed to elect some and reprobate others, then decreed creation and the Fall as the means to that end. This was defended by Calvin's successor Theodore Beza (1519–1605).
- **Infralapsarianism:** God first decreed to create, then to permit the Fall, and only afterward to elect certain fallen humans to salvation. This was Calvin's position.

No matter how this is answered, to include begging the question (as we will see below), the determinist structure shows itself to be internally inconsistent—irrational and thus false.

The Moral Problem of Supralapsarianism

The supralapsarian claim—that God decreed election and reprobation prior to creation—implies God not only foresaw but *willed* the Fall to occur in order to display His mercy toward the elect and His justice toward the damned. The moral problem is obvious. If the Fall had not yet taken place, there were no sinners; thus, to ordain damnation before sin existed portrays God as arbitrary, unjust, and the source of evil.

If every human act is predetermined by divine decree, then moral evil itself must originate in the divine will. This would make God the author of sin—something Calvin explicitly denied yet could never logically avoid (*Institutes* III.xxiii.2; Helm 2004, 71–75). Supralapsarianism therefore threatens the very holiness of God by implying that evil serves as an instrument of His predestined plan, and so Calvin chose the next option.

The Infralapsarian Attempt and Its Contradictions

To avoid saying God is the real source of evil Calvin and later Reformed thinkers proposed *infralapsarianism*, which places election after the decree to create and permit the Fall. Here, God first created free beings (Adam and Eve), then allowed their fall into sin, and only afterward elected some of the fallen to salvation. Calvin affirmed Adam's genuine pre-Fall freedom by writing, "Adam possessed freedom of will by which, had he chosen, he might have obtained eternal life" (*Institutes* 2.1.8).

This solution, however, fails to solve the problem. If God "permits" what He fully foreknows and predetermines, permission becomes indistinguishable from causation. The Fall remains divinely authored. Conversely, if God's decree to elect follows His knowledge of sin, He appears to *react* to human rebellion—a position Calvinists reject as limiting divine sovereignty (Frame 2010, *The Doctrine of God*, 144–48). **Either option absolutely undermines one of Calvin's** assumed core attributes of God: either God's goodness or God's immutability have to be denied.

The Return to Eden

Calvinists often accuse Free-Will theologians of "returning to Eden," yet it is precisely there that determinism collapses most obviously. If election comes *after* the Fall, then the original creation must have included genuine libertarian freedom. Adam's freedom was not illusory; even Reformed orthodoxy concedes he had the ability to choose good or evil (Calvin, *Institutes* 2.1.8; Bavinck, *Reformed Dogmatics*, 3:50–52). Thus, God's intention for human freedom is woven into creation itself.

The problem becomes visible when tracing Augustine's interpretation of Paul. Reading Romans 5:12 through the Latin Vulgate—*in quo omnes peccaverunt* ("in whom all sinned")—Augustine concluded that all humanity literally sinned *in Adam*. The Greek text, however, reads ἐφ' ᾧ πάντες ἥμαρτον ("because all sinned"), meaning each person sins by imitation, not by participation (Metzger 1994, 516–17; Wilson 2019, 90–92). On this misreading Augustine constructed the doctrine of inherited guilt, foreign to the early Christian defenders[93].

Pelagius saw the inconsistency immediately. He argued that if all are condemned *in Adam*, then logically all must be saved *in Christ*—which Paul clearly does not teach. If all are condemned for one man's sin it follows that all are justified by Christ's righteousness. Since this is not so, the comparison must be understood to be about possibility, not necessity (*Commentary on Romans* 5:18–19; Augustine, *De Natura et Gratia* 70.84). The Apostle Paul's point is that Adam introduced death to all humanity, while Christ *offers* resurrection life to all who believe (1

---

[93] Augustine. *De Natura et Gratia*. In *Nicene and Post-Nicene Fathers*, First Series, Vol. 5.

Cor 15:21–22). The symmetry is moral and redemptive, not mechanical or universal.

When Both Systems Collapse

Both lapsarian schemes implode under scrutiny. Supralapsarianism implicates God in moral evil; infralapsarianism compromises divine immutability by depicting God as revising His plan after human rebellion. Sensing this impasse, modern Calvinists have begged the question by proposing a metaphysical escape: all divine decrees are "logically simultaneous" in God's eternal mind. Yet as Richard Muller explains, this maneuver "erases the very notion of sequence, rendering the concept of 'before' and 'after' meaningless, and thus emptying the lapsarian distinctions of content" (Muller 2003, 58–60). If everything happens simultaneously in God's mind, then Calvinists cannot coherently discuss any sequence of events.

In trying to escape the clear fallacy inherent in both infralapsarianism and supralapsarianism, these modern Calvinists have inadvertently stumbled upon the truth. If there is no order among decrees, then one cannot claim election precedes foreknowledge—as Calvin had to do to protect his system[94]. Once sequence is abandoned, it is obvious that God's foreknowledge would inform His decisions— He could see who would repent and choose faith—so that would be a part of His calculus from eternity.

Paradoxes, Mysteries, and "God's Good Pleasure"

When confronted with reason Calvinists often respond by acting like people outside their belief system cannot possibly understand because they do not have enough faith or enough theological training. Since in their view faith is something God gives us rather than

---

[94] Calvin, John. *Institutes of the Christian Religion.* Trans. by Ford L. Battles. Edited by John T. McNeill. 2 vols. Philadelphia: Westminster Press, 1960, III.xxi.5–7.

something we choose, they do not try to explain themselves but rather they can feel humbled God has given them sufficient faith to believe despite incongruities. One good friend even told me I was using the "world's reasoning" whereas he was using "biblical reasoning." I was using Scripture, which seems biblical, and there is only one kind of reason--the opposite of which is being unreasonable.

The Reformed position often declares things are a "mystery" (or, if Lutheran, "a paradox"). For example, "Ultimately, the cause of sin must remain mysterious, for sin is the undoing of all reasonability"[95] and "God is sovereign over all things, and his sovereignty extends even to the sin of man, but in mysterious and noncausal ways."[96] When they cannot justify the many Scriptures supporting free will, they just call it a mystery. They even have developed the Black Box of God's Good Pleasure. Anytime they are asked why God does things that seem unreasonable, such as why God chooses some and not others, or why He wants to torture some aborted babies for eternity, or why He feels the need to impress humans with His justice, they retreat into claiming it is because of "God's Good Pleasure." These questions were not about whether something makes God happy—they are legitimate concerns that Reformed doctrine puts God in a poor light and demands an inconsistent vision of God's character from that revealed in the Bible.

This kind of reasoning began with Calvin himself. When writing about why God would elect some and not others he said God "deemed it meet" that Adam fall. "Why he deemed it meet, we know not." He goes on to say it displayed God's glory and that, "man...falls, divine providence so ordaining, but he falls by his own fault." Calvin believes we should look to human corruption rather than "a cause hidden and

---

[95] Robert A. Peterson and Michael D. Williams, *Why I Am Not an Arminian* (Downers Grove, IL: InterVarsity Press, 2004), 30.

[96] Robert A. Peterson and Michael D. Williams, *Why I Am Not an Arminian* (Downers Grove, IL: InterVarsity Press, 2004), 31.

almost incomprehensible in the predestination of God," and "submit our judgment" to God's wisdom, admitting "Ignorance of things which we are not able, or which it is not lawful to know, is learning; the desire to know them is a species of madness." *Institutes* III.xxiii.8

Admittedly the above paragraph had to be heavily edited or else it would have been even more convoluted, so the reader is encouraged to look up the passage and read it in its entirety[97]. In short, Calvin both asserts divine ordination of the Fall and then declares the rationale "unknown", "hidden", and even "unlawful to know", saying any inquiry beyond that as "madness." This is exactly the "mystery shield" his adherents continue to wield today.

When it comes to claiming something is a mystery, we should strive to at least recognize why it is mysterious. When the Bible uses the word "mystery", and it is very rare, it is usually saying something is "marvelous" or beyond reason in its graciousness—such as the incarnation. We can also accept mystery when Scripture leaves something in tension because it cannot be explained in human words, such as the nature of the Trinity[98]. Mystery is not a legitimate claim to escape an uncomfortable position when there is a logical contradiction (e.g., "A is non-A") such as "you have non-free free will."

As Alvin Plantinga notes, there is a logical contradiction in both causing a free act and calling it free (*God, Freedom, and Evil,* 1974). Compatibilism and Reformed theology in general is rife with these types of logical incompatibilities. For example to "permit irresistibly" is self-contradictory, as is any kind of coerced "freedom" or forced love.

---

[97] Calvin, John. *Institutes of the Christian Religion,* Book III, Chapter 23. In *The Institutes of the Christian Religion of John Calvin,* trans. Henry Beveridge. Bible Study Tools. Accessed October 25, 2025. https://www.biblestudytools.com/history/calvin-institutes-christianity/book3/chapter-23.html

[98] I'd argue understanding can be approached using String Theory and our knowledge that there are ten dimensions instead of just four. See my devotional book *Etched in Eternity* for details.

The Greatest Good Glorifies God Most

The preponderance of both Scripture and church history firmly support a Free Will, or synergistic, understanding of salvation. Yet, for the sake of fair-minded dialogue, let us grant that each side can challenge the other Scripturally and that, to some, the debate may appear inconclusive. Let us then take the hypothetical one step further and assume the Calvinist premise—that God's ultimate purpose in creation is His own glory. If that is true, then the question becomes decisive: which vision of God actually glorifies Him more? Which view better exalts His character and more effectively motivates His people toward love, holiness, and evangelism?

The Calvinist position, when examined closely, gains God nothing. It does not, in fact, ascribe to Him more glory, for as both Scripture and experience testify, one gains greater glory precisely when one does not seek it (Phil. 2:5–11; John 13:31–32). Neither does it display greater power, for both perspectives affirm God's omnipotence. Rather, it confines His majesty within the narrow logic of control.

By contrast, the Free Will perspective magnifies God's glory fully. It attributes to Him the most radiant of His qualities—love freely given, justice truly fair, mercy genuinely merciful. It depicts not a cosmic puppeteer but a perfect Father who dignifies His children with freedom while surrounding that freedom with moral boundaries for their good. It produces greater assurance of salvation, for the believer knows that love, not arbitrary decree, governs the universe. It infuses prayer and evangelism with meaning, for our cooperation with God truly matters. And it inspires holiness, since obedience arises from willing love, not coercion.

St. Anselm of Canterbury (1033–1109) famously argued in the *Proslogion* that God is "that than which nothing greater can be conceived." From this, he reasoned that because existence in reality is greater than existence in thought alone, God must exist in reality as the summum bonum—the greatest conceivable good.[99] Building upon Anselm's insight, we might add one more premise for theological reflection:

Since God is the greatest good, any true theology about Him will portray His goodness, love, and justice in their highest possible light.

Therefore, if we are to describe God as the greatest conceivable being, the theology that most exalts His moral beauty and relational love must be the truest. By that standard, Free Will theology (synergistically attained) best displays the glory of God, for it shows Him as both sovereign and self-giving, powerful and patient, transcendent yet tender—the God who wins our hearts, not our helplessness.

This is why C.S. Lewis wrote that to love and be loved is the highest good of creatures,[100] and why Alvin Plantinga argued free will is necessary for moral goodness—because "a world containing free creatures who can do moral good is more valuable than a world containing no free creatures at all."[101] The same principle that justifies the existence of moral freedom also illuminates the nature of divine glory: God's greatness is magnified by His willingness to share genuine freedom and love with His creation.

As philosopher-theologian Dr. Jerry Walls observed, a God who creates free beings capable of rejecting Him takes a greater risk, but achieves a greater good. The freedom to love is the very image of God's own goodness mirrored in us.[102] The Calvinist model of determinism, by contrast, leaves no such reflection of divine love in human hearts. True glory belongs not to the God who coerces, but to the God who woos.

---

[99] St. Anselm, *Proslogion*, trans. Thomas Williams (Indianapolis: Hackett, 2001), chaps. 2–3.

[100] C.S. Lewis, *The Problem of Pain* (New York: HarperOne, 2001), 128.

[101] Alvin Plantinga, *God, Freedom, and Evil* (Grand Rapids: Eerdmans, 1974), 30.

[102] Jerry L. Walls, *Heaven, Hell, and Purgatory: Rethinking the Things That Matter Most* (Grand Rapids: Brazos Press, 2015), 67.

God's Foreknowledge is the Key to Freedom

As we saw in Chapter Three, Scripture does not teach an eternal "election" without using God's foreknowledge. God does not make Himself blind to the future exactly when it most matters (determining who to save). The key to reconciling divine sovereignty with human responsibility is not paradox/mystery/The Black Box of God's Good Pleasure -- but *foreknowledge.*

The Church Fathers consistently taught God's eternal knowledge encompasses every human choice without coercing it. God foresaw humanity's rebellion and suffering, yet He also foresaw those who would freely respond to His love. In His wisdom, He judged that creating such beings—capable of love, repentance, and communion—was worth the cost of freedom.

God created free will and *allowed* sin; He did not *cause* sin. He then sent Christ as the propitiation "for our sins; and not for ours only, but also for those of the whole world" (1 John 2:2, NAS). Salvation is universally offered yet freely received. The elect are those whom God foreknew would respond to grace in repentance and faith (Rom 8:29). In this way, divine love and goodness and justice remain intact. God's sovereign purpose is not thwarted as He operates through His foreknowledge. Human freedom is preserved, God's holiness is defended, and the harmony between divine will and human response is perfectly explained.

Divine foreknowledge, rather than divine deterministic power, perfectly reconciles divine will with human will. God's redemptive plan honors the human freedom to repent and still fulfills His ultimate purpose to create a loving family for eternity. **By permitting freedom even when He knew it would be abused, God demonstrates a greater sovereignty—one that triumphs through redemption rather than coercion.** As Jesus taught, those forgiven much love much (Luke 7:47); thus, redeemed humanity will ultimately love and glorify God more deeply than unfallen humanity ever could.

Calvinism's deterministic scaffolding—its hidden will, decrees, compatibilism, and secret dualism—may sound philosophically tidy, but they are alien to Scripture and self-contradictory in logic. The God of the Bible does not hide one will behind another. He reveals His heart in Christ, who is "the image of the invisible God" (Col 1:15), saying plainly: "Whoever will may come" (Revelation 22:17).

Calvinist In Name Only

Reformed theology stems from a good desire to protect God's sovereignty, but it quickly becomes a philosophical lens through which all is interpreted, such that everything is seen as for or not for TULIP. With this logic it becomes self fulfilling--verses saying "ALL" can be saved are said to only be directed at the elect, whereas verses saying you can reject salvation are said to only be valid for the un-elect. This happens even when the Bible in no way suggests a doctrine of election in the pericope.

Many modern Protestants who identify as "Calvinists" are, in practice, far removed from Calvin's full theological system. American Evangelicals from the Baptist tradition often embrace a softened or partial Calvinism that affirms *salvation by grace through faith alone* without endorsing strict determinism, limited atonement, or unconditional reprobation.[103] In this respect, their beliefs are much closer to pre-Augustinian historic Christianity and to the free-will reformers such as Erasmus, Arminius, and Wesley, than to the Genevan confessions.

Unaware of Calvinism's deeper Augustinian roots, these believers label themselves "Calvinist" chiefly to emphasize divine grace in salvation. Yet this conviction—**that salvation is initiated and sustained by grace, not by human merit—is not uniquely Calvinist. It stands as the common inheritance of the entire Reformation and indeed of all orthodox Christianity,** shared

---

[103] (e.g., Lifeway 2017, Pew 2015)

(though differently articulated) by Protestants, Catholics, and Eastern Orthodox alike. As Reformed advocate D. A. Carson observes, "All Christian confessions affirm that salvation is of grace; the debate turns not on *whether* grace is necessary but on *how* it operates in relation to human responsibility."[104]

While doing a poor job of it in the sixteenth century, the Catholic Church today teaches that salvation begins with grace and cannot be earned.[105] It teaches God's grace precedes, accompanies, and follows every human act of faith and love (Council of Trent, Session VI, Canon 4). Eastern Orthodoxy has always rejected Augustinian thought and teaches the primacy of divine grace working synergistically with human freedom. The key difference lies not in whether grace is necessary for salvation, but whether it is irresistible (Calvinist), prevenient (for everyone) but resistible and synergistic (Arminian/Wesleyan), or synergistic alone as God's image affords initial faith and God's grace makes it saving faith (Catholic/Orthodox). (See comparisons in Appendix 3)

Some "Calvinists in name only" recognize God's foreknowledge as the key to meshing human will with God's will, which makes them much closer to free will and historic Christianity than to Augustinian-Calvinism. Others simply drop or deny the more clearly unbiblical outcomes of Calvin's thoughts such as the need for infant baptism or that God predestines people to Hell (double predestination) without trying to justify the omission within a Calvinist framework.

Many who wear the Calvinist label today affirm grace, not determinism. Such faith belongs to the wider historic Christian consensus that salvation is by grace, through faith, freely given and freely received. That is not Calvinism—it is Christianity. To all brothers and sisters formerly-known-as-Calvinists let me be the first to

---

[104] D. A. Carson, *Divine Sovereignty and Human Responsibility: Biblical Perspectives in Tension* (Eugene, OR: Wipf and Stock, 2002 [orig. 1981]), 17–18.
[105] Council of Trent, Session VI, *Decree on Justification* (1547).

welcome you to the Free Will ranks. I hope you will consider changing your terminology from being a follower of Augustinian-Calvinism to being a follower of Christ and His teachings as passed down through the early Church and inherited by the vast majority of Christians today.

Chapter 4 Summary

Reason is not the enemy of revelation; it is its ally. The God of Scripture is consistent, truthful, and rational—never double-minded. The Calvinist scaffolding of hidden decrees and paradoxical freedoms may seem tidy, but it collapses under its own contradictions. The glory of God shines not in determinism but in love freely given and freely received. God's invitation remains open: 'Whoever will may come.'

In this chapter we looked at many of the debates within Calvinism as it struggles to reconcile determinism with logic. Ultimately, when a theology must retreat perpetually into mystery to sustain itself, it ceases to be faith seeking understanding and becomes faith avoiding understanding. The Word of God is rational, historic, and internally consistent. Because God is its Author we must have a system that makes sense of *every* Bible verse. It is the fulsome inerrant/infallible Word of God.

In the next chapter we will look at the practical outcomes of the two views about how God works out His sovereignty. What are the implications on motivation and holiness? Is there any data that can help us know which belief leads to the best outcomes?

---

[1] Edwards, Jonathan. Sermon *"The Final Judgment; Or, The World Judged Righteously by Jesus Christ."* Ch1.1

Chapter 5: Fruits of the Faith: Evidence from Outcomes

"You will know them by their fruits. Grapes are not gathered from thorn bushes, nor figs from thistles, are they?" — Matthew 7:16 (NAS)

"The doctrine of original sin, or of a sinful constitution, and of necessary sinful actions, represents the whole moral government of God, the plan of salvation by Christ, and indeed every doctrine of the gospel, as a mere farce. Upon this supposition the law is tyranny, and the gospel an insult to the unfortunate." Charles Finney, Presbyterian minister, *Lectures on Systematic Theology* (Oberlin, 1846), Lecture 40.8, "Moral Depravity."

This chapter examines how the lived fruits of different theologies—Calvinist determinism versus Free Will synergism—manifest in prayer, evangelism, holiness, and social liberty. Every theology plants seeds in the soil of the human heart, shaping how we see God, others, and ourselves. Doctrines are not sterile abstractions; they bloom into worship, witness, and will. Jesus said, "You will know them by their fruits" (Matt. 7:16 NAS). Thus, the question is not only which doctrine seems more consonant with creation, history, the Bible and reason, but also which one inspires us to be more like Jesus. While fruit alone does not falsify a doctrine, consistently barren outcomes invite scrutiny of the root.

The Fruit of a Theology Matters

The true test of theology lies not in its symmetry but in its sanctity—whether it produces love, holiness, and hope. As A.W. Tozer observed, "What comes into our minds when we think about God is the most important thing about us.[106]" Our theology ultimately becomes our biography; our view of God shapes our lives.

Our theology ultimately becomes our biography; our view of God shapes our lives.

It is important from the outset to distinguish that here we are discussing the logical and sometimes historic outcomes of belief systems: we are not saying these generalities apply to every individual. There are some fantastic Christians who have believed Calvinism is what God's word intended to teach, and they have persevered with determination to both act as if their choices mattered while denying human will and action has any true impact on the outcome of God's plan. Instead of seeing the Christian life as a partnership, they have believed life is something to endure as God's will unfolds. While they may have the feeling they are completely irrelevant, they at least retain the comforting blanket that God will always get every detail of His will done on earth as it is in Heaven.

The Calvinist Garden is one of beauty in order, but it can also be barren of purpose and compassion. It is consistently applied and so can be said to be symmetrical; all flower petals are preordained, all fences rise high above, and the rows are admirably straight and narrow. However, its soil can feel dry. A theology rooted in determinism, however intellectually rigorous, risks producing resignation, elitism, and fear rather than joy, evangelism, and holiness.

Because Scripture presents grace as God's empowering partnership (Phil 2:12–13; Rom 8:13), theological systems that collapse sovereignty

---

[106] Tozer, A. W. *The Knowledge of the Holy.* New York: Harper & Brothers, 1961.

into determinism tend, over time, to yield pastoral resignation (prayer), programmatic proclamation (evangelism), and positional rather than practical holiness. In contrast, free-will theology—understood as Spirit-enabled cooperation—predictably cultivates intercessory expectancy, missionary urgency, and moral transformation.

Fruit of Fatalism: Withering Prayer, Evangelism, & Holiness

It is worth noting from the outset that Calvinism is not a monolith. It can be divided into (a) classical Reformed confessionalism (Westminster, Dordt) (b) "hard determinism" versions (supralapsarian rigor), and (c) contemporary "New Calvinism." Of these groups, the critiques below apply least to the New Calvinists who explicitly deny the fatalistic entailments of their doctrines. However, the logic still holds that Reformed theology leads to motivational erosion despite incoherent doctrinal declarations attempting to prevent the decay.

If every event is eternally decreed, prayer and evangelism lose purpose while the pursuit of holiness languishes. Why plead with God to change what He has already fixed? Why evangelize if God already irresistibly saved or damned everyone? Why strive for holiness if we are absolutely depraved and so destined to fail? Why worry about staying the course of salvation if once we are saved we are always saved? Simon Sinek in his bestselling book *Start with Why* explains convincingly that all human motivation starts with knowing why.[107]

Calvinism effectively robs that motivation. Simply "do what you are told" is hardly motivational. In fact, there is no motivation to live the Christian life when you deprive it of the all the important reasons "why" we should act.

Scripture portrays the Christian life far differently than determinism describes it. A free will theology naturally provides far more motivation

---

[107] Sinek, Simon. *Start with Why: How Great Leaders Inspire Everyone to Take Action*. New York: Portfolio, 2009.

to partner with God to actually accomplish things that would not have been done otherwise. We are to be about our Father's work just as Jesus was as a young boy in the temple. God's redemptive love cannot just be absorbed by the saved; it must be reflected and even overflow from a heart of joy onto others. Love is both the goal and the mechanism of God's transformation.

Demotivated Prayer

For Calvin, the true purpose of prayer is not to move God but to move us. He says prayer is training the soul to depend on God and align our desires with his will. About prayer he writes:

> *Those who argue thus attend not to the end for which the Lord taught us to pray. It was not so much for his sake as for ours...*

> *No better is the frivolous allegation of others, that it is superfluous to pray for things which the Lord is ready of his own accord to bestow; since it is his pleasure that those very things which flow from his spontaneous liberality should be acknowledged as conceded to our prayers. Institutes of the Christian Religion, (Institutes, 3.20.3)*

In his haste to support Augustine's a-historical beliefs that were counter to the early patristic consensus, Calvin's system, though sincere in honoring divine sovereignty, unintentionally narrows the biblical portrait of prayer as genuine participation. Prayer in the Bible is not portrayed as some kind of static thing that helps us acknowledge what God already decided, but rather is a clear partnership with God to move this world from His permissive will into His good or highest will. The Bible teaches our prayers are heard by God and effective to bring His power to bear on our circumstances. "The effective prayer of a righteous man can accomplish much" (James 5:16, NAS).

Jesus makes it clear when He is asked how to pray that the purpose of prayer is to get God's will done on earth as it is in Heaven. We are told to pray, "Your kingdom come. Your will be done, On earth as it is in heaven" (Matt. 6:10, NAS). This is also a powerful refutation of the entire Reformed TULIP system that says God's will is always done on earth as it is in Heaven. Every Christian who has faced persecution on earth or tragedy due to sin is hoping God's perfect will is more accomplished there than it is here!

Even Calvin's sleight-of-hand attempt to give prayer purpose is logically flawed. Just as Calvin thinks God has determined external things, he should also believe God determined internal things to remain consistent. In his paradigm, God should already have decided to "align our will" with Himself or not, regardless of whether or not we pray.

Determinism by definition destroys all purpose for action—everything was predetermined. Love invites collaboration; determinism cancels it. God desires partnership, not puppetry, for prayer is the intimacy of co-laboring with the divine. Under any system teaching exhaustive decree, means (our actions) simply lack genuine contingency, and that reduces rational motivation.

Calvin's pedagogical view of prayer captures dependence but misses the participatory dimension evident in Scripture. Reformed believers often say "prayer works" so that they do not have to confront the truth that prayer moves God to action. Any religion can believe "prayer works." *Christian* prayer involves speaking to God and in faith believing He hears and acts on our behalf. Prayer doesn't work—God answers because we pray. Prayers from doubt are of little or no value—God demands prayers of faith and He intervenes on our behalf when we pray (James 1:6).

More than Alignment: Effective Christian Prayer in a Fallen World

Christian prayer is not a faith in words alone to change our reality but rather it is a faith that there is a good Heavenly Father, that He hears and loves us, and that He moves in our world in a way He would not otherwise. When we pray we always do so "in Jesus' name" as what we want is not our will but His will to be done. J.I. Packer in his *Praying the Lord's Prayer* notes, "…the purpose of prayer becomes plain: not to make God do my will (which is practicing magic), but to bring my will into line with his (which is what it means to practice true religion)" (57–58). Yes, prayer aligns our wills with God's, but it also moves the heart of God *to accomplish what He wants* instead of allowing the evil and pain that a fallen world deserves.

Prayer is like laying the tracks for God's response—He is the engine and His Spirit directs where the tracks are laid, but we get to be a part of the process. God restricts His perfect will from being done because His just nature recognizes we deserve the results of our iniquity, pain often calls us toward repentance, and because He wants to afford us opportunities to be about His business. Of course praying has effect and failing to pray has a different effect. We are literally told Moses' prayer changed God's mind. "So the LORD changed His mind about the harm which He said He would do to His people" (Exod. 32:14, NAS).

How does prayer relate to life in a fallen world? Imagine a master mechanic teaching his daughters how to rebuild an engine. He provides them with the proper tools and a detailed manual. He stands beside them, encouraging their progress and observing their work. When they make small mistakes, he doesn't rush to stop them. He may note the error, but he allows it to happen, knowing that failure is part of the learning process. If they were to pause and ask, he would gladly show them the right way—but he doesn't need to intervene at every turn. After all, he can repair the engine himself at any time. Yet that isn't the point. He isn't there to get an engine built; he's there to train his daughters.

While minor errors are permitted, the master would step in immediately if his children were about to do something truly dangerous. His permissive will allows ordinary mistakes that lead to growth; his masterful oversight ensures no lasting harm comes. The daughters' safety is guaranteed by his wisdom—but their progress depends on their willingness to ask for help.

This is how prayer functions in a fallen world. God sees all that we do and even allows our missteps, not because He is indifferent, but because He is forming us. He is not after a perfect world in the present—if that were His goal, it would already exist. Rather, He desires mature children who have learned His trade of love. He intervenes when eternal danger threatens, for He will not allow His children to be tempted beyond what they can bear. Yet when the matter is a teaching moment, He patiently uses it for our good, weaving even our mistakes into His redemptive purpose. For a fuller exploration of this theme—and of how prayer participates in God's training of His children—see my book *Love Above Glory*.

Demotivated Evangelism

The Reformed deterministic framework, though often defended as evangelistically compatible, logically undermines the motivation to evangelize as well. If God eternally decreed who will be saved and who will be damned, then human persuasion, prayer, or preaching cannot alter those outcomes. Evangelism becomes a duty without causal efficacy—a necessary formality in a drama whose ending is already written. Many Calvinists feel the conviction that they should share their faith but they fail to do so because they lack an explanatory reason why such sharing should be done when it can ultimately have no effect on who does and who does not accept Jesus as their Savior.

The New Calvinists have developed a counter claim, saying evangelism is the *means* God ordains to call the elect, but this does not change the fact that the result is predetermined. Whether one obeys or not, the same number of people will be saved or lost. This fatalistic implication saps evangelistic urgency, replacing a sense of rescue with one of ritualistic obedience. All this is certainly not to say there have been no great Calvinistic missionaries (Carey and Judson come immediately to mind), but rather it is to claim the *TULIP system* removes any real alternative possibilities and that tends to depress evangelistic urgency.

Attempts by New Calvinists to reconcile election with evangelism by asserting God ordains both the ends and the means cannot fully escape the problem of motivational loss. If every outcome is certain, then evangelism cannot alter it; if it cannot alter it, then its urgency is psychological, not rational. The logic of determinism turns the missionary cry of "Come to Christ!" into an echo of what has already been decreed. As my Asbury Theological Seminary professor and advisor Dr. Jerry Walls wrote, "If God's saving love is withheld from some by eternal decree, then it cannot serve as the model of the universal love that motivates Christian mission" (Jerry L. Walls and Joseph R. Dongell, *Why I Am Not a Calvinist*, 2004, 192). A theology that portrays God as withholding grace from most of humanity cannot kindle the same passion to save as one that believes grace is offered to all.

The early Reformers themselves felt this tension. If God's eternal decree is exhaustive—encompassing not only who believes but whether they can believe—then the preacher's words function merely as instruments of confirmation, not transformation. The sinner's response is not contingent upon hearing or believing in a truly open sense, but rather upon whether God has unchangeably decreed regeneration.

Even for the Compatibilist if both the elect and the means of election are eternally fixed, evangelism's success is guaranteed—but not because of human agency; hence, the human role becomes instrumental rather than cooperative. J. I. Packer acknowledges this tension in his *Evangelism and the Sovereignty of God* (1961) but then dismisses it as a mystery.

Scripture portrays evangelism as a genuine invitation that can be accepted or refused: "We are ambassadors for Christ, as though God were making an appeal through us; we beg you on behalf of Christ, be reconciled to God" (2 Cor. 5:20, NAS, emphasis mine). Appeals, by nature, assume freedom of response. God is the one making the appeal—so clearly He did not predetermine the response. Evangelism is sharing God's love, partnering with the Spirit, being about the Father's work. In many ways it is the training ground that teaches our hearts, words, and deeds to mirror our loving Father's. Under strict determinism, that appeal becomes a simulation, and the emotional energy of pleading for souls is replaced by cold proclamation of a fixed outcome.

As we turn to look at history I acknowledge my argument may overstep my evidence. There simply is no way to boil all history down and compare that which has been accomplished by Calvinists and that which has been accomplished by Free Will Christians—both by the power of the Spirit. Therefore this is put forth tentatively, and the point remains to compare which doctrine *logically* leads to the most good rather than to conclusively demonstrate one has led to more positive outcomes that the other.

Historically, determinism led Calvinist communities to excel in doctrinal formulation and precision over missionary fervor. As the historian Kenneth Latourette observed, it was not from the Geneva tradition but from the Wesleyan and Moravian awakenings that the great modern missionary expansion arose (*A History of Christianity*, 1953). For the 18th–19th centuries, the main propulsion of Protestant missions derived less from classical Reformed confessionalism and more from Moravian/Wesleyan revivalism—Methodist and allied evangelical networks supplying a disproportionate share of new societies and workers.[108] Historian David Bebbington explicitly roots modern Evangelicalism in the eighteenth-century Methodist revival (1730s) and identifies "activism" as intrinsic to its character; he then

---

[108] See Latourette, *History of Christianity*, 2:1134; Bebbington, *Evangelicalism in Modern Britain* (1989), esp. on "activism" and the voluntary society tradition.

notes that from the 1790s the movement poured out missionaries worldwide (Bebbington, *Evangelicalism in Modern Britain*, 2–3, 11).

Where Calvinism taught God would save His elect with or without human participation, Free Will preachers believed their obedience could truly make an eternal difference. The latter view naturally produces zeal, compassion, and persistence, while the former tends toward introspection and resignation.

While I cannot name the source out of respect for his privacy, I know a godly man who has traveled to more than 120 countries. He has been a missionary and served as an advisor to hundreds of Christians doing Business as Mission and Business For Transformation. In a private conversation he confided in me that "not one—NOT ONE person" he met who was actively doing missions around the world fully subscribed to TULIP. Even the ones sent from Presbyterian and other denominations who profess full Calvinism did not believe in the full Reformed deterministic system.

This may be because people who believe it do not feel compelled to be sent, or it may be that after they are sent they see God in action and revise their theology, or a mix of both causes. In any case, the testimony of history and the testimony of this anecdotal interview both evidence that it is Free Will theology that creates zeal to preach the Good News.

It is important to not entirely discount the evangelistic activities of believers from Reformed traditions. They certainly have also contributed to world missions, but the point here is that it is despite their theological convictions rather than because of them. In his book *Killing Calvinism: How to Destroy a Perfectly Good Theology from the Inside*, Reformed pastor Greg Dutcher rightly points out that good Calvinism follows God in His fulness of revelation to include witnessing. "This world desperately needs to see a robust, healthy Calvinism that celebrates the fullness of God's ways and works—not a lopsided Christian who cannot get off of the hobbyhorse of God's sovereignty" (43).

The more Christians, both Calvinist and Arminian, seek God and grow into mature believers who put their faith into action, the more they will also realize and represent the same God who is reconciling the world to Himself. Orthodoxy (correct teaching) leads to orthopraxy (correct doing) and orthopraxy leads to orthodoxy. It should be a fly-wheel in a positive direction, but it can also go in the opposite direction. Anyone who is bored at Church, uninspired to read the Bible, and critical of the things of God needs to start putting God's Word into motion. Actively evangelizing and using Scripture creates a hunger for more of God's Word and transforms spiritually-fat milk-drinking babies into powerful doers for the Kingdom.

If Christ "tasted death for everyone" (Heb. 2:9) and God "desires all men to be saved" (1 Tim. 2:4), then every person we meet is a potential child of God. This conviction animated John Wesley's evangelistic fire and the missionary awakenings that followed. Grace's universality ignites urgency—no one is beyond redemption.

Demotivated Holiness

As evangelistic urgency wanes under determinism, so too does the pursuit of holiness, for the two share the same moral logic. Calvinism, though motivated by a desire to exalt God's sovereignty, logically diminishes the pursuit of holiness by redefining human moral capacity and the nature of sanctification. Total depravity asserts every part of human nature is corrupted by sin to the extent that no one can do or even desires genuine good apart from divine regeneration. Even after regeneration most Calvinists expect a life trapped in a constant cycle of sin and repentance.[109] While Scripture indeed testifies to human

---

[109] See Sproul, R. C. *What Is Reformed Theology?: Understanding the Basics.* Grand Rapids, MI: Baker Books, 2016. He thinks even the pharisee of pharisees, the man whose personal discipline allowed him to say "as to the righteousness which is in the Law, found blameless" (Phil 3:6) is referring

sinfulness, Calvin's interpretation goes much further: it portrays the will as permanently enslaved to sin, incapable of cooperating with grace in any sense.

In *Institutes of the Christian Religion*, Calvin declares, "Man is said to have free will, not because he has free choice of good and evil, but because he acts voluntarily and not by compulsion. This is perfectly consistent with his being under the necessity of sinning" (2.2.8). By defining freedom as "voluntary necessity," Calvinism makes sin inevitable even for the believer—a condition that, if taken seriously, renders holiness aspirational rather than attainable. This starkly contrasts with the New Testament's position that evangelism is propelled by participatory imperative and results in real moral potency (see Rom. 6; 8; and Gal. 5).[110]

The Calvinist doctrine of *perpetual sinning* compounds this problem. The *Westminster Confession of Faith* (1646) asserts, "the most sanctified have only small beginnings of obedience" (XIII.2), and Reformed teachers such as R.C. Sproul have echoed the claim that we continually sin. One of his more frequent lines is, "We are not sinners because we sin; we sin because we are sinners."[111] If believers remain bound to continual moral failure by divine decree, the moral exhortations of Scripture lose their genuine force. Commands to "be holy, for I am holy" (1 Pet. 1:16 NAS) or to "put to death the deeds of the body" (Rom. 8:13 NAS) become mere reminders of what God has already rendered impossible. The believer is encouraged to confess depravity rather than overcome it.

---

to himself in Romans 7. We'll look at the truth about that chapter later in this book.

[110] See the Dordt articles on perseverance/election; WCF XIII.2 on sanctification. See Calvin's *Institutes* 3.20.3 on prayer and 2.2.8 on "voluntary necessity."

[111] See Sproul, R. C. *What Is Reformed Theology?: Understanding the Basics.* Grand Rapids, MI: Baker Books, 2016

How many times have you heard pastors and other Christian leaders say they are "sinners saved by grace." They think they are being humble when in truth they are

The believer is encouraged to confess depravity rather than overcome it.

denying the power of God and justifying their refusal to partner with the Spirit and be regenerated. The New Testament nowhere defines us by our past sins. Once united with Christ, believers are no longer slaves to sin but slaves to righteousness! (Rom. 6:18).

God declares believers are His saints or "holy ones" (1 Cor. 1:2), new creations (2 Cor. 5:17), and children of God (1 John 3:1). To continue defining oneself by past rebellion is to deny the Spirit's regenerating power and to minimize the victory of the cross. God does not merely forgive sinners; He transforms them into saints who walk in the freedom and holiness that His grace provides. You are not given life insurance to enter Heaven; you are saved from the need to sin while still on earth.

> *No temptation has overtaken you but such as is common to man; and God is faithful, who will not allow you to be tempted beyond what you are able, but with the temptation will provide the way of escape also, that you may be able to endure it* (1 Cor. 10:13, NAS).

Reformed theology often emphasizes *positional* holiness—righteousness imputed rather than imparted—so that sanctification risks being viewed as a declaration rather than a deep participation in the divine life. We are credited righteousness rather than actually being transformed into Christ's likeness. This produces a subtle but pervasive moral defeatism. When Christians are taught their every act remains tainted by sin and that perfection is unattainable in this life, they often cease striving for the sanctified life that the New Testament consistently describes. Why strive toward a goal you are told you cannot obtain, especially when there are no consequences since "once saved always saved"? Even if few reason this way directly, the doctrine certainly fortifies ennui rather than energizing activity.

repentance becomes acknowledgment of helplessness rather than transformation of character. Rev. Charles Finney, Presbyterian Pastor and key figure of America's Second Great Awakening, said, "The theory of the mixed character of moral actions, is an eminently dangerous." He taught people have freedom to sin and freedom not to sin, and that emphasizing a "sin nature" was an excuse to sin that leads to antinomianism. "It is erroneous to say that Christians sin in their most holy exercises, and it is as injurious and dangerous as it is false. The fact is, holiness is holiness, and it is really nonsense to speak of a holiness that consists with sin" (*Systematic Theology*, Lecture 14.3 and 14.6, "Moral Government").

John Wesley critiqued this very tendency, lamenting that "the doctrine of original sin carried too far tends to drive men either into despair or into careless living" (*A Plain Account of Christian Perfection*, 1766, 17). Calvinism's emphasis on the incurable corruption of the will leads to resignation: "I sin because I am depraved."

Maybe even worse yet, Calvinism's anthropology leaves little room for moral growth. If every human action, even post-conversion, is predetermined, then ethical progress becomes illusory. The believer's sanctification is not a partnership but a performance, already written into the eternal decree. Consequently, repentance becomes acknowledgment of helplessness rather than transformation of character. As theologian Donald Bloesch observed, "When divine sovereignty is interpreted as divine determinism, human responsibility and the call to holiness are effectively nullified" (*Essentials of Evangelical Theology*, 1978, 1:153). Calvinism's insistence on perpetual depravity undermines both the promise of transformation and the incentive to pursue it. The inevitable result is a Christianity defined more by confession than by conquest—an identity of sinners saved by grace rather than saints empowered to live free from sin.

By contrast, the biblical model of sanctification assumes the cooperation of grace and human will—"if by the Spirit you are putting to death the deeds of the body, you will live" (Rom. 8:13 NAS). Holiness, in this synergistic framework, is both commanded and empowered. A theology of free grace understands the believer's will as liberated by the Spirit, not erased. Grace does not merely cover sin; it cures it. The Spirit enables believers to cooperate with God's work of renewal, restoring the image of Christ in real moral change.

Wesley defined holiness as "perfect love"—a will wholly united to God's will. Love does not excuse sin but expels it. "We all… are being transformed into the same image from glory to glory" (2 Cor. 3:18 NAS). Calvinism often ends in resignation—"I sin because I am depraved"—whereas Free Will theology leads to transformation—"I love because He first loved me."

Learned Helplessness: Slave to Sin or to Righteousness

There is a stark difference in how Reformed theology portrays holiness and the possibility of victory over sin and what the Bible really teaches. Calvinists frequently insist believers sin constantly—every minute of every day. I once asked a Calvinist professor whether he had sinned in the previous hour while teaching theology. He replied, "I'm sure I did, though I'm not sure how." Such thinking betrays a tragic confusion between humility and hopelessness. True humility admits dependence; false humility denies empowerment.

When Free Will believers speak of living days, weeks, or even months without conscious sin, such testimonies are often dismissed as prideful exaggerations rather than as evidence of the transforming power of the Holy Spirit. Yet Scripture calls such freedom not arrogance, but sanctification.

Paul wrote, "Thanks be to God that though you were slaves of sin, you became obedient from the heart… and having been freed from sin, you became slaves of righteousness" (Romans 6:17–18, NAS). The apostle does not describe a theoretical position but a lived reality of freedom. Jesus Himself declared, "Everyone who commits sin is the slave of sin... but if the Son makes you free, you *"... but if the Son* will be free indeed" (John 8:34–36). This freedom *makes you free, you* is not future—it is now. Through union with *will be free indeed"* Christ, the believer is "crucified with Him, so that the body of sin might be done away with, so that we would no longer be slaves to sin" (Romans 6:6).

The gospel of grace is not the gospel of defeat. It is not a perpetual confession of depravity but the proclamation of deliverance. When I returned from a mission trip to Calcutta, where our team had witnessed healings and other miracles through prayer, I shared these testimonies with a senior Reformed Christian leader. He admitted he believed such things possible but confessed unease with "anything related to the Spirit." Like many Western Christians, he lacked categories for the Spirit's ongoing work. His faith was intellectual, not experiential—a reflection of how theology can become so cautious that it leaves no room for God's power.

Determinism goes so far as to breed learned helplessness. If sin is inevitable, why strive for holiness? Yet Scripture continually calls us to strive, to overcome, and to be perfect as our Father in heaven is perfect (Matthew 5:48). Peter exhorts us, "As obedient children, do not be conformed to the former lusts... but like the Holy One who called you, be holy yourselves also in all your behavior" (1 Peter 1:14–15). John insists that those who truly know God do not live in habitual sin: "No one who abides in Him sins; no one who sins has seen Him or knows Him" (1 John 3:6). This is not sinless perfectionism, but Spirit-enabled transformation. "Whoever is born of God overcomes the world; and this is the victory that has overcome the world—our faith" (1 John 5:4).

When I presented these truths to my Calvinist colleague, I offered him six pages filled with biblical evidence for freedom from sin's dominion. In return, he cited two common texts—Psalm 51:5 ("in sin my mother conceived me") and 1 John 1:8 ("if we say we have no sin, we deceive ourselves"). Yet even a simple examination shows these cannot mean believers must continue sinning after salvation.

The inevitable consequence of Christ in us is not perpetual failure but progressive victory.

Psalm 51 describes David's repentance prior to the cross and before regeneration. It is also full of hyperbole (such as saying he had "broken bones" to mean great pain) and is poetic rather than prose. As for 1 John 1:8, the Greek tense allows the translation "if we say we have never sinned," which fits the context of conversion. In the very next chapter, John clarifies: "My little children, I am writing these things to you so that you may not sin" (1 John 2:1) and a little later we find, "No one who abides in Him sins; no one who sins has seen Him or knows Him" (1 John 3:6). The inevitable consequence of Christ in us is not perpetual failure but progressive victory.

This brings us to the heart of the debate—Romans 7. Many misread Paul's lament ("the good that I want, I do not do...") as describing the normal Christian life and Paul's personal struggles. However, that interpretation fails under the weight of context. Romans 6 and 8 surround chapter 7 like bright pillars proclaiming freedom: "Sin shall not be master over you" (6:14) and "the law of the Spirit of life in Christ Jesus has set you free from the law of sin and of death" (8:2).

The middle section (7:14–25) depicts not the Spirit-filled believer but the moral man striving under law. The first-person singular ("I") in Greek often functions generically like the third person in English. Thus, in English this chapter should read "one does what one hates." It is not Paul confessing his own experience but Paul dramatizing the human inability apart from grace. Never forget the Apostle Paul was:

> *Circumcised the eighth day, of the nation of Israel, of the tribe of Benjamin, a Hebrew of Hebrews; as to the Law, a Pharisee; as to zeal, a persecutor of the church; as to the righteousness which is in the Law, found blameless* (Phil 3:5-6)

He does not conclude the passage chained to sin and in despair but rather in in triumph as he declares:

Wretched man that I am! Who will set me free from the body of this death? Thanks be to God through Jesus Christ our Lord! (Rom. 7:24-25).

The metaphor of "the body of death" (7:24) evokes a gruesome Roman punishment described by Virgil[112]. The murderer was chained to his victim's corpse to allow the decay from the corpse to kill the murderer. Paul uses this image to depict humanity's bondage to the flesh. Through Christ, that corpse is cut away—we are free from sin's decay! We may still feel its lingering stench and sores, but we no longer live under its dominion. Every day we should be becoming successively free and healed from the body of death.

This is the crucial difference between determinism and cooperative grace. In Reformed monergism, the Spirit irresistibly regenerates but does not require human participation. In biblical synergism, the Spirit empowers willing cooperation: "If by the Spirit you are putting to death the deeds of the body, you will live" (Rom. 8:13). As Clement of Alexandria wrote, the Spirit is "co-worker with those who are willing" (*Stromata* 2.4). Grace is not mere pardon but power. As Donald Bloesch explained, it is "the dynamic presence of God that enables obedience" (*Essentials of Evangelical Theology*, 1978).

To be "under grace" is to be under transformation. The Holy Spirit renews not only our status but our nature: "You have put off the old self... and have put on the new self, which is being renewed in knowledge after the image of its Creator" (Colossians 3:9–10). The free-will view celebrates this ongoing cooperation—where divine power meets human willingness, where holiness becomes not theoretical but experiential.

---

[112] "The living and the dead at his command; Were coupled, face to face, and hand to hand, Till, chok'd with stench, in loath'd embraces tied; The ling'ring wretches pin'd away and died." The *Aeneid*, Book 8, starting on line 485

Thus, the fruit of learned helplessness is paralysis, but the fruit of faith is freedom. Believers are not doomed to perpetual failure; they are invited into continual victory. The Spirit who justifies also sanctifies, making us not slaves to sin but slaves to righteousness. If Adam can mar the image of God by sin, our Christ can fully restore it within us through His sacrifice.

Spiritual Paralysis

In practice, determinism often yields *spiritual paralysis*—a waiting on God instead of working with God. These are the churches that perpetually sing about "fighting on our knees" and "waiting on the Lord" rather than being the Body of Christ and actively being a part of God's transformative power. When all events and moral outcomes are viewed as eternally fixed by divine decree, human striving can seem futile. Believers may feel growth, prayer, and obedience are merely tokens in a cosmic play already written. As Methodist theologian William Burt Pope observed, "The denial of the will's cooperation with grace makes all exhortations to holiness unreal and all divine warnings illusory" (*A Compendium of Christian Theology*, 1875, 2:58).

Our best examination of history bears out his warning: deterministic revivals burned bright but brief, producing seasons of intense introspection yet little sustained missionary zeal. Then Free Will movements such as Wesleyan Methodism and the Moravian missions reignited the call to active holiness and evangelistic compassion (Latourette, *A History of Christianity*, 1953, 2:1134). Even today outbreaks of revival are far more likely to occur at holiness Wesleyan schools like Asbury University than at Reformed schools like Calvin University.

Scripture presents a vision of dynamic *synergy* between divine and human will. Paul captures this beautifully in *Philippians 2:12–13*:

> So then, my beloved, just as you have always obeyed, not as in my presence only, but now much more in my absence, work out your

167

salvation with fear and trembling; for it is God who is at work in you, both to will and to work for His good pleasure (NAS).

Salvation is not described as a completed decree but as an ongoing cooperation. The believer is commanded to "work out" what God "works in." The two verbs (*katergazesthe* and *energon*) form a reciprocal pattern: divine energy empowers human effort, and human obedience expresses divine indwelling. As Thomas Oden explains, "Grace does not act apart from the believer's freedom but restores it. God's prevenient working enables our responsive working" (*The Transforming Power of Grace*, 1993, 92).

The Apostle Paul's words affirm both divine initiative and human participation in sanctification. God's grace is not passive nor coercive; it is participatory. The Holy Spirit energizes the believer's will without annulling it. As we saw the 4th-century theologian John Chrysostom preached, "God draws, but He draws the willing… It is ours to choose, His to assist" (*Homilies on Romans* 18). This ancient insight captures the balance that deterministic systems lose: love requires freedom, and holiness requires cooperation.

Modern theologians such as Thomas Oden and Donald Bloesch described this same biblical balance. Oden summarized: "Grace does not act apart from freedom but restores it. God's prevenient working enables our responsive working" (*The Transforming Power of Grace*, 1993, 92). Bloesch agreed, calling grace "the dynamic presence of God that enables obedience" (*Essentials of Evangelical Theology*, 1978, 1:153). In this framework, the Holy Spirit is not merely the agent of justification but the enabler of sanctification—the co-worker/partner/*paraklete* who empowers believers to walk in holiness and love.

The Greek word "παράκλητος" (parakletos) occurs five times to describe the Spirit who works with us. The word comes from *para* ("beside") and *kaleo* ("to call"). Literally, it means "one called alongside" someone. In Greek legal and social contexts, it referred to a helper, advocate, intercessor, comforter, or counselor—someone who stands beside another to offer aid or defense (*BDAG*, s.v. "παράκλητος"; *LSJ*, s.v. "παράκλητος"; *TDNT* 5:800–810).

Such cooperation does not diminish God's sovereignty; it reveals its true majesty. Only an all-powerful and all-loving God can endow His creatures with real freedom and then redeem that freedom when misused. The synergy of divine initiative and human response produces the richest fruit: authentic obedience, love freely chosen, and holiness that flows from relationship rather than compulsion.

When believers misunderstand sovereignty as determinism, they risk collapsing obedience into observation. The result is a Christianity of spectators rather than stewards—souls waiting for God to act instead of volunteering themselves as "fellow workers with Him" (2 Cor. 6:1). But when we understand grace as partnership, the spiritual life becomes vibrant, creative, and morally responsible. God works in us *so that* we may work with Him; His sovereignty is not a barrier to action but the foundation of it.

Fruit of Calvinist Historical Systems vs. Relational Faith

While dispensationalism is often less determinist than covenantal Calvinism, both views grow from the same root—the conviction that God's decrees exhaustively determine all events. The Westminster Confession declared that God "unchangeably ordains whatsoever comes to pass,"[113] establishing a metaphysical certainty that defines both systems. Covenantal Calvinism reads history through the "Covenant of Works" and "Covenant of Grace," the first broken by Adam, the second fulfilled in Christ—but both predetermined. Humanity's moral story thus becomes an illustration of God's decree rather than a drama of genuine response.

Dispensational Calvinism, emerging later with John Nelson Darby and C. I. Scofield, preserved the same determinism while dividing

---

[113] *The Westminster Confession of Faith* (1646), III.1.

history into successive "economies" or tests—Innocence, Law, Grace, and so on—each foreknown to end in failure.[114] Charles Ryrie described a dispensation as "a distinguishable economy in the outworking of God's purpose,"[115] yet in both systems, the "purpose" unfolds necessarily, not relationally.

The practical fruit of these theologies often reflects the structure that birthed them: **reverence without responsiveness, zeal without intimacy**. When all outcomes are prewritten, prayer risks becoming observation, not partnership. Evangelism turns into the unveiling of election rather than the pleading of love. Even moral striving, stripped of contingency, becomes evidence of grace rather than the exercise of it. Philosophers like Alvin Plantinga and Richard Swinburne have shown that such determinism erases moral responsibility—if a person could not have done otherwise, then praise and blame lose meaning.[116]

Societal Fruit: Freedom of Religion and Thought

Theological ideas bear social fruit. Doctrines about God and human will inevitably shape how societies view authority, conscience, and liberty. Where determinism prevailed, faith became enforced; where human freedom was affirmed, conscience and democracy flourished. The contrast between Calvinist determinism and the free-will tradition thus extends beyond the pulpit into the fabric of Western civilization.

---

[114] J. N. Darby, *Synopsis of the Books of the Bible* (London: Morrish, 1857–1862).

[115] Charles C. Ryrie, *Dispensationalism* (Chicago: Moody Press, 1995), 33

[116] Alvin Plantinga, *God, Freedom, and Evil* (Grand Rapids: Eerdmans, 1974), 29–30; Richard Swinburne, *The Coherence of Theism*, rev. ed. (Oxford: Clarendon, 1993), 144.

Calvinism's Deterministic Theology: Quest for Control

Classical Calvinism taught both belief and action were predetermined by God's eternal decree. Rooted in Augustine's anti-Pelagian writings, Calvin's system subordinated the human will entirely to divine determination. As historian Perez Zagorin observed, "Predestinarian theology, by subordinating the human will entirely to divine determination, provided little room for freedom in thought or religion."[117]

This theology readily aligned with confessional coercion. John Calvin's Geneva became not only a model of moral discipline but also of doctrinal enforcement. As we have seen, Michael Servetus's execution in 1553 for heresy reveals how tightly orthodoxy was bound to civil authority. Quentin Skinner remarks, "The Reformed churches became in practice among the least tolerant… since they treated heresy not as error but as rebellion against God's sovereign decree."[118]

The logical outcome of such determinism was a fusion of church and state designed to protect God's "glory" through control. A worldview in which every act was preordained left little space for conscience, persuasion, or debate. When faith is viewed as something irresistibly imposed, freedom of belief becomes not a virtue but a threat.

The Free-Will Tradition and the Birth of Liberty

By contrast, the Free Will Christian traditions linked divine sovereignty with human moral agency. Desiderius Erasmus's *De Libero Arbitrio* (1524) argued that moral choice is essential to both justice and love: "To take away free choice is to destroy the very essence of human

---

[117] Perez Zagorin, *How the Idea of Religious Toleration Came to the West* (Princeton, NJ: Princeton University Press, 2003), 91.

[118] Quentin Skinner, *The Foundations of Modern Political Thought*, Vol. 2 (Cambridge: Cambridge University Press, 1978), 248.

righteousness and responsibility." [119] Jacob Arminius (1560–1609) later reaffirmed "love cannot exist without liberty," grounding faith in voluntary cooperation with grace rather than irresistible decree.[120]

This theological shift had profound political implications. If God respects human freedom, so must rulers. If faith must be voluntary to be genuine, coercion becomes sacrilege. Historian Joseph Lecler explains how the Protestant roots of modern religious liberty lie less in the rigor of Geneva than in the humanist and Arminian stream of Protestantism that upheld free inquiry and voluntary faith. He argues that the promising roots of religious toleration in the Reformation lay with Erasmian humanism and the Dutch Remonstrant/Arminian tradition, rather than with rigorist Calvinist models such as in Geneva (Lecler, *Toleration and the Reformation*, 2:256, 385–423).[121]

The early advocates of religious toleration in England and Holland—John Milton, John Locke, and Hugo Grotius—were heirs of this Arminian-humanist synthesis. Milton's *Areopagitica* (1644) declared truth must be tested by freedom: "He that can apprehend and consider vice with all her baits, and yet abstain, is the true way of liberty." Milton's theological writings reveal an anti-predestinarian foundation rooted in moral freedom and the dignity of conscience.

John Locke, who was one of the primary influences upon America's Founding Fathers, was educated in Arminian-influenced Oxford circles and explicitly rejected Calvinist determinism[122]. In his *Letter*

---

[119] Desiderius Erasmus, *On the Freedom of the Will*, trans. E. F. Winter (New York: Frederick Ungar, 1969), 25.

[120] Jacob Arminius, *Declaration of Sentiments* (1608), in *The Works of James Arminius*, Vol. 1, trans. W. Nichols (London: Longman, Hurst, Rees, 1825), 659.

[121] Joseph Lecler, *Toleration and the Reformation*, Vol. 2 (London: Longmans, Green & Co., 1960), 287.

[122] Diego Lucci, *John Locke's Christianity* (Cambridge: Cambridge University Press, 2020), notes that Locke's religious views "denote various similarities

Concerning Toleration (1689), he grounded freedom of religion in moral agency before God, arguing that **coerced faith is no faith at all**. Locke's landmark text further made explicit the link between Christianity and religious liberty:

The one guarded power; the other guarded persuasion of conscience.

> *Since you are pleased to inquire what are my thoughts about the mutual toleration of Christians in their different professions of religion, I must needs answer you freely, that I esteem that toleration to be the chief characteristic mark of the true church.* (21).

As Jeremy Waldron notes, "Locke's defense of toleration depends on a voluntarist conception of faith as a free act of the will."[123]

These thinkers did not sever Christianity from liberty—they drew liberty from Christianity's truest roots. Where Calvinist theocracies sought uniformity, the Arminian stream sought integrity of conscience. The one guarded power; the other guarded persuasion of conscience. Anglican patriot Patrick Henry is often quoted as saying, "It cannot be emphasized too strongly or too often that this great nation was founded, not by religionists, but by Christians; not on religions, but on the gospel of Jesus Christ. For this very reason peoples of other faiths have been afforded asylum, prosperity, and freedom of worship here."[124] Free Will Christians believe in free thought and free debate, and they trust God will lead people to the truth of the gospel.

Human freedom is not a threat to divine sovereignty but a necessary condition for genuine faith. This theological conviction proved fertile

---

with heterodox theological currents such as Socinianism and Arminianism, which Locke knew well."

[123] Jeremy Waldron, *God, Locke, and Equality: Christian Foundations in Locke's Political Thought* (Cambridge: Cambridge University Press, 2002), 53.

[124] Patrick Henry, *The Trumpet Voice of Freedom: Patrick Henry of Virginia*, p. iii. (as cited in "7 Founding Fathers' Quotes on Religion, God & the Bible," LearnReligions) Thus, this could be apocryphal.

ground for civil liberty. England's movement toward toleration was deeply rooted in Christian voluntarism, dissenting conscience, and the conviction that faith compelled by power is not true faith.[125]

Theological systems that subordinate human will entirely to divine decrees—while maybe intellectually consistent—often produce social structures in which religious uniformity is enforced rather than invited. The result is a model of faith that aligns more readily with state power than with genuine liberty.

By affirming the divine dignity of free response, the free-will stream of Christian theology laid the conceptual foundation for religious liberty, pluralism, and the modern ethos of conscience. Its fruit is not simply freedom *from* coercion, but freedom *for* witness, love, and responsible community.

Particularly in the United States, Wesleyan revivalists carried this theology into the social sphere. John Wesley proclaimed, "Where the Spirit of the Lord is, there is liberty… liberty both of the soul and of the body."[126] Methodism's emphasis on prevenient grace and moral responsibility nurtured democratic and abolitionist movements. In the new colonies, revivalist voluntarism produced churches independent of the state yet passionately moral—religion without coercion.

Alexis de Tocqueville observed voluntarist Protestantism sustained America's religious vitality without compulsion: "Religion in America… is mingled with all the national habits and all the feelings to which the native country gives rise."[127] Liberty of conscience, far from weakening faith, strengthened it by rooting belief in genuine conviction.

---

[125]See John Coffey, *Persecution and Toleration in Protestant England, 1558–1689* (Harlow, UK: Longman, 2000).

[126] John Wesley, *Sermons on Several Occasions* (London: 1771), Sermon 17, "The Lord Our Righteousness."

[127] Alexis de Tocqueville, *Democracy in America*, (New York: Vintage Classics, 1990 [1835]), Book 2 Chapter 9.

Methodism was the most influential religion in the United States in the 1800s[128]. Methodism then merged various denominations and in so doing watered down their doctrine and lost their biblical moorings[129]. In the twentieth century the Southern Baptists became the largest denomination, but they have slowly been turning toward the doctrines of TULIP[130] and commensurately are seeing declining adherents. The fastest growing denominations tend to be holiness and Wesleyan oriented, such as the Assemblies of God and the newly formed Global Methodist Church (GMC). The GMC broke away from the United Methodist Church with just a few churches in 2022, and today it lists more than 6000 Bible-believing (and Free Will) churches worldwide.

The Fruit of Freedom and Implications for Politics Today

While Calvinism strove for disciplined moral order, its determinism often yielded control and suppression of dissent. Free-will theology,

---

[128] See https://hirr.hartfordinternational.edu/articles/4438/?utm_source=chatgpt.com. Historians routinely call the 1800s "America's Methodist Century."

[129] Critics within the tradition have argued that such institutional consolidation, combined with 20th-century ecumenism, thinned doctrinal clarity. John Wesley himself warned that Methodists could become a "dead sect, having the form of religion without the power" if they lost "doctrine, spirit, and discipline," and Methodist theologian William J. Abraham famously diagnosed U.S. Methodism with "doctrinal amnesia."

[130] In the late 20th and early 21st centuries, the Southern Baptist Convention (SBC) became the largest Protestant denomination in the U.S. Recent SBC membership has declined to ~12.7 million (2024 data reported in 2025). There has been a measurable shift toward Calvinist soteriology among SBC leaders (2007–2012 LifeWay research) probably spearheaded by Al Mohler who told this author it was his personal objective to bring back Calvinism so as to maintain purity of practice. Journalistic and academic coverage labeled this movement in young Baptists as the "Young, Restless, and Reformed." *Christianity Today*

grounded in moral responsibility and voluntary love, cultivated liberty of conscience, freedom of inquiry, and respect for human dignity. As Dutch Historian of Theology Heiko A. Oberman concluded, the real seed of Western liberty was sown not in Geneva but in the conviction that faith must be free—an insight preserved by Erasmus, Arminius, and their heirs.[131]

The two divergent streams of Christian thought continue to impact today's political landscape. Calvinists want to force their religious views upon the masses whereas Free Will theologians are more apt to seek another way that is voluntary and respectful. Often Free Will Christians are lumped in with the militant Calvinists and called haters of diversity or radical religious social engineers. On the other extreme, some Free Will denominations such as the United Methodists often believe more like Unitarian churches than like Bible-believing Christians. Free Will practitioners who follow the Bible have struggled to maintain a winsome witness while also affirming the fundamentally biblical values the Calvinists wish to impose by force.

A way forward can be found in Colorado Christian University business professor Kevin Miller's book *Freedom Nationally, Virtue Locally —Or Socialism*. Miller's central thesis is that contemporary Christian-conservative politics should **pursue freedom at the national (federal) level, and entrust virtue to the local (community and civil-society) level.** He warns that when the federal government takes on the role of legislating virtue, it inevitably expands government power—and in doing so it undermines freedom and gives rise to socialism. This system of socialism is not merely political but also economic, depriving people of liberty and the general blessings of a free market capitalistic system.

Miller also provides a clarion warning to Christian political activists: beware of the "Haman strategy." He describes that in the Book of

---

[131] Heiko A. Oberman, *The Dawn of the Reformation* (Grand Rapids: Eerdmans, 1992).

Esther Haman was a scheming power-broker who built gallows for his enemy only to be hanged himself upon them. In the same way, Christians need to fight against the machinery of national governance that imposes "virtue" from above using regulatory, fiscal and administrative levers. If Christians support these coercive means, these means will eventually be used to persecute Christians and create powerful governmental centralized control of society. Instead of the government empowering citizens to live out virtue in free local communities, Americans will become subject to top-down mandates that suppress the very freedom the Christian political movement was meant to defend.

The Free-Will or Relational Theology

The free-will tradition—found in the early fathers, Arminius, and Wesley—begins not with decree but with relationship. God's sovereignty is revealed through love, not control. He initiates, empowers, and invites, but never coerces. As Scripture declares, "I have set before you life and death... so choose life" (Deut 30:19, NAS). Jesus laments over Jerusalem, "How often I wanted... and you were unwilling" (Matt 23:37, NAS). Paul affirms that God "desires all people to be saved" (1 Tim 2:4, NAS).

This theology produces different fruit altogether. It cultivates responsibility, repentance, and responsive love—a moral partnership in which God's prevenient grace enables human cooperation without abolishing choice. The early church spoke this language instinctively. Justin Martyr wrote, "Each man goes to everlasting punishment or salvation according to the value of his actions."[132] Irenaeus affirmed that God "made man a free agent from the beginning."[133] Origen

---

[132] Justin Martyr, *First Apology* 43.
[133] Irenaeus, *Against Heresies* 4.37.1.

taught that when we "will and run" *then*
God's mercy comes to our aid.[134] Their
faith was dynamic, relational, and
expectant.

Its adherents work with God, not merely for Him,

Because this system honors both divine initiative and human freedom, it yields a spirituality of hope and engagement rather than resignation. Prayer becomes co-labor; obedience becomes covenantal love; history becomes a genuine dialogue between Creator and creation. C. S. Lewis summarized its heart: "God created things which had free will... because mere automata could never love Him freely."[135]

Comparing the fruit, we see the determinist systems, for all their intellectual elegance, tend to produce either passivity or pride—passivity in those resigned to their fate, pride in those convinced they are the elect. The free-will model produces contrition, compassion, and cooperation—the living fruit of love. Its adherents work *with* God, not merely *for* Him, and see divine sovereignty as a Father's guiding hand, not a puppeteer's string. The relational view alone explains the biblical picture of a God who grieves (Gen 6:6), relents (Exod 32:14), and rejoices (Luke 15:7). The moral fruit testifies to the truth of the tree: a theology that honors love and liberty bears love and liberty in its people.

Conclusions on the Fruit of the Two Views

The New Testament consistently portrays grace as God's empowering partnership with human agency rather than an all-encompassing determinism that renders human participation illusory (Phil 2:12–13; Rom 6:14; 8:13; Gal 5:16). When sovereignty is evolved into decree-determinism, prayer tends toward observation rather than petition, evangelism toward formality rather than pleading love, and

---

[134] Origen, *On First Principles* 3.1.21.
[135] C. S. Lewis, *The Problem of Pain* (New York: Macmillan, 1940), 48

holiness toward perpetual confession without conquest. By contrast, when sovereignty is understood as covenantal love that restores freedom, intercession regains expectancy, mission regains urgency, and sanctification regains moral realism.

This is not a judgment on every Calvinist believer but on the tendency of systems. Where moral outcomes are said to be fixed from eternity, motivation erodes over time—even when adherents verbally affirm the importance of means. If nothing could have gone otherwise, then "appeals" (2 Cor 5:20) function as disclosures of destiny rather than authentic invitations; petitions (Matt 6:10; Jas 5:16) become exercises in alignment rather than instruments by which God truly acts in history; exhortations to "be holy" (1 Pet 1:15–16) risk being heard as ideals that grace never enables. In practice, this breeds resignation, scrupulosity[136], or spiritual elitism.

Free-will (synergist) theology yields different fruit because it tells a different story of God. God initiates, enables, and invites—never coerces. He "desires all people to be saved" (1 Tim 2:4), Christ "tasted death for everyone" (Heb 2:9), and the Spirit empowers believers to "put to death the deeds of the body" (Rom 8:13). Here grace is not only pardon but power; it both forgives and transforms. The Christian life is neither passive waiting nor self-reliant striving but responsive cooperation: God "works in" so that we may "work out" (Phil 2:12–13).

The question, then, is not merely which scheme is more symmetrical on paper, but which one reliably cultivates the fruits Jesus

---

[136] Scrupulosity is a type of obsessive-compulsive disorder (OCD) characterized by an obsessive fear of being sinful or morally wrong, leading to repetitive compulsive rituals and reassurance seeking. It involves excessive guilt and anxiety over perceived moral or religious failings, which can be caused by genetic and environmental factors. Symptoms include intrusive thoughts about sin, a fear of offending God, and rituals like repeated prayers or confessions.

commends (Matt 7:16): love that casts out *Calvin's gospel is not really* fear (1 John 4:18), holiness that is more than *"Good News" for anyone* positional (Rom 6:17–18), hope that refuses fatalism (Rom 15:13), and a gospel that is genuinely good news for all (John 3:16–17).

Calvin's gospel is not really "Good News" for anyone: It is not "news" the "elect" need to hear because they were destined to salvation already, and it is not "good" for everyone else who were chosen to destruction. Compatibilist freedom (acting according to strongest motives ordained by God) cannot ground the sort of interpersonal love Scripture requires (1 Cor 13; Deut 30:19). Deterministic systems tend to harvest order without life, while synergistic faith—rooted in Scripture's calls and promises—regularly bears repentance, courage, compassion, and persevering mission.

Two gardens remain before us. The decree-centric garden prizes tidy rows and high fences; it often yields fear, guilt, and control. The freedom-centric garden prizes life and responsibility; it tends to produce liberty of conscience, genuine repentance, and love chosen rather than compelled. In God's field, love must be chosen to be real, and freedom is the soil in which that love grows.

Freedom was not God's gamble but His glory. Determinism produces symmetry; love produces life. The true test of theology is not its internal logic but the living fruit it yields—prayer that moves heaven, mission that redeems the lost, and holiness that reflects divine love.

Chapter 6: Replanting The Flower of Love: Intro. to ROSES

꽃

"It is a trustworthy statement: For if we died with Him, we shall also live with Him; If we endure, we shall also reign with Him; **If we deny Him, He also will deny us***; If we are faithless, He remains faithful; for He cannot deny Himself. Remind them of these things, and solemnly charge them in the presence of God* **not to wrangle about words***, which is useless, and leads to the ruin of the hearers. Be diligent to present yourself approved to God as a workman who does not need to be ashamed,* **handling accurately the word of truth***"* 2 Tim. 2:11-15, NAS, emphasis added.

"You represent God as worse than the devil, more false, more cruel, more unjust. But you say, you will prove it by Scripture. Hold! What will you prove by Scripture? That God is love? Love in the ordinary sense of the word? No; that God is hate." Rev. John Wesley (1703-1791), *Free Grace* (1740), §8.

Every gardener knows that when a plant grows in the wrong soil it can become stunted or toxic. The same is true of theology. Augustine and Calvin sought to honor God's greatness, but when Calvin magnified omnipotence to combat the corrupt Catholic Church he reduced love as due to only a special few and lost God's goodness. While Calvinism began as a protest against the weeds of corruption, it ended up not only pulling the weed of works-based

A truly sovereign God can even limit the direct influence of His sovereignty to achieve His ultimate ends salvation but also removed all human willpower and in so doing destroyed the "why" for living a Christian life and the synergy that comes when humans freely cooperate with God to accomplish His purposes.

The main motive of most modern faithful Calvinists is to ensure God gets all the glory, and this is absolutely laudable, but it does not require a deterministic framework. All glory belongs to God—but He has chosen that glory to be revealed through love freely given, not fate forcibly imposed. The history of Calvinism reminds us that theology must be pruned by Scripture used in context and watered by love, lest we mistake sovereignty for goodness or control for grace.

Only an infinitely sovereign God can afford to govern through freedom rather than compulsion. A truly sovereign God can even limit the direct influence of His sovereignty to achieve His ultimate ends. What He wants is love, and love cannot be gained any other way than in the soil of free choice. God's ultimate desire is not to glorify Himself on the present earth, but rather it is to cultivate a loving family to enjoy in eternity. **He has no need to impress humans by showing His justice or glory.** Instead, God gains far more glory by restraining His irresistible will and cultivating the hearts of humanity.

When we started this book we looked at the Bible's definition of love—it starts with "love is patient" because that must ultimately be God's greatest expression of love toward His creatures. God is not getting what He wants when He wants it as Calvinists declare. Instead, He is waiting for humans to repent, and partnering with His people to teach them love. He limits the full force of His will now so that he can grow the precious flower of love to be enjoyed in eternity. God encourages our development, prunes our excesses, and wants no one to reject His love and therefore need to be tossed into the fire.

As we have seen, the Reformation's motive was wonderful but its roots reached only back to the somewhat polluted stream of Augustine instead of returning the Church to the beliefs held by Christians during the first 400 years of Christianity. The time has come to complete the Reformation by replanting the flower of God's grace—to move from the rigid petals of TULIP to the living fragrance of ROSES. The following synthesis proposes a constructive alternative within the bounds of orthodox Christian theism, recovering the pre-Augustinian consensus on human freedom and divine love.

In this replanted garden, God's sovereignty is not deterministic control but covenantal faithfulness; His justice is not cold decree but burning mercy; His glory is the natural bloom of His eternal love for all people whom He created. God's true garden will always bloom with the fragrance of freedom, the beauty of redemption, and the eternal life of love.

From TULIP to ROSES

For centuries, theological debate has often revolved around the five points of Calvinism, remembered by the acronym TULIP—Total Depravity, Unconditional Election, Limited Atonement, Irresistible Grace, and Perseverance of the Saints. While the Reformers rightly sought to magnify God's sovereignty, the resulting system champions divine control at the expense of divine love. The ROSES model— Redeemable Creation, Open Invitation, Surrender to Salvation, Empowered Decision, and Secure in Relationship—offers a more biblical and relational framework. It preserves God's sovereignty while honoring His character of love and humanity's genuine moral freedom.

The early church pretty much unanimously affirmed human responsibility and freedom. Origen wrote, "God compels no one to good; for the power of choice has been bestowed by God upon man" (*On First Principles* 3.1.2). Likewise, Irenaeus taught, "God made man free from the beginning...for God never uses force" (*Against Heresies* 4.37.1). This emphasis on voluntary love and relational grace dominated Christian theology for the first four centuries before

Augustine's later determinism reshaped Western thought (Wilson, *The Foundation of Augustinian-Calvinism*, 2019).

R - Redeemable Creation: Deserving Death but Offered Life

The early Church (pre-Augustine) taught it is the remnant of the image of God that gives us the ability to choose to repent. God protected the ability to love and repent from the consequences of the Fall and therefore we either choose to repent or we become responsible for our own perdition.

John Wesley believed in a more severe marring of the image of God, saying that though humans are grievously flawed by sin, after Jesus' atonement the Spirit empowers everyone with the ability to repent. He frequently cites Jesus' proclamation, "And I, if I be lifted up from the earth, will draw all men to Myself" (John 12:32, NAS).

Scripture presents salvation as a cooperative reality: God initiates, and humanity responds in faith. Paul's exhortation captures this divine-human partnership: "Work out your salvation with fear and trembling, for it is God who is at work in you" (Philippians 2:12–13). This synergy between grace and faith does not diminish divine sovereignty; it magnifies divine generosity.

The Calvinist view of monergism—that God unilaterally determines who believes—fails to account for Scripture's constant calls to repentance, faith, and perseverance. Synergistic salvation affirms that God's prevenient grace restores moral freedom and enables a genuine human response without rendering it inevitable (Arminius, *Declaration of Sentiments*, 1608). Salvation is "by grace through faith" (Ephesians 2:8), yet faith is not a mechanical effect of grace—it is a trusting, willing response. Clark Pinnock captured this dynamic well: "Grace does not abolish freedom; it restores and perfects it." (*Grace Unlimited*, 1975, 25).

O – Open Invitation: All Invited, Not All Will be Saved

While Calvinism teaches God's saving choice is *limited* to certain people and *unconditional,* the gospel teaches God's invitation is *universal* but its application is *conditional*—we must repent. The God revealed in Scripture is not a distant sovereign who selects a few by hidden decree, but a loving Father who genuinely invites all people into relationship with Himself. If He *created* for love, He also offers that love to all rather than reserving some people to automatically be sent to perdition. From Genesis to Revelation, God's call resounds with open-handed grace: "Turn to Me and be saved, all the ends of the earth" (Isaiah 45:22); "Come, all who are thirsty" (Isaiah 55:1); "Whoever will may come" (Revelation 22:17). Salvation is not reserved for a preselected elite but freely offered to the world through Christ's redeeming work.

Instead of Unconditional Election, Scripture reveals an Open Invitation—a divine summons extended to every person, accompanied by *prevenient grace* that empowers the human will to respond. Humanity, though fallen, is not abandoned to fatalism. The Holy Spirit goes before, awakening conscience, softening hearts, and restoring our capacity to choose. God's desire is not exclusion but reconciliation, not compulsion but cooperation.

The "O" in ROSES does double duty, also responding to Calvinism's *L*—Limited Atonement. This doctrine, which claims Christ died only for the elect, lacks clear biblical grounding and stands as one of the most widely rejected points of TULIP, even among evangelicals with Reformed sympathies. Nearly all major denominations affirm Jesus' blood was shed for all people and that the Father's heart beats for the salvation of the world. Scripture repeatedly declares the atonement's universal reach: "He Himself is the propitiation for our sins; and not for ours only, but also for those of the whole world" (1 John 2:2). The author of Hebrews adds that Jesus "tasted death for everyone" (Hebrews 2:9), and Paul affirms that God "desires all men to be saved and to come to the knowledge of the truth" (1 Timothy 2:3–4).

Even Calvin, in a rare departure from his more rigid Augustinianism, conceded while commenting on Romans 5:18 that "It is certain that through the goodness of God, the benefit of Christ is common to all."[137] The text itself proclaims: "So then as through one transgression there resulted condemnation to all men, even so through one act of righteousness there resulted justification of life to all men" (NAS). Though Calvin later sought to narrow its meaning, the verse stands as a clear affirmation of universal atonement—Christ's redemptive act as broad in scope as Adam's fall.

John Wesley later articulated the evangelical heart of this truth with elegant simplicity: "The grace or love of God, whence cometh our salvation, is free in all, and free for all" (*Sermon 128: Free Grace*). Likewise, Roger Olson observes that *universal atonement* "best reflects God's universal salvific will" (*Arminian Theology: Myths and Realities*, 2006, 197).

Thus, Open Invitation proclaims what might be called Omni-available Atonement—the truth that God did not merely *offer* salvation to all without first *purchasing* salvation for all. Christ's death on the cross paid the full price of sin—sufficient for every person, effective for those who believe. This universal redemption does not guarantee universal acceptance, but it does guarantee the sincerity of God's call. The open invitation of grace ensures "whosoever will" (John 3:16) can come.

Moreover, this doctrine honors the breadth of divine love while calling believers to holy gratitude. If Christ "tasted death for everyone," then sin should taste bitter to those who claim His name. We live in righteousness not to earn His favor but because His sacrifice, made for all, compels us to honor the One who bore the world's burden. The atonement's scope is as wide as humanity itself;

---

[137] Calvin, John. *Commentaries on the Epistle of Paul the Apostle to the Romans.* Translated by John Owen. Edinburgh: Calvin Translation Society, 1849.

the question is whether we will freely respond to the God who opens His arms to all.

S – Surrender for Salvation: More Glorifying than Coercion

Since Limited Atonement was also dealt with in the above section on Open Invitation, here we can go into more detail about how the act of salvation works. Calvinists argue people do not *surrender* to God at all, but that God unilaterally imposes salvation upon the elect-- *irresistibly*. They claim since the Bible calls us "dead in sin" we lack the capacity to make any spiritual choice. This interpretation fails under the weight of biblical language and logic. "Dead" in Scripture never means "incapable of volition." It means alienated from God—the source of life—not metaphysically volitionally paralyzed.

In Hebrew thought, to be "dead" often meant "separated from covenant life" or "worthy of death," whereas to be "alive" meant to "walk in God's commands" and enjoy fellowship with the One who is Life Himself (Deut. 30:19–20; Ps. 119:88; Wright 2012, 842–43[138]). Thus, Paul's statement that we were "dead" in our sins (Eph. 2:1) should be read exactly as Jesus used the term "dead". In the parable of the prodigal son, the father declares, "This son of mine was dead and has come to life again; he was lost and has been found" (Luke 15:24, NAS). The son's being "dead" to his father clearly did not prevent him from choosing repentance and returning home (Lewis 1952, 122[139]).

The determinist motive in denying human capacity to surrender is well-intentioned: they wish to give God all the glory. Yet it tragically misunderstands *what kind of glory* most befits God. God is far more glorified by the willing surrender of a repentant sinner than by the coerced compliance of an automaton. Divine love is magnified not

---

[138] Wright, N. T. *Paul and the Faithfulness of God.* Minneapolis: Fortress Press, 2012.

[139] Lewis, C. S. *Mere Christianity.* New York: Macmillan, 1952.

Surrender never glorifies the one surrendering; it glorifies the One to whom we yield. through overpowering human will, but through persuading it—through grace that invites rather than compels (Wesley, Sermons on Several Occassions, 115). Salvation is participation in the very life of God, not mere submission to an irresistible decree (Chrysostom, *Homilies on Romans* 16.2).

To illustrate this, imagine yourself as a Confederate general in the American Civil War. You realize your position is hopeless. If your opponent were an honorable man—say, General George B. McClellan—you might agree to surrender and trust his terms. But if you faced General William Sherman, known for burning cities, you might fight to the last man. Surrender honors the victor because it acknowledges both his strength and his trustworthiness. Likewise, when a sinner surrenders to God, it exalts His goodness, not the sinner's resolve. Surrender never glorifies the one surrendering; it glorifies the One to whom we yield.

The Old Testament offers little to no support for Calvinism, and if we affirm its divine authority, neither should we. From Genesis to Malachi, we see a God who speaks, invites, and pleads—a God who reasons with humanity and calls us to choose life. "I call heaven and earth to witness against you today," God says, "that I have set before you life and death, the blessing and the curse. So choose life in order that you may live, you and your descendants, by loving the LORD your God, by obeying His voice, and by holding fast to Him" (Deut. 30:19-20a, NAS). This is not the language of compulsion; it is the language of relationship[140].

When we freely surrender to God, we are infused with His grace. We receive not only forgiveness but also participation in His holiness,

---

[140] Origen. *Commentary on Romans*. Translated by Thomas P. Scheck. Washington, DC: Catholic University of America Press, 2001. 7.13–16

drawing near to Him so that we may learn righteousness. **Grace does not bleach us white through irresistible chemical force; it transforms us gradually and relationally.** It is the reorientation of the soul—learning to see through God's eyes, to feel His heart, and to give His love. We begin to share His nature and become His children not merely in name, but in character and truth (Wesley 1765, 84–85).

E - Empowered Decision making: The Grace to Repent

Scripture declares "the grace of God has appeared, bringing salvation to all men" (Titus 2:11). The Calvinist concept of "Irresistible Grace" is easily refuted in Scripture as we find God's grace is universal and persuasive but never coercive. "Irresistible Grace" is far more founded upon the shifting sands of human philosophy than upon the bedrock of Scripture. God empowers our decision to repent and accept His grace, but He never forces us into compliance.

God's grace is often resisted in the Bible, with Stephen testifying: "You always resist the Holy Spirit" (Acts 7:51). Jesus' lament over Jerusalem is also indicative: "How often I wanted to gather your children together... and you were unwilling" (Matthew 23:37). God's divine love appeals to us and is often persistent -- but can be shunned.

Father of the Church John Chrysostom explained: "God draws, but He draws the willing... All depends indeed on God, but not so as to deprive our free will" (*Homilies on Romans* 18). This reflects a theology of resistible grace—God's love draws with sincerity but allows freedom to refuse. Thomas Oden summarized the same truth: "Grace works not by compulsion but by cooperation; not by negating freedom but by healing and fulfilling it" (*The Transforming Power of Grace*, 1993, 27). God's glory is not found in irresistible control but in love freely received and freely returned.

It is Satan and the demons who strive to force and overpower and possess. The Father *waits patiently* wanting none to perish, the Spirit is *grieved* by our sin, and our Lord *invites* us to His table. There was a forbidden fruit in the garden that gave Adam and Eve a choice—they could stay in God's grace or leave it. **Even when writing the Bible, the very inerrant word of God, we see a guiding not a dictating as each author brings their particular vocabulary, thinking patterns, and literary style to God who then weaves it into His unassailable Word.** God doesn't even assume our continued choice but rather asks that we take up our crosses *daily* and follow Him.

S -Secure in Relationship: Sealed with the Holy Spirit

Finally, our salvation is sealed by the Holy Spirit so we can be secure in our relationship to God. This is not due to a fatalistic decree but to persisting in our faith in Jesus. Jesus said, "Abide in Me, and I in you… apart from Me you can do nothing" (John 15:4–5). Those who remain in Christ are secure, for "no one will snatch them out of My hand" (John 10:28–29). Peter likewise assures believers that they "are protected by the power of God through faith" (1 Peter 1:5).

The Reformed perspective often claims it has the market cornered on assurance of salvation when in fact it gives none at all. Every year or so it seems like

We are saved not due to good works, but we do good works because we are saved.

a great Calvinist leader gets revealed as a fraud, and they go from being on the roster of the "elected saved" to the column of "never saved in the first place." Calvinists cannot know they are saved because salvation is a mysterious selection. Christianity teaches that we can know we are saved—we simply choose faith, God empowers our faith and our lives to live out that faith, and then we trust God will do the saving as He promised. Your continued walk with and toward the Lord, your life producing spiritual fruit, is evidence you are saved. We are saved not due to good works, but we do good works because we are saved. Ultimately the Holy Spirit is the true seal of our salvation, the guarantee that we are in God's gracious hands (Eph 1:13).

While no one can tear us from God's hands and we do not lose something as valuable as salvation, Scripture does say we can give it back by going down the road of sin (Hebrews 6). In fact, Scripture repeatedly warns against apostasy. "If we deny Him, He also will deny us" (2 Timothy 2:12); "If anyone does not remain in Me, he is thrown away like a branch" (John 15:6). Salvation is relational and covenantal, not mechanical. As Athanasius taught, "It is they who persevere in faith to the end who shall be saved" (*Festal Letters* 10, NPNF 2nd Series, Vol. 4). Wesley echoed this truth, warning that believers must "continue in faith, or they cannot continue in salvation." True perseverance is the perseverance of ongoing trust and love. All the believer must "do" is choose to trust God, and like the Old Testament Saints before them, their faith will be counted as righteousness and God will apply His atoning blood for their salvation.

Many verses warn us to think of salvation as the beginning of our lessons on love rather than as some kind of finished act. Jesus did not teach us that we can relax once we are saved, but rather He repeatedly warns that only those who overcome (live out the love of God) will be saved.

To paraphrase a Wesley sermon, to argue that salvation can never be lost requires ignoring or reinterpreting a host of clear warnings in Scripture. According to this view, no lamp can go out (Matt. 25:8), no fruitful branch can ever become barren and be cut off (John 15:2,6), no pardon forfeited (Matt. 18:32–35), and no name ever erased from the Book of Life (Rev. 3:5).

You would have to insist that no salt can lose its flavor (Matt. 5:13), no one can "receive the grace of God in vain" (2 Cor. 6:1), "bury his talent" (Matt. 25:25–30), "neglect so great a salvation" (Heb. 2:3), or "look back" after putting his hand to the plow (Luke 9:62). You would need to deny that anyone can "grieve the Holy Spirit of God" (Eph. 4:30), "quench the Spirit" (1 Thess. 5:19), or resist Him until He no longer strives (Gen. 6:3). You would insist none can "deny the Master who bought them" or "bring swift destruction upon themselves" (2 Pet. 2:1).

You would need to believe the church can never become so lukewarm that Christ would "vomit them out" (Rev. 3:16). You would need to show how if one is lost, he was never found (John 17:12); if he falls, he never stood (Rom. 11:20–22); if cast out, he was never truly in (John 15:6); if he draws back, he never had anything to retreat from (Heb. 10:38–39); if he falls away into darkness, he was never enlightened (Heb. 6:4–6); if entangled again in the world's defilements, he never truly escaped (2 Pet. 2:20); if he "puts salvation away," he never possessed it; and if he shipwrecks his faith, he never had a ship to begin with (1 Tim. 1:19).

In short, the argument must be if you are saved, you cannot lose it—and if you appear to lose it, you never had it. Such mental gymnastics, however clever, twist Scripture to fit a system that is simply not the gospel. May we never embrace a doctrine that must survive by denying so many sober warnings from the Word of God.

While it may be true that warning passages are means God uses to keep the elect and so they don't *prove* actual loss of salvation is possible, to include so many performative exhortations seem excessive. These warnings frequently state real possibility (e.g., "cut off," "fallen from grace," "erase his name") and so reading them as real possibilities best honors the plain force of the text as well as supports the relational nature of salvation.

The popular slogan "once saved, always saved" is neither biblical nor linguistically accurate. It rests on a misunderstanding of the Greek verbs that describe salvation. As any first-year Greek student learns, Greek verbs are based on *aspect*—the kind or quality of action—rather than simple tense or time of action. Consequently, Scripture portrays salvation as a process with past, present, and future dimensions.

Believers have been saved from the penalty of sin through faith in Christ, as well as from the compulsion to sin. "For by grace you have been saved through faith; and that not of yourselves, it is the gift of

God" (Ephesians 2:8–9, NAS). The verb "you have been saved" (*sesōsmenoi este*) is in the perfect tense, emphasizing a completed act with ongoing results.

We are also *being saved* in the present as we live out our faith through obedience and perseverance. Paul exhorts believers, "Work out your salvation with fear and trembling; for it is God who is at work in you, both to will and to work for His good pleasure" (Philippians 2:12–13, NAS). Salvation here is an ongoing, cooperative relationship with God's transforming grace.

Our salvation will be fully consummated when Christ returns. As Paul writes, "Now salvation is nearer to us than when we believed" (Romans 13:11, NAS). Similarly, Peter says believers "are protected by the power of God through faith for a salvation ready to be revealed in the last time" (1 Peter 1:5, NAS). Thus, the believer's final deliverance remains future, contingent on persevering faith.

Salvation, therefore, is not a one-time transaction but a dynamic relationship. A past confession must be confirmed by a present faith and evidenced by a life transformed by the Spirit. As Jesus warned, "The one who endures to the end, he will be saved" (Matthew 24:13, NAS).

New Testament scholar I. Howard Marshall summarized it well: "Security in Christ is never apart from continuing faith in Christ" (*Kept by the Power of God*, 1969, 210). The believer's confidence rests not in an impersonal decree but in a living union with the risen Lord—abiding in Him daily, trusting His grace continually, and awaiting the full revelation of His salvation.

Theological Summary

The ROSES model envisions salvation as a divine love story rather than a legal decree. God's sovereignty is not that of a cosmic puppeteer but of a loving Father who governs by wisdom and relationship. The image of His imprint remains and teams with prevenient grace to allow human repentance and faith, the invitation to salvation is open and universal but constrained by human rejection, salvation is best understood as surrendering to God's calling, humans are empowered to accept or reject God's redemptive love, and we can feel security in our salvation as we live in relationship with God and are sealed by the Holy Spirit.

This relational model aligns with the early church's understanding of moral freedom and with modern evangelical scholars who reject determinism. The ROSES framework reclaims the biblical portrayal of a God whose glory is revealed not in control but in communion. The Reformed TULIP, by contrast, reflects a metaphysic of necessity; ROSES reflects a theology of love. As C.S. Lewis observed, "If a thing is free to be good, it is also free to be bad... free will, though it makes evil possible, is also the only thing that makes possible any love or goodness or joy worth having" (*Mere Christianity*, 1952, 47). God is most glorified not when humans are irresistibly programmed to worship Him, but when they freely choose to love Him.

The free-will (Arminian, Wesleyan, or "classical") position begins not with abstract power but with God's *relational nature*: "God is love" (1 John 4:8). Love, by definition, requires freedom—the possibility to respond or resist. Scripture's moral commands, invitations ("choose this day," "whosoever will"), and judgments presume real human agency.

This view interprets divine foreknowledge as perfect awareness of free choices, not predetermination of them (Romans 8:29, 1 Peter 1:2). God's sovereignty is understood as providential and persuasive rather than coercive: He works all things for good without willing evil (Genesis 50:20, James 1:13).

Philosophically, it preserves moral responsibility: if God unchangeably decrees every act—including unbelief and sin—then human accountability becomes incoherent. Biblically, seeing foreknowledge rather than decree aligns better with the tenor of the prophets and the teachings of Jesus. Jesus even lamented over

Jerusalem's unwillingness to come to Him, which would make no sense if their willingness was somehow decreed (Mat. 23:37).

A God who creates sentient beings for the sole purpose of tormenting them in Hell forever is evil. God does not damn by decree but honors the freedom of those who persist in rejecting His love. C. S. Lewis put it this way: "The doors of hell are locked on the inside." (*The Problem of Pain*, 1940, 130)

The free-will interpretation—properly understood as *grace-enabled freedom*—faithfully expresses the scriptural balance that declares God sovereignly initiates and empowers (Phil 2:13) yet humans genuinely respond (Phil 2:12). It preserves both the majesty and moral beauty of God as well as the responsibility and dignity of humanity. God's sovereignty is not domination but the power to create truly free beings and still accomplish His good purposes. That is a higher, not lesser, sovereignty—one that produces love rather than puppetry. God's omnipotence is not that of a tyrant who must control, but of a Father so infinitely wise that He can grant freedom without fear of losing the outcome.

The garden of ROSES thus restores what the Reformation began but did not complete: a vision of divine sovereignty radiant with love. From this soil, unity and mission can grow anew.

Two Gardens, Two Spirits

Aspect	TULIP Garden	ROSES Garden
Root	Divine control	Divine love
Soil	Determinism	Freedom
Motive of God	Glory	Love/Relationship
Human Role	Passive recipient	Cooperative partner
Evangelism	Limited purpose (the elect only)	Universal invitation, selective surrender
Prayer	Declarative or resigned	Dynamic, relational
Emotion	Fear and awe	Hope and joy
Fruit	Intellectual order	Relational transformation

PETER A. KERR

Chapter 7: The Missing Terrace: Recovering Sheol/Hades

"Now it came about that the poor man died and he was carried away by the angels to Abraham's bosom; and the rich man also died and was buried. And in Hades he lifted up his eyes, being in torment, and saw Abraham far away, and Lazarus in his bosom" (Lk. 16:22-23, NAS).

"Thus, since there are two capacities in fire, one of burning and the other of illuminating, the fierce and scourging property of the fire may await those who deserve to burn, while its illuminating and radiant warmth may be reserved for the enjoyment of those who are rejoicing." St. Basil the Great (330–379) *Homily on Psalm 28(29):7* 'The voice of the Lord divides the flames of fire'

At the start of this book was a comment by James Orr that good theology is anchored in the past and so we want to build upon it rather than depart from it. While to this point the main contention has been to decry a belief system that diverged from historic Christianity, this chapter involves recovering something that theology lost but that was commonly believed and confessed by Christians prior to the fifth century[141].

---

[141] There is an exception as Eastern Orthodoxy retained an understanding of the intermediate state that is much closer to biblical/historic Christianity.

Including this more speculative chapter in a heavily researched book that is mostly about determinism and historic Free Will (synergistic) theology may seem ill-advised. However, this chapter is no less researched, it supports my thesis that God created out of His love for all people, and it advances my real objective of recovering/restoring/reforming Christian doctrine to the relational faith believed in the first three Christian centuries.

In a way, this chapter demonstrates the kind of research that we must do if we wish to someday have a united Body of Christ on earth. We must judiciously discern truth primarily through Scripture and then through the lenses of history/tradition, reason and experience in order to recover the fulsome truth God intended and hopefully with that eventually unite our divided Church[142]. We cannot shy from criticism—we must invite it in good faith and believe God's truth shining like pure gold will rise above the dross.

This chapter discusses what happens between death and resurrection—the intermediate state. It is important from the outset to explain the levels of confidence we can have about the topic. All conclusions must rest on Scripture as the final authority. The early Christian writers should be heard and treated as faithful historical interpreters but not necessarily as infallible sources of doctrine.

With this in mind we can be *certain* there is a conscious existence after death and that after dying on the cross Christ descended into Hades/Sheol. It is *probable* that Hades exists as a temporary realm of the dead divided into some partitions and that a post-mortem proclamation of the gospel was made at least to the Old Testament faithful. It is *possible* Hades continues to exist and the Gospel continues to be preached there to all who do not hear it while among the living.

Furthermore, it is certain that all men will not be saved (universalism), that salvation can only happen by faith through grace,

---

[142] Some will recognize the four elements of the "Wesleyan quadrilateral" used here

and that there will be a Day of Judgement when people are sent to Heaven or Hell and Hades will be thrown into the Lake of Fire. **The purpose of this chapter is not to reinvent but rather to recover the early Church's hope that exalts Christ's justice, mercy, and victory over death.**

In the earliest era of Christian thinking, theology was not speculative philosophy but a proclamation of divine rescue: Christ saved us from sin, first in the here and now, and later for all eternity. God gave us His holiness that we might draw near to Him, learn from Him, and be the Holy ones (saints) of God.

Furthermore, Jesus Christ is "Lord both of the dead and of the living" (Rom. 14:9b, NAS). The early Church firmly confessed Jesus "descended into Hades," preached salvation even to the dead, conquered death, and rose again. By gospel proclamation, the Church participates in His victory, but the keys are His (Mat 16:19; Rev.1:18).

Not only does the Apostle Paul mention this multiple times, but Christian art has celebrated the harrowing of Hell throughout the centuries, and the act of Christ in the intermediate state was enshrined in the Apostle's creed—a confession of faith recognized by all branches of true-believing Christianity today. Speaking of Jesus Christ it says He:

> *was crucified, died and was buried;*
> *He descended into hell [Hades];*
> *on the third day He rose again from the dead*[143]

Recovering a biblically grounded account of the intermediate state recalls an ancient Christian hope: the dead await resurrection under the reign of the risen Christ. By recovering the historic doctrine of the

---

[143] Philip Schaff, ed. *The Creeds of Christendom: With a History and Critical Notes.* Vol. 2, *The Greek and Latin Creeds.* 6th ed. Grand Rapids: Baker Book House, 1983, 45–46. The creed was the reason English had to pick up a word for Hades. Interestingly, linguistically the word "Hell" is from Norse mythology.

intermediate state, we rediscover a faith at once more ancient and more understandably just—a gospel that truly reaches all people—and a further testament that salvation is only had by grace through faith.

The Problem of the Unevangelized

From its beginning, Christianity has proclaimed salvation is offered to all who believe in Christ. Yet an uncomfortable question arose and has lingered: what of the billions who never have a chance to hear His name? This question was important to the early Church because they needed a way to understand how Christ's atoning work on the cross applied to the Old Testament heroes of the faith. In our day, "what about the people in Africa/China" is questions God's fairness and the ubiquity of His offer of salvation.

Philosophers and skeptics have pressed this moral tension. John Stuart Mill, though admiring Jesus' ethics, rejected the idea of a God who would damn the unevangelized, declaring, "I will call no being good who is not what I mean when I apply that epithet to my fellow-creatures; and if such a being can sentence me to hell for not so calling him, to hell I will go" (*An Examination of Sir William Hamilton's Philosophy*, 103).

Many pastors tacitly share Mill's concern if not his belligerent attitude. When officiating funerals for unbelievers, they often say, "God knows the heart" or "He will do what is right" rather than outright proclaiming the deceased are damned.

Such words reflect a deep instinct of faith: that God's judgments, though fearsome, are never unjust. The question is not whether God desires all to be saved (He does, see 1 Tim. 2:4), but how such desire can be realized when so many people never hear the gospel. The answer should also be balanced by the fact that thousands of faithful Christians have heard and heeded God's call to go on missions, with most of Jesus' own disciples dying in distant lands as they spread the word of Christ's resurrection. Surely their calling and acts of sacrifice were not in vain. The answer lies in the intermediate state—a teaching known by the early church, obscured by later dogma starting with Augustine, and urgently needed to be regained today.

Biblical Foundations of Sheol and Hades

Scripture consistently affirms conscious existence after death in Sheol (Hebrew: שְׁאוֹל) or Hades (Greek: ᾅδης). The psalmist confesses, "If I make my bed in Sheol, behold, You are there" (Ps. 139:8). The Septuagint translates Sheol as Hades (ᾅδης), confirming conceptual continuity. We must overcome the many fantasies we learned while studying Greek mythology and think of Hades as the Greek word for the biblical Sheol—the waiting abode of the dead between death and resurrection.

Intertestamental noncanonical writings such as 1 Enoch 22 depict Sheol as divided into compartments—bright for the righteous, dark for the wicked—awaiting final judgment. Jesus affirms at least one division in the parable of the rich man and Lazarus (Luke 16:19–31). It is a long passage but the full parable needs to be seen since its implications have been so often overlooked:

> *"Now there was a certain rich man, and he habitually dressed in purple and fine linen, gaily living in splendor every day. And a certain poor man named Lazarus was laid at his gate, covered with sores, and longing to be fed with the crumbs which were falling from the rich man's table; besides, even the dogs were coming and licking his sores. Now it came about that the poor man died and he was carried away by the angels to Abraham's bosom; and the rich man also died and was buried. And in Hades he lifted up his eyes, being in torment, and saw Abraham far away, and Lazarus in his bosom. And he cried out and said, 'Father Abraham, have mercy on me, and send Lazarus, that he may dip the tip of his finger in water and cool off my tongue; for I am in agony in this flame.' But Abraham said, 'Child, remember that during your life you received your*

good things, and likewise Lazarus bad things; but now he is being comforted here, and you are in agony. 'And besides all this, between us and you there is a great chasm fixed, in order that those who wish to come over from here to you may not be able, and that none may cross over from there to us.' And he said, 'Then I beg you, Father, that you send him to my father's house--for I have five brothers-- that he may warn them, lest they also come to this place of torment.' But Abraham said, 'They have Moses and the Prophets; let them hear them.' But he said, 'No, Father Abraham, but if someone goes to them from the dead, they will repent!' But he said to him, 'If they do not listen to Moses and the Prophets, neither will they be persuaded if someone rises from the dead.'" (Lk. 16:19-31, NAS)

Interestingly, this does not follow Jesus' classic parable formulation because Jesus gives the people proper names (instead of just saying "a man" or "a farmer"). This may suggest He is relating something that is more than just a parable. Notice that in Hades/Sheol both men are conscious; both await resurrection; and between them a great chasm is fixed.

Several leading interpreters treat Luke 16:19–31 primarily as a parable of moral reversal and repentance, not a literal place in the afterlife. My former seminary professor Dr. Joel Green reads Luke 16 primarily as moral exhortation about wealth and repentance, as well as an exhortation to heed Moses and the prophets, rather than a cartographic tour of the afterlife; Bock agrees on the parabolic setting but notes that Luke's use of afterlife motifs still presupposes recognizable categories for Jesus's hearers. [144]

While I understand their caution, Luke's sustained detail (Abraham's bosom, fixed chasm, conscious dialogue) and congruence

---

[144] See Joel B. Green, The Gospel of Luke, New International Commentary on the New Testament (Grand Rapids: Eerdmans, 1997), 596–604. And Darrell L. Bock, Luke 9:51–24:53, Baker Exegetical Commentary on the New Testament (Grand Rapids: Baker, 1996), 1357–75.

with contemporary beliefs about Sheol plausibly suggest real categories of an intermediate state. Richard Bauckham and Klyne Snodgrass claim the story draws on "Jewish folklore" to dramatize the urgency of repentance before death[145].

The pericope certainly serves the purposes these commentators claim, but I believe it does far more as Jesus is not inventing a location but actually explaining His understanding of where people go immediately after death. John Wesley, in his sermon *The Rich Man and Lazarus*, accepted the story's realism and location as it appears in its plainest sense, using the passage to stress there is "a great gulf is fixed" which means there is no second chance at salvation after death[146].

I agree with Wesley that, especially in the light of Patristic writings and beliefs we will discuss below, we should prefer the more plain reading and real existence of Hades. Jesus was using what He and others in His day understood would happen in the afterlife to deliver an important moral warning.

Interestingly, after His resurrection Jesus never corrects the common understanding that the dead go immediately to Hades/Sheol. I agree with Wesley's main point that there is no second chance doctrine, but I think he missed the idea that Hades may be where those who never had a chance to hear the gospel are held, and that the "fixed chasm" may be dissolved at the Day of Judgement before Hades is tossed into the lake of fire (Hell).

Hades is the missing piece that can transform our understanding of divine judgment as arbitrary punishment upon the lost who never hear

---

[145] Richard Bauckham, "The Rich Man and Lazarus: The Parable and the Parallels," *New Testament Studies* 37, no. 2 (1991): 225–46. And Klyne R. Snodgrass, *Stories with Intent: A Comprehensive Guide to the Parables of Jesus* (Grand Rapids: Eerdmans, 2008), 428–36.

[146] John Wesley, "The Rich Man and Lazarus," Sermon 112 in *The Works of John Wesley*, 3rd ed. (London: Wesleyan Methodist Book Room, 1872), 4:326.

the Good News into the fulfillment of Jesus' offer of mercy to all who will repent. If in Hades people may respond by faith through grace to Christ's self-revelation, we should expect people held there to be welcomed into eternal life at the Day of Judgement. Certainly those who persist in rebellion—along with Satan, the beast, and the false prophet—will face final separation in the lake of fire (Rev 20:10, 14).

The Threefold Structure of Hades

A number of Jewish and early Christian sources picture Sheol/Hades in differentiated terms. While Scripture does not provide a formal taxonomy, the following model summarizes common ancient depictions drawn primarily from biblical references, but also using intertestamental (primarily the Book of I Enoch) and patristic evidence:

Upper Hades (Paradise/Abraham's Bosom)—A place of comfort for the righteous awaiting resurrection (Phil. 1:23) and a place where God's presence dwells.

Middle Hades (the default, so just "Hades")—A place of weeping and gnashing of teeth, of frustration, outer darkness and disembodiment—not a place where you want to be. It is where all the Old Testament heroes of the faith go (Sheol) until Jesus' resurrection. It may also be where those without knowledge of the law or gospel go and they may hear there the good news of salvation before the Day of Judgement (Eph. 2:12; Rev. 1:18).

Lower Hades (Tartarus)—Where all who hardened their hearts in rebellion go, as well as demonic spirits from Noah's day remain chained (2 Pet. 2:4). This is the abode of those who rejected Christ in life (either knowing His name or His law on their hearts and grievously rejected His character of truth and goodness). See the below discussion on sin that leads to death.

Christ's Descent and the Gospel Among the Dead

Although it is often overlooked, when Jesus tells the repentant thief on the cross beside Him, "Today you will be with Me in Paradise" (Luke 23:43), He does not say "Heaven" (Greek: *Ouranos*). Paradise—from the Persian *pairidaeza*, meaning "garden"—was the blessed section of upper Hades, also called Abraham's bosom. Thus, even on the cross, Jesus was expecting to see Hades in the afterlife

After His crucifixion, Jesus entered the realm of the departed. Peter declares He "was put to death in the flesh but made alive in the spirit, in which also He went and preached to the spirits in prison" (1 Pet. 3:18–19). Later he explains, "For the gospel has for this purpose been preached even to those who are dead, that though they are judged in the flesh as men, they may live in the spirit according to *the will of* God" (1 Pet. 4:6).

Many conservative interpreters read 1 Pet 3:19 as Christ proclaiming victory to hostile powers or as Spirit-enabled preaching in Noah's day. I acknowledge these options, but I do not see Christs' character as one that gloats over those being punished nor do I think a comment about Christological time-travel to Noah's day fits well here. It is far more likely that Jesus was revealing Himself as the Savior of the world, and "Lord of both the dead and the living" (Rom. 14:9).

The verb *kērussō* means to proclaim good news, not merely to mock the damned. Furthermore, the parallelism in 4:6 and the baptismal context of 3:18–22 (the flood serving as a type of baptism), together commend a reading in which Christ's saving proclamation reaches the departed without implying universal success. Christ's descent, therefore, was not spectacle but salvation—His gospel announced to those who never heard it in life.[147]

---

[147] For more discussion on this and the alternative meanings see: Karen H. Jobes, 1 Peter, Baker Exegetical Commentary on the New Testament

Not only was the criminal on the cross going to paradise on the day of Jesus' crucifixion, but all the Old Testament faithful heard Jesus' preaching and were released from Middle Hades as the first fruit of the Resurrection. They could not precede Jesus into paradise because, "it is impossible for the blood of bulls and goats to take away sins" (Heb. 10:3-4). The blood of animals was sacrificed by faith looking forward to Jesus' sacrifice that could pay for sin. Old Testament saints were only writing checks by faith—Jesus was the cashing of the checks because He was the *Agnus Dei*, the "Lamb of God who takes away the sin of the world!" (Jn. 1:29).

When Jesus died we are told, "And behold, the veil of the temple was torn in two from top to bottom, and the earth shook; and the rocks were split, and the tombs were opened; and many bodies of the saints who had fallen asleep were raised; and coming out of the tombs after His resurrection they entered the holy city and appeared to many" (Matt. 27:51-53). This was the outcome of Jesus' preaching in Hades. Souls came alive and the Old Testament faithful followed Jesus and migrated from Middle Hades/Sheol to Upper Hades (Paradise). This is also how Clement of Alexandria (c. AD 150–215) understood the passage as he wrote:

> *Further the Gospel Matthew 27:52 says, that many bodies of those that slept arose,— plainly as having been translated to a better state. There took place, then, a universal movement and translation through the economy of the Saviour. (The Stromata 6.6)*

(Grand Rapids: Baker Academic, 2005), on 3:18–22, canvasses the major options and judges the "Noahic preaching" reading most likely. and Thomas R. Schreiner, 1, 2 Peter, Jude, New American Commentary 37 (Nashville: B&H, 2003), 178–86, prefers a triumphal proclamation to hostile powers but acknowledges the difficulty of the passage. and Richard J. Bauckham, Jude, 2 Peter, Word Biblical Commentary 50 (Waco, TX: Word, 1983), on 1 Pet 3:19 as cited in intertextual discussions, highlights Jewish traditions about imprisoned spirits that shape Petrine imagery.

Jesus led the first fruits of the Resurrection, the Old Testament faithful, into Paradise or Upper Hades, as described in I Cor. 15:16-24:

> *"For if the dead are not raised, not even Christ has been raised; and if Christ has not been raised, your faith is worthless; you are still in your sins. Then those also who have fallen asleep in Christ have perished. If we have hoped in Christ in this life only, we are of all men most to be pitied. But now Christ has been raised from the dead, the first fruits of those who are asleep. For since by a man came death, by a man also came the resurrection of the dead. For as in Adam all die, so also in Christ all shall be made alive. But each in his own order: Christ the first fruits, after that those who are Christ's at His coming,"* (NAS).

This may also be why in John 20:17 Jesus told Mary not to touch her, "…for I have not yet ascended to the Father; but go to My brethren, and say to them, 'I ascend to My Father and your Father, and My God and your God'" (NAS). We hear from the Apostle Paul:

> *Therefore it says, "When He ascended on high, He led captive a host of captives, And He gave gifts to men." (Now this expression, "He ascended," what does it mean except that He also had descended into the lower parts of the earth? He who descended is Himself also He who ascended far above all the heavens, that He might fill all things.)* Eph. 4:8-10, NAS

Jesus led the captives free, fulfilling Ps. 68:18, and made a place for the redeemed to await His second coming. The early Church inherited, believed, and propagated the truth of Hades. Irenaeus taught, "The Lord descended into the regions beneath the earth, announcing the glad tidings of His coming and remission of sins to those who believe in Him" (*Against Heresies*, 4.27.2). Clement of Alexandria affirmed that the Lord preached the gospel to those in Hades, so that they might be saved (*Stromata*, 6.6). Even Augustine, though later developing a different soteriology, affirmed Christ's descent[148].

---

[148] See Ep. 164; Enchiridion 110; City of God 20

Both Scripture and the Ante Nicene Church Fathers affirmed it was Christ's descent into Hades that made a way for the Old Testament faithful to hear the Gospel of Jesus Christ and be saved by the only name under Heaven given to men that can save (Acts 4:12). But does this gospel continue to be preached in Hades? Does Hades exist even after Jesus' ministry there? Did the early Church know more about Hades that was subsequentially buried in history but that we can recover through diligent exegesis of the Bible and thorough examination of the beliefs of the early Church?

The Church Fathers on Hades

Before Augustine invented his doctrines of Original sin and Purgatory, the Ante Nicene Church Fathers agreed Hades was temporary and redemptive. They taught Christ's descent opened Paradise to humanity and proclaimed freedom to the captives, and some even talked about the gospel continuing to be taught in Hades after Jesus' resurrection.

The Apostles' Creed enshrined the doctrine of Jesus' descent into Hades to preach: "He descended to the dead." Eastern Christianity, maintaining this heritage, still celebrates Christ's going to Hades on the Saturday before Easter declaring: "Christ is risen from the dead, trampling down death by death" (Alfeyev 2009, 35).

While the Fathers are not uniform, a significant stream—from Irenaeus through Chrysostom—affirms a real intermediate state distinct from final judgment, and several witness to Christ's effective proclamation of the Gospel there. Perhaps it is best to allow some of the Church Fathers to speak for themselves:

Irenaeus of Lyons (c. 130–202)

Irenaeus affirmed all souls descend to an intermediate realm, not immediately to Heaven or Hell, and that it was the gospel that was preached there:

The Lord descended into the regions beneath the earth, announcing the glad tidings of His coming and remission of sins to those who believe in Him. (Against Heresies 4.27.2; cf. Ps. 16:10; Acts 2:31)

Clement of Alexandria (c. 150–215)

Clement taught God's mercy extends even into Hades, where the Gospel is preached to those who never heard it in life, to include gentiles.

> *If, then, the Lord descended to Hades for no other end but to preach the Gospel, as He did descend; it was either to preach the Gospel to all or to the Hebrews only. If, accordingly, to all, then all who believe shall be saved, although they may be of the Gentiles, on making their profession there; since God's punishments are saving and disciplinary, leading to conversion, and choosing rather the repentance them the death of a sinner; and especially since souls, although darkened by passions, when released from their bodies, are able to perceive more clearly, because of their being no longer obstructed by the paltry flesh… **Not only then the believer, but even the heathen, is judged most righteously.** (Stromata* 6.6; 6.14 bold mine; cf. 1 Pet. 3:19; 4:6)

Tertullian (c. 160–225)

Tertullian described Hades as a divided realm where there is comfort for the righteous, torment for the wicked, and where all souls are shut up within Hades until the day of the Lord. He writes:

> *Why, then, cannot you suppose that the soul undergoes punishment and consolation in Hades in the interval, while it awaits its alternative of judgment, in a certain anticipation either of gloom or of glory?" (A Treatise on the Soul,* chapter 58).

He goes on to reject soul sleep in the intermediate state, saying:

> *What, then, is to take place in that interval? Shall we sleep? But souls do not sleep even when men are alive: it is indeed the business of bodies to sleep, to which also belongs death itself, no less than its mirror and counterfeit sleep (A Treatise on the Soul,* chapter 58)

Tertullian also defended the existence of both pain and pleasure in Hades, despite us not having bodies there. He concluded:

> ...*no one will hesitate to believe that the soul undergoes in Hades some compensatory discipline, without prejudice to the full process of the resurrection, when the recompense will be administered through the flesh besides.* (*A Treatise on the Soul*, chapter 58)

Hippolytus of Rome (c. 170–235)

In his vivid cosmology, Hippolytus described Hades as a vast subterranean place with distinct regions. There are some who are awaiting the Day of Judgement in pain and others, in "Abraham's Bosom" await it in pleasure.

> *But the righteous shall obtain the incorruptible and un-fading kingdom, who indeed are at present detained in Hades, but not in the same place with the unrighteous..* (*Against Plato on the Cause of the Universe* Ch. 1; cf. Luke 16:26)

He also clearly saw Hades as existing until the end, writing:

> ...*on the subject of Hades, in which the souls of all are detained until the time which God has determined; and then He will accomplish a resurrection of all, not by transferring souls into other bodies, but by raising the bodies themselves* (*Against Plato, On the Cause of the Universe*, Ch. 2)

Origen (c. 185–253)

Origen emphasized Christ's descent and preaching in Hades is salvific and restorative, and even suggested Jesus knew who would better accept the gospel while alive and who would be more open to it after death:

> ...*he went to Hades to gain over those who were there. But whether he like it or not, we assert that not only while Jesus was in the body did He win over not a few persons merely, but so great a number, that a conspiracy was formed against Him on account of the multitude of His followers; but also, that when He became a soul, without the covering of*

the body, He dwelt among those souls which were without bodily covering, converting such of them as were willing to Himself, or those whom He saw, for reasons known to Him alone, to be better adapted to such a course. (Against Celsus 2.43)

Athanasius of Alexandria (c. 296–373)

Athanasius stressed Hades was decisively conquered because God's word triumphs in every realm:

> *or by the Word revealing Himself everywhere, both above and beneath, and in the depth and in the breadth — above, in the creation; beneath, in becoming man; in the depth, in Hades; and in the breadth, in the world — all things have been filled with the knowledge of God (On the Incarnation, 16)*

> *But if a man is gone down even to Hades, and stands in awe of the heroes who have descended there, regarding them as gods, yet he may see the fact of Christ's Resurrection and victory over death, and infer that among them also Christ alone is true God and Lord. For the Lord touched all parts of creation, and freed and undeceived all of them from every illusion. (On the Incarnation, 45)*

John Chrysostom (c. 347–407)

Chrysostom distinguished Hades' compartments and emphasized moral consequences. He saw part of the pain of the wicked in Hades was being able to see the righteous people in Abraham's Bosom, and used Luke 16 to refute the false belief in wandering spirits haunting things after death (*Homily on Lazarus and the Rich Man* 2; cf. Luke 16:19–31). He also saw Christ's sacrifice on the cross as opening the gates of Hades as he wrote:

> *For if it [the cross] opened the gates of hades, and threw wide the archways of Heaven, and made a new entrance into Paradise, and cut away the nerves of the devil; what marvel, if it prevailed over poisonous*

drugs, and venomous beasts, and all other such things. (Homily on Matthew 54.7)

Augustine (354–430)

Augustine also believed in Hades, but then while condemning Pelagius he started transforming the common belief into Purgatory complete with the need to pay indulgences. He taught souls go to Hades where there are those who are afflicted and those who enjoy peace:

> *The State of the Soul During the Interval Between Death and the Resurrection: During the time, moreover, which intervenes between a man's death and the final resurrection, the soul dwells in a hidden retreat, where it enjoys rest or suffers affliction just in proportion to the merit it has earned by the life which it led on earth. (Enchiridion* 109; cf. Luke 16:22)

We'll get back to how Augustine was instrumental in reworking the common understanding of Hades into the doctrines of Purgatory and indulgences.

The witness of the early Church affirms Hades/Sheol is neither the final Hell nor an empty metaphor, but a real and temporary realm in which the souls of the dead first awaited Christ's victory and may now be awaiting His return. From Irenaeus of Lyons to Chrysostom, for the first three centuries the Church Fathers proclaimed a redemptive narrative that stretched beyond the grave—a descent that became deliverance.

In the ancient Church, the Gospel was truly "good news to the dead" (1 Pet. 4:6), proclaiming no corner of creation was beyond the reach of divine love. This understanding not only reconciles God's justice with His mercy but also restores the original Christian hope: that life triumphs over death, love descended even into Hades, and that every human is valuable and is offered not only a chance to be righteous (which we universally fail to achieve) but also access to the blood of Christ and His atoning work on the cross.

The Biblical Bedrock: Is there Salvation After Death?

There are many opaque passages in the Bible that become clear when we understand Sheol/Hades as the early Fathers did. Most of the Scriptures that point to Sheol/Hades were coopted and absorbed into Catholic doctrines that Protestants reject. These verses have hence been mistrusted instead of seen as the early Church saw them.

The verse that first made me start studying the intermediate state was Jesus saying, "but whoever shall speak against the Holy Spirit, it shall not be forgiven him, either in this age, or in the *age* to come" (Matt. 12:32b, NAS). This naturally implies some sins can be forgiven in the age to come. What is the age to come?

When I read this at 14 years-old I thought we die and then go to Heaven or Hell. It did not take much research to see we cannot go to Heaven or Hell until the Day of the Lord (1 Thess. 5:1-4; Acts 17:31; II Tim 4:8), and so when we die we must go somewhere to await the Judgement Day.

Hades is where Jesus taught we go (Luke 16) and Hades exists until the end. It also cannot be the same as "Hell" because it will be thrown into Hell as we read in Revelations 20:13-15:

> *And the sea gave up the dead which were in it, and death and Hades gave up the dead which were in them; and they were judged, every one of them according to their deeds. And death and Hades were thrown into the lake of fire. This is the second death, the lake of fire. And if anyone's name was not found written in the book of life, he was thrown into the lake of fire.* (NAS)

As a quick aside that is somewhat germane, further study of Matthew 12 had me trying to understand blaspheme of the Holy Spirit, or speaking against the Holy Spirit (so I could avoid it!). I believe it is linked to the Hebrew 6 admonishment (covered earlier in Chapter 3).

213

In Matthew 12 Jesus is speaking to pharisees who are declaring the Spirit's activity is Satan's activity. These men should have recognized Jesus as the Savior—they had all the evidence of goodness in front of them and yet they called Him evil anyway. They had fully "tasted of the Heavenly gift" (v.4), knew the truth, but had decided to reject it because they preferred self-righteousness.

The very existence of an unforgivable sin should give pause to the "once saved always saved" crowd. What happens if you are saved then you commit this sin? In my understanding, it cannot be done by accident, and it cannot be done by anyone who is not fully invested in the faith. It can only be done intentionally and knowingly by a mature believer declaring what is of God is of the devil. This is most consonant with the plain meaning of Hebrews 6 and 10.

Sin that Does not Lead to Death?

Moving away from a sin that cannot be forgiven, let's look at sin that does not lead to death. Many Protestants have heard at least one sermon about how "all sin is equal" and have quoted "For the wages of sin is death, but the free gift of God is eternal life in Christ Jesus our Lord" (Rom. 6:23 NAS). If sin were all "equal" in the sense of equally morally repugnant to God then why does God give different punishments for different sins? Even the Ten Commandments are listed starting with the most offensive to God and ending with the least (Aquinas, *Summa Theologiae*, I–II, q.100, a.6). It seems the more a sin breaks down relationship the worse it is, with murder pretty much destroying all relationship. If all the law is summed up in loving God and loving others, then all sin is summed up in doing the opposite, and the more you act to break relationship the more you are culpable.

Catholicism categorizes sins into the venial (not as bad and can be worked off in Purgatory) and the mortal (deserving Hell) sins. Protestants reject this division because they see any single sin deserves separation from God and they do not see any evidence of Purgatory in

214

Scripture. They especially do not wish sin to be seen as ranging from those that are less to those that are more financially costly to be forgiven by the Church. However, there is a biblical reason for the Catholic division of sins that could suggest assist our understanding of the intermediate state.

The Bible distinguishes between sins that "lead to death" and "sins that do not lead to death," as the Apostle John writes:

> *If anyone sees his brother committing a sin not leading to death, he shall ask and God will for him give life to those who commit sin not leading to death. There is a sin leading to death; I do not say that he should make request for this. All unrighteousness is sin, and there is a sin not leading to death.* (1 Jn. 5:16-17, NAS)

Here the word "death" can be understood as "separation from the One who is Life," which is to say separation from God. How can there be a sin that doesn't LEAD to death? With the understanding of Hades, this pericope makes perfect sense. The sin *"leading* to death" is the sin leading straight to Lower Hades and then to Hell. It is a rejection of God's love and salvation. A sin that doesn't *lead* directly to death is a sin that is not a rejection of Christ.

This passage has so many poor commentary interpretations that it is not worthwhile to even describe them here. Many of them even think "sin leading to death" means physical death, but that seems nonsensical—if their sin leads to physical death it would be more important to pray for the friend's salvation. The plainest interpretation is hard to see unless we understand John's readers in the ancient near east expected to go to a tiered Hades and so understood that some sins could be forgiven in Hades whereas rejection of the Savior leads to Lower Hades.

Early Christians believed in far more continuity between the dead and the living than is taught today. They certainly believed their actions on earth could impact and bless the dead below the earth.

The Apostle Paul mentions baptism for the dead without denouncing it, writing, "Otherwise, what will those do who are baptized for the dead? If the dead are not raised at all, why then are they baptized for them?" (1 Cor. 15:29, NAS). While the Apostle is not recommending it, if nothing else this shows baptizing for the dead was practiced in Corinth and the early Church.

It is vital we do not allow this reference to confuse us into giving credibility to modern cults like Mormonism. The Mormons saw this verse was in the Bible, but rather than seeking a return to the true faith, they did the same thing they did with all Scripture and twisted it into their own modern beliefs that are only a shadow of the true Gospel.

Not only did the early church baptize for the dead, but they also prayed for the dead. Prayer between the living and the dead has been a contentious topic, with most Protestants at least agreeing the *faithful dead can pray for the living* because there is a "cloud of witnesses" (Heb 12:1) who are actively interceding on our behalf (Rev 5:8; 8:4).

The Eastern Orthodox Church and the Catholic Church recognize prayer also can go in the other direction; the living can pray for the deceased because of passages in 2 Maccabees (which Catholics claim as Scripture but which is noncanonical for Protestants):

> *For if he were not expecting that those who had fallen would rise again, it would have been superfluous and foolish to pray for the dead. But if he was looking to the splendid reward that is laid up for those who fall asleep in godliness, it was a holy and pious thought. Therefore he made atonement for the dead, so that they might be released from their sin.* 2 Maccabees 12:44–46 (NRSV)[149]

Why do Protestants reject praying for the dead? There is nothing in Scripture that forbids it, but rather people have believed they go straight to Heaven or Hell after death and so there is no reason to pray. A biblical understanding of the intermediate state encourages prayer for the dead as it opens up the possibility of praying for ancestors and loved ones who never heard the Good News. Later in his life C.S.

---

[149] Also see Metropolitan Philaret (Drozdov) of Moscow, *A Longer Orthodox Catechism*, Q. 376–377 (Jordanville, NY: Holy Trinity Monastery, 1975), 135.

Lewis affirmed the instinct to pray for the dead, writing, "Of course I pray for the dead. The action is so spontaneous, so all but inevitable, that only the most compulsive theological case against it would deter me" (*Letters to Malcolm, Chiefly on Prayer*, 107).

1 John 5 may be saying that we cannot effectively pray for those who hear and reject Christ (sins that lead to death) but that we can intercede on behalf of those who whose sins do not lead to death. Admittedly, this is not strong proof of Hades and how people might still be there hearing the Good News. Is there other Scripture that clearly indicates salvation is possible after life?

The Gates of Hades will Not Prevail

The most powerful verse to that effect lies right in the middle of the most contested passage between Protestants and Catholics. It is when Jesus says, "And I also say to you that you are Peter, and upon this rock I will build My church; and the gates of Hades shall not overpower it" (Matt. 16:18, NAS). Catholics claim this established the Church with Peter and his successors as its head, whereas Protestants claim Jesus did not say "Cephas" (Peter's name meaning something like "pebble") but rather "Petras" (meaning "big boulder") and so Jesus was referring to Himself as the Rock and the confession as the foundation of the Church.

What is relevant here is that some Bibles also mistranslate this passage and erroneously put "Hell" instead of "Hades." That would make no sense—the gates of Hell are locked permanently—people in Hell will be there for eternity (unless you believe in annihilation, which is another topic for another day).

This also leads to the whole misunderstanding in which people think Hell is a metaphor for Satanic forces or that Satan rules in Hell. That error arose because the Church preached in Latin so few understood the Bible being read or the homilies. Instead, they gained much of their theological training by looking at stained glass windows and Christian art. It is hard to depict people being tortured without torturers, so the artists put Satan and the demons as the ones dolling out the punishment. Nothing could be farther from the truth: Hell was made to torment Satan and the demons (Mat 25:41), and humans who follow them will also be there. No one sent to Hell will get out.

It is not the *gates of Hell* but the *gates of Hades* that the Church can invade. Upper Hades is paradise and Lower Hades is Tartarus, so that means specifically Middle Hades is where people can still come to salvation. It can only be by grace through faith and it can only be due to the blood of Christ, but all of those things can logically be had even in Hades.

There is even some evidence that Hades can be reformatory. In Luke 16 the rich man is no longer only thinking of himself. Instead of just asking for water, he also asks that Abraham visit the land of the living to warn his brothers of their upcoming fate. That certainly looks like Hades is not only about punishment but also possibly about reforming the soul.

There are other hints of Hades having a reformative effect upon the souls waiting there. The Apostle Paul writes, "Or do you not know that the saints will judge the world? And if the world is judged by you, are you not competent to constitute the smallest law courts?" (1 Cor. 6:2–3, NAS). The word *judge* (*krinō*) here does not merely mean "to condemn," but "to decide, to evaluate, or to pronounce an opinion concerning right and wrong." According to BDAG, *krinō* carries a semantic range that includes "to separate, distinguish, select, or determine" and "to judge, evaluate, or rule" but not solely "to condemn."[150]

If final judgment involved only condemnation of people who have not heard of Jesus, the saints' participation would be decidedly

---

[150] *A Greek-English Lexicon of the New Testament and Other Early Christian Literature*, 3rd ed., rev. and ed. by Frederick W. Danker (Chicago: University of Chicago Press, 2000), s.v. "κρίνω."

superfluous. Instead, Paul's language suggests a more comprehensive role—one that reflects the righteous discernment and mercy of Christ Himself. As believers are conformed to His likeness, as they become increasingly *in* Christ, they are entrusted to share in His just and merciful governance. One can even imagine a martyr standing beside Christ, affirming His gracious verdict toward a former persecutor now redeemed from Hades. This may also be why our forgiveness requires us to forgive (Mat. 6:14-15).

To conclude this section, it might be good to note that the Eastern Orthodox tradition, heir to the Greek language and better eschewing Augustine's influences, never lost the doctrine of Hades and potential salvation there (although it is slightly different than the three tiers version explained here). Metropolitan Hilarion Alfeyev summarizes: "The descent into hell [Hades] signifies that salvation was extended to all people and all times... even those who had died before Christ could hear the gospel and believe" (*Christ the Conqueror of Hell*).

Addressing Objections

The two most common objections when given so much evidence about the intermediate state are discussed below. See my upcoming book *Resurrecting Hades* for a more fulsome account of this topic, but for now I can address these very reasonable objections.

First, some people claim Hebrews 9:27 precludes an intermediate state. It reads, "It is appointed for men to die once, and after this comes judgment." However, this verse affirms the certainty of judgment, not its immediacy. The same passage points beyond death to Christ's return and the final resurrection (v. 28). Judgment follows death, but *after* the gospel has accomplished its universal reach (Rev. 20:13–15). There is no need to read immediacy into the Greek—it is speaking of sequence, not insisting "and immediately following death is judgement."

Second, some may worry this doctrine could lessen the urgency for evangelism and missions. Yet, if one holds to a strictly Reformed view, that concern seems misplaced—for in that system, God has already decreed who will be saved or lost, regardless of human effort or location. Missions for the Reformed are not necessary to change outcomes but are acts of obedience to God's command. To the question, "Why do missions?" the most consistent Reformed answer would be, "Because God said so." Compatibilists would add that they are the means that God uses to gain His end of salvation.

The Free Will (synergy) believer has much more motivation to support missions and that is why they have historically launched many more agencies and sent more Christians abroad (see Chapter Five). Missionaries do not only work to get souls to Heaven; they are concerned about full-life flourishing and they desire to introduce the lost to their Heavenly Father.

My wife makes my life so much better that I wish I would have met her in college, or High School, or better yet, grade school. In the same way, it is hugely beneficial to meet Jesus in this life. To know Christ now is to enter life's purpose (*telos*)—worship, transformation, service—rather than to defer joy to after the grave. Furthermore, we do not know how effective evangelism is in the afterlife, and we do know Middle Hades is an extremely uncomfortable place best avoided.

We also may believe missionaries are effective in guiding the truly reprobate to the throne of Christ—those who would have gone to Tartarus (Lower Hades) may gain faith through their witness in this world. In this way missionaries retain all of their vital purpose of introducing people to the one and only Lord Jesus Christ who can transform them in this life and dwell with them into eternity. "And there is salvation in no one else; for there is no other name under heaven that has been given among men, by which we must be saved" (Acts 4:12, NAS).

Beyond retaining the original motivation for evangelism and missions, this doctrine increases our motivation and gives clarity of purpose. We are told we can "hasten the Day of the Lord's coming" (2 Peter 3:12). This comment is just after 2 Peter 3:9 that speaks of God waiting because He wishes none to

God will not return until everyone has heard the Good News and had a chance to repent.

perish, leading many to link "hastening the day" with missions. God will not return until everyone has heard the Good News and had a chance to repent.

Consider this: thus far we have discussed a possible mechanism for some of the living and all of the dead to hear the Good News. But what about the final generation living upon the earth—do they all hear the Good News too, even without going to Hades? Absolutely! The last generation cannot hear God's call to repent in Sheol/Hades, so they must all hear it while still living. They will hear the joyous proclamation of truth and freedom from the chains of sin as the Bible declares, "And this gospel of the kingdom shall be preached in the whole world for a witness to all the nations, and then the end shall come" (Matt. 24:14, NAS).

Missions are essential to God's plan: They hasten the Day of the Lord. They may also be seen to cut short the tribulation, and Matthew 24:22 reads, "And unless those days had been cut short, no life would have been saved; but for the sake of the elect those days shall be cut short" (NAS). Missions are the way Christians usher in the reign of Christ[151]. Every soul is loved, Jesus' blood was shed "once and for all," and all are invited by the power of God's grace to partake of salvation. Post-mortem disclosure does not reduce missions motivation; if anything, it makes missions even more vital, and all the more so as we see the last days approaching.

---

[151] Whereas nineteenth century zeal proclaimed triumphalism: that all would believe and then Christ would appear, this is the belief that all will be told of God's grace (and most will probably still not believe).

An Invitation to All: Optimal Opportunity

An historic and fulsome doctrine of Hades makes more sense of many Bible verses and conflicts with none of them. It also provides a way to understand the grace pastors at funerals instinctually apply. God's love for people knows no bounds, and even physical death and the grave cannot separate us from the love of God.

Jesus Himself grounds the hope that the unevangelized will still encounter His saving voice: "Truly, truly, I say to you, an hour is coming and now is, when the dead will hear the voice of the Son of God, and those who hear will live" (John 5:25, NAS). If even "the dead" hear and some "live," then divine revelation and response extend beyond bodily death without negating human freedom[152]. The verse does not imply inevitability, only availability: the same gospel that summons faith now is heard then, and those who truly hear will live.

This is not a "second chance" doctrine. No one gets a second chance.

This is not a "second chance" doctrine. No one gets a second chance. The revelation in Hades is the *first genuine chance* (or "optimal opportunity") for those who never had one. Those who knowingly rejected grace in life are chained in Tartarus until they are judged and placed in the Lake of Fire (Hell).

---

[152] When explaining Matthew 5, Carson and Köstenberger emphasize inaugurated eschatology: the "now is" points to spiritually dead people believing in the present; yet both also note the future resurrection in 5:28–29. My reading allows a both/and: John 5:25 announces present new birth and anticipates a coming disclosure in which "the dead will hear" prior to the eschatological judgment, keeping 5:25 in literary tension with 5:28–29. See D. A. Carson, The Gospel according to John, Pillar New Testament Commentary (Grand Rapids: Eerdmans, 1991), 255–60 and Andreas J. Köstenberger, John, Baker Exegetical Commentary on the New Testament (Grand Rapids: Baker Academic, 2004), 182–87.

If God truly wills that all be saved, then His justice (fairness) requires every soul receive a morally sufficient revelation of Christ. Philosopher Jerry Walls in *The Logic of Hell* argues that Hell is only coherent if those condemned have freely and persistently rejected divine love in full awareness of its offer. To be damned in ignorance would indict divine goodness. The intermediate state, therefore, is not a sentimental loophole but a moral necessity: it guarantees the "unreached" encounter Christ before the final judgment, thus preserving the integrity of free will being offered universally.

Paul's teaching supports this moral logic: "Sin is not imputed when there is no law" (Rom. 5:13). Degrees of light determine degrees of guilt (Luke 12:47–48). Thus the doctrine of Hades vindicates both divine equity and human accountability. Every human God creates will receive an "optimal opportunity" – a real presentation of the truth and an ability to repent or harden their heart. Before the final verdict on the Day of Judgement, the truth of Christ will be heard by all so that salvation or separation corresponds to a free and informed response to the Lord of the living and the dead.

Some have questioned why a person in Hades would reject Christ, to which I respond "Why would a person in life reject Christ?" It is not just because of ignorance. In Hades they only have the testimony of pain whereas in life we have pain acting as God's megaphone to a dying world and we have His glorious artistry in nature and testimony of love in the hearts of believers. The freedom to reject God remains real even post-mortem, and it still stems from the love of self over others, the desire to sin instead of obey, the drive to rebel rather than surrender to God's love.

From Jesus' Hades to Augustine's Purgatory

The Catholic doctrine of Purgatory developed gradually from the earlier Christian understanding of Hades / Sheol. This devolution was not abrupt but unfolded over centuries, shaped by philosophical influences, pastoral concerns, and shifts in eschatological focus. What began as a neutral realm of waiting became a moralized process of purification for those pronounced saved by Rome but not good enough to enter through Heaven's gates. In fact, Purgatory and the requisite indulgences to escape it was one of the primary reason's Luther recognized true Christian doctrine had been corrupted and so he launched the Reformation.

How was the knowledge of Hades/Sheol lost? Augustine of Hippo contributed decisive conceptual elements to change the early Church's understanding of Hades into what became the Catholic Church's doctrine of Purgatory.

Before Augustine's role is explained, it is important to see how Origen of Alexandria's (c. 185–253) thinking may have been an influence. Origen was one of the most powerful and creative minds to ever wrestle with God's Word. In his work *De Principiis* he developed a theology of divine fire (in Hell not Hades) that differed sharply from both earlier and later conceptualizations (2.10.4). For Origen, God's eternal fire was not just punitive but also purifying. He interpreted biblical references to fire in 1 Corinthians 3:13–15 and Malachi 3:2–3 not as literal flames of torment, but as metaphors for the spiritual purification of the soul. The "fire" of God's presence and truth would burn away sin and ignorance so that the soul may be restored to its intended likeness to God (apokatastasis). This "restoration" meant that, while some would go to Hell, they might be reformed in Hell, and everyone would eventually be saved (based in part on Col. 1:19–20). This "long way" of being a universalist was harshly condemned by the Church at the Council of Constantinople II in AD 553.[153]

---

[153] In Hades, Christ may be continuing His mission of reconciliation. Colossians 1:19–20 states: "For it was the Father's good pleasure for all the fullness to dwell in Him, and through Him to reconcile all things to Himself, having made peace through the blood of His cross; through Him, I say, whether things on earth or things in heaven." (NAS) Universalists

Augustine inherited the early Church's understanding of Hades (or Sheol) as a divided realm of the dead and absorbed Origen's concept of divine fire as purifying rather than merely punitive. He mixed these ideas with his developing framework of sin, grace, and satisfaction to lay the groundwork for Purgatory.

By *satisfaction*, Augustine meant some sins are remitted in this life, while others must be paid for "in the age to come" (Matt. 12:32). In his *City of God* (21.13) Augustine explicitly taught that some *believers* suffer temporary punishments after death for lesser sins, and in his *Enchiridion* (110) he urged the living to pray and make offerings for the departed Christians to ease their suffering.

What the Greek Fathers had envisioned as Hades—a realm of pain but also potential pedagogical purification so that the Gospel was made available to all—was transformed into a temporary post-mortem state *reserved only for believers* who die imperfectly purified. Augustine transported Origen's purifying fire from Hell to Hades, merged Hades' redemptive function with his own notion of temporal satisfaction, and created the conceptual groundwork for what would become Purgatory and indulgences (Kelly 1978, 482).

---

argue "all things" (τὰ πάντα) means Christ reconciles not just all people, but all creation (also where Origen created his Restoration theology). It is possible Paul had Hades in mind. Extending the pericope slightly we find, "…the hope of the gospel that you have heard, which was proclaimed in all creation under heaven" Col. 1:23 NAS. "All creation under Heaven" includes Hades, and we know in the lowest level of Hades there are demons who are chained. Perhaps "reconciling all things to Himself" is not universalism but means giving everyone a chance to recognize His Lordship—humans who know Him in Paradise, humans can learn of Him for the first time in Middle Hades, and both humans and demons in Tartarus are "reconciled" in the sense that they acknowledge His divinity and just punishment.

Augustine absolutely understood the Ante Nicene Father's belief in Hades as a place where even those who have not heard the gospel in life get to hear it preached. He explained their view while writing against it in AD 414:

> *They say that all those who were found in hell [Hades]*[154] *when Christ descended there had never heard the gospel, and that that place of punishment or imprisonment was emptied of all these, because the gospel was not published to the whole world in their lifetime, and they had sufficient excuse for not believing that which had never been proclaimed to them; (Letter 164, 4.12).*

And he goes on to write about how the early Church Fathers believed Hades continued to be a place for people to hear the gospel even after the Resurrection of the first fruit:

> *those also who since the Lord's resurrection have died or are now dying without the gospel having been proclaimed to them, may have heard it or may now hear it where they are, in hell [Hades], so that there they may believe what ought to be believed concerning the truth of Christ, and may also have that pardon and salvation which those to whom Christ preached obtained; for the fact that Christ ascended again from hell [Hades] is no reason why the report concerning Him should have perished from recollection there for from this earth also He has gone ascending into heaven, and yet by the publication of His gospel those who believe in Him shall be saved; moreover, He was exalted, and received a name that is above every name, for this end, that in His name every knee should bow, not only of things in heaven and on earth, but also of things under the earth. But if we accept this opinion, according to which we are warranted in supposing that men who did not believe while they were in life can in*

---

[154] Augustine's Latin *inferos* often corresponds to the idea of "the lower regions" or "the abode of the dead" (akin to Hades/Sheol) rather than exclusively "hell" in the modern English sense of eternal torment.

hell believe in Christ, who can bear the contradictions both of reason and faith which must follow? (*Letter 164*, 4.13, in A.D. 414)

Augustine knew what the early Church Fathers taught about Hades, but a God who offers salvation to all (even in Hades) went against his understanding of original sin and a God who only elected a few and so had no need of extending an invitation to eternal life into Hades. Instead of agreeing with the early Church Fathers, he rejected their doctrine of a place where everyone can hear the gospel for the first time, reasoning it meant we didn't need grace before death or to preach the good news in life. This objection has already been addressed above as it amounts to the same question of why we need missionaries.

Having rejected the historic understanding, he twisted the ancient conceptualization of Hades into his doctrine of Purgatory so that people on earth had to pay money to the Church to assist their tortured *believing* relatives in the afterlife:

> *The Benefit to the Souls of the Dead from the Sacraments and Alms of Their Living Friends: Nor can it be denied that the souls of the dead are benefited by the piety of their living friends, who offer the sacrifice of the Mediator, or give alms in the church on their behalf. But these services are of advantage only to those who during their lives have earned such merit, that services of this kind can help them. For there is a manner of life which is neither so good as not to require these services after death, nor so bad that such services are of no avail after death; there is, on the other hand, a kind of life so good as not to require them; and again, one so bad that when life is over they render no help.* (*Enchiridion* 110)

Just like with his invention of Original Sin and the doctrines that led to Calvinism, Augustine was instrumental in burying the early Church's understanding of Hades and creating the erroneous ideas of Purgatory and indulgences. He is not only the father of Christian determinism/fatalism, the father of "Original sin" that teaches people are sinful at birth and babies deserve Hell unless they are baptized by believing parents, but he is also the reason God's love for everyone and provision for all to hear the gospel was obfuscated. Augustine never learned Greek well, mixed his Manichean and Greek philosophical ideas with the Bible, and turned the redemption possibility in Hades into Purgatory. This lead to the Church requiring payments for its spiritual blessings (indulgences), an influence that corrupted true religion for centuries to come.

Pope Gregory the Great (540–604) converted Augustine's theological reflections into a pastoral and institutional doctrine. In his *Dialogues* (4.39), Gregory affirmed believing souls "are purified by the purgatorial fire after death." He linked this process to the intercession of the living through masses and prayers for the dead, asserting some souls could be released from purgation through the merits of the faithful (Le Goff 1984, 62–68). Gregory thus transformed speculative theology into ecclesial teaching, marking the birth of Purgatory as a defined part of Latin Christianity.

In the medieval church, Purgatory became intertwined with a growing system of sacramental control and penance, which unintentionally obscured the original hope of Hades as divine mercy awaiting fulfillment. They asserted salvation comes through the Church's sacramental system, i.e. "holy" baptism and "Holy" communion[155]. But what happens when someone is morally reprehensible but still in the good graces of mother Church, having been baptized and taking communion? Those individuals are saved but must serve their time in painful Purgatory.

By the twelfth century, the doctrine of Purgatory became more formalized through scholastic theology. Peter Lombard distinguished purgatorial fire from the eternal fire of Hell (*Sentences* IV.21). Thomas Aquinas (1225–1274) gave it its mature form, defining Purgatory as a place where "souls are detained for a time" to satisfy divine justice

---

[155] The Bible nowhere teaches baptism, communion, or even matrimony are "holy." This terminology was created to garner the Church more power. This is why these are often called "ordinances" by Protestant denominations.

(*Summa Theologiae*, *Suppl.* Q71–72). This scholastic synthesis united moral, metaphysical, and sacramental dimensions—making Purgatory central to medieval piety and penance (*McGrath* 2020, 221).

Dante's *Divine Comedy* (1308–1320) later gave imaginative depth to this vision, portraying the ascent of the soul through purifying love rather than punitive suffering. By the sixteenth century people were not only offering prayers for their dearly departed, they were also earning indulgences to get them out of Purgatory by taking pilgrimages to holy sites (a precursor of modern tourism), fighting crusades, repeating the hail Mary prayer, and of course paying money. It is little wonder the Reformers tossed out most teachings regarding the intermediate state.

Summary of the Evolution from Hades to Purgatory

Period	Conceptual Focus	Representative Figures	Theological Shift
1st–3rd centuries	Hades as intermediate state (comfort and torment)	Irenaeus, Tertullian, Hippolytus	Awaiting resurrection and judgment
3rd century	Purification as spiritual progress	Origen	Fire as purifying rather than punitive
4th–5th centuries	Moralization of Hades; Purgation replaces waiting	Augustine of Hippo	Post-mortem purification for believers
6th century	Institutionalization of doctrine Purgatory	Gregory the Great	Purgatorial fire and intercession
12th–13th centuries	Scholastic refinement	Peter Lombard, Thomas Aquinas	Defined place and process of purgation
14th century onward	Artistic & doctrinal consolidation	Dante, Council of Florence, Trent	Purgatory institutionalized as dogma

Modern Catholic Development of Hades

From a theological standpoint, Purgatory was a greatly altered (or even twisted) understanding of Hades. While the early fathers viewed

Hades as a temporary place of waiting, Augustine and Gregory reframed it as a purgative process of sanctification. This shift maintained belief in divine justice but introduced a quasi-meritorious system that seemed to extend human participation in salvation beyond death.

As the Western church's theology shifted under Augustine's influence, the vibrant and hopeful doctrine of Hades—a temporary realm of waiting and purification—was gradually replaced by more manipulative constructs. What the early Church Fathers had seen as a terrace of hope between death and final judgment became, under Augustinian logic, a way to inflict punishment upon the saved. His insistence that all humanity inherited Adam's guilt left no place for the intermediate state the apostles and earliest Christians had described. Without that terrace, theologians were forced to invent new compartments—Purgatory for the baptized who were not yet pure enough for heaven, and Limbo for the unbaptized who were not wicked enough for Hell. Both arose as substitutes for the lost understanding of Hades as a dynamic and redemptive domain awaiting Christ's return.

The doctrine of Limbo represents another theological innovation that arose from Augustine's increasingly juridical understanding of original sin and salvation. Unable to envision an intermediate state of waiting or mercy, Augustine taught even unbaptized infants shared Adam's guilt and were excluded from heaven (cf. *On Merit and the Forgiveness of Sins and the Baptism of Infants* 1.9). This view was unpopular as it did not point to a merciful God and it failed to comfort bereaving families during a time of high infant mortality. Later scholastics such as Peter Abelard and Thomas Aquinas softened this stance, describing a *limbus puerorum*—a state of natural happiness but without the beatific vision, free from suffering yet outside heaven (Aquinas, *Summa Theologiae* III, q.68, a.11; Suppl., q.71, a.7).

Scriptural support was thin and largely inferential but the concept endured for centuries as a way of safeguarding both divine justice and mercy. The Catholic Catechism (CCC §633) still affirms that before Christ's descent the righteous dead were kept in *Abraham's bosom*, a "state of all the dead, evil or righteous, awaiting the Redeemer," which theologians called *limbus patrum*—the "limbo of the fathers"—later emptied by Christ's victory (cf. 1 Pet 3:19; Eph 4:8–9). By contrast, the *limbo of infants* (*limbus puerorum*) was never defined as dogma. Modern Catholic theology, following the *International Theological Commission's* 2007 statement *The Hope of Salvation for Infants Who Die Without Being Baptized*, now entrusts these souls to God's mercy rather than to an imagined borderland of exclusion (CCC §1261).

With the recovery of Hades we may understand that aborted babies and people who die in childhood may still receive God's grace. Either it is true that God does not punish them because they have not sinned (the Free Will view) or we can see Hades as a reformative place wherein they might still hear the gospel and be saved (for a Reformed believer). In either case, the recovery of this doctrine provides us an understanding of how God can live out His loving and just nature rather than simply condemning sentient beings to Hell or Limbo for being created and thereby excluding them from God's glorious presence in eternity.

Conclusion

The Reformation rightly rejected Purgatory and Limbo for lacking clear biblical support and for undermining the sufficiency of Christ's atonement (Calvin 1960, III.xxi.5–7). The Reformers also undermined the authority of the Catholic Church by demonstrating its unbiblical doctrines and challenging its claim that baptism into mother church was what led to salvation. However, instead of returning to the earlier doctrine of the intermediate state they tossed it all out and Protestants started believing the unsubstantiated (biblically) idea that after death people get their individual day in court and then go directly (or after souls sleep) to Heaven or Hell.

Martin Luther tried to account for the time between death and resurrection by developing *soul sleep* (*Seelenschlaf*). He said the dead are truly at rest until the resurrection, experiencing no passage of time or conscious suffering in the interim. Luther wrote, "The dead lie there, accounting neither days nor years; but when they are awoken, it will seem to them as though they had slept but an hour" (*An Exposition of Solomon's Booke Called Ecclesiastes*, 1526). For Luther, this imagery upheld both the reality of death and the certainty of bodily resurrection—death was not a Purgatory but a rest, a sleep in Christ from which believers would awaken instantly, from their own perspective, into the presence of God at the last day.

As seen above, soul sleep fails to do justice to far too much evidence from the Bible and early Church Fathers. Recovering the ancient doctrine of the intermediate state restores coherence to the gospel that is open to all, supporting the heart of *ROSES* theology. The possibility of everyone hearing the gospel, if not in this age then in the age to come, reveals the Open Invitation of God, whose love reaches beyond death and offers all an optimal invitation. It harmonizes justice and mercy, freedom and sovereignty, without resorting to fatalism or universalism.

The damned are not unlucky; they are those who freely and knowingly resist our God who is love. The saved are not the fortunate few; they are all who, having encountered that love—whether in this world or the next—embrace it by grace through faith. Hell is not divine cruelty but a just desert and possibly even a merciful exile from God's awesome direct presence. Heaven is love freely received for those who have Christ in them and so learned to freely give it to others. As Archbishop of Constantinople Gregory of Nazianzus (380–381) summarized:

> *If He descend into Hell, (1 Peter 3:19) descend with Him. Learn to know the mysteries of Christ there also. What is the providential purpose of the twofold descent? To save all men absolutely by His manifestation, or there too only them that believe.* (*Oration*, 45.24).

The early church preached a Christ who not only died for all but who also descended for all—a Savior who preached the Good News even to the deceased and established a Church that could prevail over the gates of Hades. The recovery of this truth returns Christian theology to its first bloom, where divine love is truly universal in scope, particular in reception, but eternal in consequence. The universal offer of salvation in Christ is absolutely sincere; **He died *once and for all*** *(Greek: "Ἐφάπαξ";* Rom. 6:10; Heb 7:27; Heb. 9:12; Heb 10:10; 1 Pet. 3:18). When we bury our dead, even those who never heard the Good News, we do not consign them to oblivion but to the pierced hands of the Savior who descended to seek them. The intermediate state reminds us that no shadow lies beyond His light.

Chapter 8: Tending the Garden: Completing the Reformation

❧❧❧

"Now the Lord is the Spirit, and where the Spirit of the Lord is, there is freedom." 2 Corinthians 3:17

"'A reformed church must always be reforming itself.' We are unfaithful to the spirit of the Reformation – as well as to all that is implied in the word "reformed" – if we ever imagine that the task of reform was finished with Luther, Calvin, Knox, and others in the sixteenth century. Ours is a glorious heritage, but if we only look back and revel in great moments in the past we negate our calling to be continually reforming." I. John Hesselink (1928-2018), in "Reformed, But Ever Reforming," *Banner of Truth USA*[156]

The story of the Reformation was never meant to end in the sixteenth century. Its true goal—a return to biblical beliefs and Spirit-empower living—remains unfinished. The Protestant Reformation recovered the authority of Scripture and the centrality of God's grace, but it left unfinished the revelation of God's relational love for all. To complete the Reformation is to let grace flower into its fullest bloom—truth perfected in love.

---

[156] The Banner article was reprinted in 2022; originally 1974 in *The Church Herald*

The Reformation furthermore reduced the power of the papal state, provoked a Catholic Counter-Reformation that purified many of its own practices, and eventually led to the Second Vatican Council that acknowledged true Christians exist outside Rome's fold.

This book may appear at first glance to be a polemic against a single branch of Christianity, yet its deeper purpose is far larger. It is a defense of God's character, a vision for rekindling motivation in the Christian life, and a theological antidote to spiritual apathy. It calls out Augustine's tragic fusion of biblical faith with pagan determinism, exposes the distortion of God's goodness such teaching produced, and affirms believers are not merely "sinners saved by grace," but *saints* being saved from sin's power through grace. Still, it is also an invitation for those within the Reformed tradition to step out of determinism's shadow and into the light of divine freedom and love.

The Reformation in Progress

It may be that when Luther and Calvin were captivated by Augustine's deterministic theology, what the enemy meant for confusion, God allowed for greater good. The Reformed system, though biblically unsupported, historically late, and philosophically indefensible, shattered the medieval illusion that salvation came through ritual or the Church's mediation. *Total Depravity* stripped away human pride and works-righteousness; *Unconditional Election* destroyed the Catholic weapon of ecclesial control. These doctrines paved the way for rediscovering grace. The Reformation's early victories— breaking papal dominance, restoring Scripture's authority, and recovering salvation by grace through faith—prepared the soil for a fuller bloom of truth.

The next flowering came through believers who embraced freedom of the will and partnership with God in mission. The Anabaptists, Wesleyans, Methodists, and Arminians in general carried forward the torch of revival, conscience, and evangelism. These movements— rooted in the belief that God's grace invites human response—birthed the modern missionary era and spread spiritual vitality across the world.

The Reformation will not be complete until Christians return to the faith of Jesus and His apostles, reclaiming the relational love that animated the first three centuries of the Church. True reform cannot afford to be static. It must continue until doctrine and Spirit are reunited, truth and love are wed, and believers stand together as one family of faith. The Reformation began with recovering the *authority* of Scripture; it will be completed when we recover the *heart* of God for His world and the fullness of shared communion in Christ.

Many in the Reformed tradition still resist this fuller bloom of truth, convinced history and Scripture imprison humanity within divine predetermination. Their zeal for the Bible is commendable, their integrity sincere, yet their doctrine confines God's love within unnecessary limits. They also have not recognized that they won the battle to see God's grace as the initiator of salvation (prevenient grace) and so now they can dismantle the theological superstructure that supported Augustine's less stable edifices.

The Reformation of the Heart

God's intention has always been partnership. He hears prayer and responds; He transforms hearts rather than merely covering sins; He imputes holiness that He might also impart it. Holiness is not a veneer but God's own life shared with His children—a spiritual family resemblance. The Christian goal is not simply *doing* right but *being* right, possessing the mind of Christ, the love of the Spirit, and the fragrance of heaven. We are not called to Christ-likeness so much as to realize and live out Christ within us.[157]

---

[157] See an interesting discussion in Hotchkiss, Jacob. *No Longer I: The Life-Changing Power of Simply Believing the Truth*. Springfield, MO: No Longer I Media, 2025. He claims 200 times we are called "in Christ" in the Bible, and only twice is "Christ likeness" mentioned.

The full Reformation will not reach completion until all who confess Christ are united in Spirit and in truth. Catholic and Orthodox traditions retain historic depth but often lack biblical fluency and personal vitality; Protestantism burns bright with zeal but often divides over doctrine. The Spirit now calls the Church to maturity—to truth joined with love, intellect joined with humility, and freedom joined with holiness.

Each petal of TULIP blooms from Augustine's fifth-century soil rather than the apostolic seed.

As global pressures mount, the world's hostility will force Christians toward unity around essentials. Doctrinal division will either be healed through patient reformation or exposed through persecution. The recent formation of the Global Methodist Church from the United Methodist Church in 2022 is a golden lesson to all: Union without shared conviction cannot endure. More than ever we need open-hearted theologians who are bold enough to recover the doctrines of the early Church in order to prepare us for the final days of tribulation we know lie ahead.

We have seen throughout this book that extreme Calvinism cannot stand on teleological (Chapter 1), historical (Chapter 2), biblical (Chapter 3), rational (Chapter 4), or practical (Chapter 5) grounds. Its system claims fidelity to Scripture but fractures logic, history, and love. Each petal of TULIP blooms from Augustine's fifth-century soil rather than the apostolic seed. The theological scaffolding is so intricate that it contradicts the gospel's simplicity: fishermen and farmers understood Jesus' message without parsing Latin paradoxes. Paul never needed to defend a God who predetermines sin, nor did he invent a "secret will" to excuse moral incoherence.

A system that can simultaneously assert both "A" and "not-A" under the banner of divine mystery ceases to be theology and becomes sophistry. Appealing to God's "hidden will" to justify contradictions could equally prove any heresy—from Gnosticism to Mormonism and possibly even Islam. The gospel of truth cannot rest on evasive logic; it rests on the Word made flesh, full of grace and truth.

The Field of Freedom: Where Love Learns to Bloom

God is not deceptive. If He had never intended humanity to choose freely, He would not have commanded all to repent and believe. No sane person lives as if his every action were coerced; experience testifies that we make real decisions daily. This freedom is not an illusion—it is the field where love learns to bloom.

Why does this matter? Because salvation itself hangs on it. If human choices make no difference, moral responsibility collapses, evangelistic zeal fades, and faith becomes fatalism. Determinism discourages prayer, blunts passion, and erodes purpose. Satan's most subtle victory has been to convince believers that their choices are irrelevant—to make them lay down arms before the battle begins.

It takes a far greater God to restrain His power than to simply overrule His creatures. As Irenaeus observed, divine omnipotence is shown not in coercion but in patience. Love, not control, is God's defining attribute. For a brief span of cosmic history, God allows true freedom that even runs counter to His own perfect will so that genuine love may emerge. Only such love can fulfill the divine command and transform creation into a family fit for eternity.

A respected colleague once asked, "If we cannot sin in Heaven, why should we have free will on earth?" He probably got the question from R.C. Sproul writing, "in our glorified state in heaven we will be unable to sin because all desire for sin and all remnants of original sin will be removed from us."[158]

---

[158] Sproul, R. C. *What Is Reformed Theology?: Understanding the Basics of the Reformed Faith.* Wheaton, IL: Tyndale House Publishers, 2005, Kindle Loc. 1,887.

Who said we *cannot* sin in Heaven? *In trying to protect divine* Scripture shows angels *did* sin in Heaven, were *sovereignty, Calvinism* cast out and made demons. The absence of *inadvertently undermines* human sin among the redeemed will not stem *divine goodness.* from coercion but from transformation— God's sanctifying grace forming hearts that freely love the good and whole-heartedly worship our Lord.

Adam sinned from a state of pure innocence in Eden, but we will be in an even better place. Luke 7:47 explains that those who have been forgiven much love much. That is the reason there will be no sin chosen in Heaven. God created and it was good; but when He redeemed us and infused His Spirit in us His sons and daughters became great! Those who have tasted sin will reject its sour fruit and aftertaste of death; those who have been forgiven much will love much and thus fulfill the full law for eternity.

The Incomplete Answers of Calvinism

Calvinism ultimately fails to answer the most profound questions of human existence: *Why does pain exist in a world made by a good God? What is the purpose of creation? What is the meaning of life itself?* A system claiming to glorify God above all should offer clarity on these, yet determinism reduces every sorrow, every evil, and every rebellion to the secret will of God. If God foreordained every act and event, then the cries of the suffering and the rebellion of the sinner both arise from His decree, making evil necessary and love meaningless. In trying to protect divine sovereignty, Calvinism inadvertently undermines divine goodness. It silences the cry of Job, flattens the poetry of the Psalms, and renders Christ's lament over Jerusalem inexplicable.

Scripture, however, portrays a different God—a Father who risks pain for the sake of love. The world's suffering finds meaning not in predestination but in redemption. Pain is permitted because it trains the will toward love, exposes sin's cost, and shapes children into

Christ's likeness. The purpose of the world is not to display power but to form a family. The meaning of life is not submission to an impersonal decree but participation in divine fellowship. Calvinism cannot explain these truths because its framework excludes the very freedom that makes love, holiness, and obedience possible.

True obedience requires free will. One cannot "submit" if there is no alternative but to obey. The very language of Scripture—commands, warnings, exhortations, and invitations—presumes choice. Likewise, love requires freedom; coerced affection is not love at all.

God desires children, not automatons. From Eden to Calvary, divine love honors human freedom even at a steep cost. Christ came not to enslave humanity to a decree, but to set it free from sin's tyranny. "Truly, I say to you, everyone who commits sin is the slave of sin. And the slave does not remain in the house forever; the son does remain forever. If therefore the Son shall make you free, you shall be free indeed" (Jn. 8:34-36, NAS).

The irony is that Calvinism, while claiming to give more glory to God, gives Him far less. It makes Him the sole actor but strips Him of relational glory—the glory of shared love, answered prayer, and voluntary worship. It offers less consistency because it must excuse its contradictions under the veil of "mystery." It has less explanatory power because it cannot reconcile divine justice with human accountability.

The Free Will (synergistic) view, by contrast, magnifies God's greatness: **He is so powerful He can endow genuine freedom without losing control; so wise He can weave human choice into His providence; so just He finds a way to offer salvation to all, and so loving that He waits patiently for our response.**

The final Reformation must therefore complete what the first began—not by discarding grace, but by deepening it. Grace is not God's unilateral override of human will; it is His persistent invitation to it. Love's victory will not come by compulsion but by consent, when every free creature, having seen the Lamb who was slain, bows before

His throne. Then, at last, the Reformation will have run its full course—from sovereignty to synergy, from decree to relationship, from law to love—and the garden of God will finally be in full bloom.

An Invitation to Freedom

Change is never easy, especially when one's convictions are deeply held and one's ministry has been built upon them. To reconsider Calvinism may feel like dismantling your own theological house brick by brick. Yet if that house rests upon a foundation laid by Augustine rather than the Apostles, then courage demands renovation. Christ Himself calls His followers to build not on sand but on rock.

Ask yourself: what kind of God is more worthy of worship—the One who ordains evil for hidden purposes, or the One who allows freedom because love cannot exist without it? Which vision of God produces more prayer, more compassion, more evangelism, and more joy? Look at the fruit of these opposing doctrines. The Calvinist system promises intellectual security but leaves hearts uncertain of God's goodness and paralyzed by fatalism. The free-will faith of the early church restores what the Reformation only began: assurance rooted in God's love, purpose anchored in genuine relationship, and holiness born of partnership rather than predetermination.

What is attractive about the Reformed position? It is possible people are afraid of the very gift they deny getting—they are afraid to choose. As Søren Kierkegaard explained, people are not frightened of failure so much as of making a choice, because choice binds freedom to responsibility. He wrote "Anxiety is the dizziness of freedom."[159]

---

[159] Søren Kierkegaard, *The Concept of Anxiety: A Simple Psychologically Orienting Deliberation on the Dogmatic Issue of Hereditary Sin*, trans. Reidar Thomte, in Kierkegaard's Writings VIII, ed. Howard V. Hong and Edna H. Hong (Princeton: Princeton University Press, 1980), 61. Paraphrase of his teaching and quote translated here by myself from *Begrebet Angest.*

Do not be afraid that you cannot act as God demands, cannot live up to His Holy standard—He knows that. Rather than believing He saved you regardless, believe He loves you regardless and that it is His power that supports all human good works. You are not losing assurance but gaining it—your only part is to choose faith—and He will always empower you to make that choice.

Yes, you cannot rest beneath a blanket of false comfort saying your salvation is completed. We must reverence/fear God and take His warnings about apostasy seriously, but we also know nothing can tear us away from His love (Rom. 8:38-39) and that "He who began a good work in you will perfect it until the day of Christ Jesus" (Phil. 1:6, NAS).

The cost of reforming your theology may be high—loss of reputation, position, or belonging—but the cost of clinging to error is far higher. To misrepresent God's character is no small matter. **To preach a gospel that limits His mercy when He Himself has declared it boundless is to obscure His glory, not defend it.** The true reformer's task is never finished; it continues wherever truth calls for courage. The invitation remains open: step into the freedom Christ purchased, and let love—not fear—define your faith.

This book has been, at its heart, an exposition of love as defined in 1 Corinthians 13:4–7. Either God created to magnify Himself through domination, or He created to share Himself through communion. Either He is a cosmic autocrat choosing a privileged few and damning the rest, or He is a patient Father yearning for all His children to come home. The latter is the gospel Jesus and the apostles proclaimed.

"Love is patient." Paul begins there because patience is God's greatest proof of love. From Eden's fall to the present age, He waits—enduring rejection, extending grace, offering Himself anew. Christ's cross is the supreme expression of that patience and the Holy Spirit's continual calling to all echoes and amplifies it. God still waits for the full harvest to come in (2 Pet 3:9).

The Reformation began by restoring grace to faith; it must now end by restoring God's love for all to grace

When the gospel has reached every tribe and nation (Matt 24:14), when it has been proclaimed even to the dead (1 Pet 4:6), and when humanity's rebellion reaches its zenith (Rev 16:14–16), then the end will come. Every knee will bow, every tongue confess (Phil 2:10–11), and creation itself will be renewed (Rev 21:1–4).

Until that day, our task is clear: to love God freely, to serve Him faithfully, and to join Him in completing His great Reformation—the renewal of the human heart in the likeness of Christ. The call to complete the Reformation is not an argument. It is an invitation. God is still writing the story of His Church. Every heart that moves from fear to freedom, from control to communion, adds another chapter to His great reform of love.

Epilogue: The Garden Restored

The story of redemption began in a garden—and it will end in paradise. What was once lost through pride and control will be restored through humility and love. The Reformation began by restoring grace to faith; it must now end by restoring God's love for all to grace. **When theology is purified of fear and control, when the gospel is heard not as decree but as invitation, when every believer lives as a partner rather than a pawn—then the flower of faith will have fully bloomed.**

Our task is not to guard the garden but to tend it—to cultivate truth, nurture freedom, and prune away whatever withers love. God is still reforming His Church, calling His children to rise above division and to dwell again in His light.

Soon the Gardener Himself will return. Every seed of faith will sprout into glory. Every tear shed for love's sake will be redeemed. The soil of history will yield its final fruit: a family restored, a world renewed, a love unending. Until that day, may we labor with joy in the fields of freedom, praying as the Spirit and the Bride together cry, *"Come, Lord Jesus."*

> *But thanks be to God, who always leads us in His triumph in Christ, and manifests through us the sweet aroma of the knowledge of Him in every place. For we are a fragrance of Christ to God among those who are being saved and among those who are perishing; to the one an aroma from death to death, to the other an aroma from life to life. And who is adequate for these things? For we are not like many, peddling the word of God, but as from sincerity, but as from God, we speak in Christ in the sight of God."* 2 Cor. 2:14-17, NASB

Author's Note

Writing this book has been both an act of research and an act of worship. I began with questions about theology and ended with wonder at the love of God. My aim has not been to win arguments so much as to help restore confidence in a God who genuinely loves, invites, and empowers His children to respond.

If this book has challenged your assumptions, I hope it has also strengthened your faith. My prayer is that every reader—whether Reformed, Catholic, Orthodox, or otherwise—will sense the Spirit's call to reform not only systems of doctrine but hearts of devotion. The true Reformation begins wherever believers rediscover the freedom and courage to love God fully and to love others freely.

I am humbled you took the time to read this book, and I appreciate your company as we pursue a lifelong journey of grace together into a faith ever reforming, a love ever deepening, and a hope ever fixed on the One who makes all things new.

Peter A. Kerr
Littleton, Colorado, 2025

About the Author

Peter A. Kerr serves as the Dean of the School of Business and Leadership at a Christian University. He is also President of KerrCommunications, providing world-class communications training for marketing, media relations, crisis planning, intercultural communications and leadership improvement. He holds degrees from the Air Force Academy, the University of Washington, Asbury Theological Seminary, and a PhD from NorthCentral University.

Peter is an ordained minister and has been published in many places including the books *Adam Meets Eve,* a chapter in *Understanding Evangelical Media,* and the sci-fi book *The Ark of Time* as well as in numerous magazines and academic journals. He has also appeared on TV programs such as *Marriage Unleashed* and *Character Matters.*

A consummate traveler, Peter has been to more than 50 countries on six continents and speaks numerous languages. He's worked with many media outlets including *CNN, NBC, FOX, BBC, NY Times, USA Today, NPR, London Times, Der Spiegel,* and *Aljazeera.* Peter led all media relations during the 2004 President Ronald Reagan State Funeral in DC, released the Air Force budget of $120B to the DC press corps, and has media trained hundreds of leaders including White House officials, generals, CEOs, and non-profit leaders. Other experiences include negotiating with U.S. embassies and foreign military leaders in the Middle East, serving as Chief Media Liaison Officer for Outdoor Games in Beijing for the 2008 Olympics, and being the primary media trainer and crisis planner for the 2010 World Equestrian Games.

Peter enjoys speaking at conferences and retreats, traveling, reading, playing sports, strategy games, and just being with his wife Rebecca and their four children.

The Author's testimony

I accepted God into my heart every Sunday from when I was five until I was seven. Well, I at least raised my hand when the Sunday School teacher asked who wanted to do so (probably greatly inflating their conversion numbers). In any case, when I was seven I was lying in the bottom bunk bed at night and I remember thinking that I loved Jesus and wanted to live my life to please Him, and that is when I really accepted God into my heart. By then I was real good at saying the prayer, admitting my sin, asking forgiveness, and promising to live from then on as He wanted me to live. While I know Christianity is not about feeling but about faith, I remember feeling God's warmth and love enter my life. I then started trying in earnest to live for Him, and began singing to God every night. My mom would sometimes listen outside my door and smile at my amateur attempts to praise God. My older brother in the bunk bed above was less amused, and would sometimes get exasperated enough to come down and rough me up some. That's why I can say I was persecuted for Christ at seven. ☺

The rest of my testimony is a story about God's guidance and faithfulness. I read the whole Bible by age 12, and I haven't stopped reading it. It's truly the word of God, a revelation of our Creator's transcendence and imminence, and if you haven't read it, I recommend you start today! -- Peter

VISIT US ONLINE

If you enjoyed this book, **please** review it on amazon.com, like it on social media, and tell others about it today. If you have comments, suggestions, or wish to invite Peter to speak at your event (live or online) you may contact the author by visiting www.kerrcommunications.com.

Appendices

Appendix 1: Contrasting Definitions: Calvinist vs. Free Will

Term	Calvinist Definition	Free Will / Classical Definition	Representative Scriptures (NAS)
Faith (pistis)	A divine gift irresistibly given to the elect after regeneration; faith is *the result* of new birth.	A relational trust freely exercised in response to God's revelation; faith is *the condition* for new birth.	Eph 2:8–9; Rom 10:17; John 1:12; Heb 11:6
Grace (charis)	Particular and effectual—grace given only to the elect and unfailingly accomplishes salvation.	Universal and enabling—grace that appears to all, awakening but not coercing the will.	Titus 2:11; Acts 7:51; John 6:37; Rom 2:4
Election (eklogē)	Unconditional—God's eternal decree choosing certain individuals for salvation apart from any foreseen faith.	Conditional or corporate—God's gracious choice of all who are "in Christ," based on foreknown faith and response.	Rom 8:29–30; 1 Pet 1:2; 1 Tim 2:4; Eph 1:4–5
Repentance (metanoia)	A gift given only to the elect after regeneration; repentance follows being made spiritually alive.	A grace-enabled but genuine act of turning to God available to all; repentance precedes forgiveness.	Acts 17:30; Luke 13:3; 2 Tim 2:25; 2 Pet 3:9
Salvation (sōtēria)	Monergistic—God alone acts to bring the elect from death to life, apart from any human cooperation.	Synergistic—God initiates and empowers, but human response of faith and perseverance is essential.	Phil 2:12–13; Rom 10:9–10; 1 Pet 1:5; Rev 22:17
Will (thelēma)	Human will is bound by sin and cannot choose God unless irresistibly regenerated by grace.	Human will is weakened but enabled by prevenient grace to choose or resist God's offer of life.	Deut 30:19; Josh 24:15; John 7:17; Acts 7:51
Perseverance	The elect are irresistibly preserved by God and cannot finally fall away.	Believers must abide and persevere in faith; security is found in continuing relationship, not a decree.	Matt 24:13; John 15:4–6; Heb 3:14; Rev 2:10
Atonement	Limited—Christ died only for the elect; His sacrifice is sufficient for all but efficient for the chosen.	Universal—Christ died for all, making salvation available to every person though effective only for believers.	John 3:16–17; 1 John 2:2; 2 Cor 5:14–15; Heb 2:9
Calling	Irresistible—God's inward call to the elect cannot fail.	Resistible—God's call goes out to all; those who respond in faith become the chosen.	Matt 22:14; Acts 7:51; John 12:32; Rom 10:21
Sovereignty	Defined as absolute control—God ordains whatsoever comes to pass, even sin.	Defined as ultimate authority—God rules over all yet allows genuine freedom and moral choice.	Gen 50:20; Matt 23:37; 2 Pet 3:9; 1 Tim 2:4

Appendix 2: Growth of Calvinism From Seed to System

Era	Historical "Soil"	Theological Development	Key Figures & Events
1st–4th Centuries	Apostolic & Patristic Christianity	Early Church Fathers emphasized free will, universal grace, and synergy between divine grace and human response. No evidence of predestinarian determinism.	Justin Martyr, Irenaeus, Origen, Chrysostom, Tertullian
Late 4th–5th Century	North African & Roman thought meets Christianity	Augustine of Hippo, influenced by Stoic and Neoplatonic determinism, redefines grace as irresistible and salvation as unconditionally predestined.	Augustine of Hippo (354–430)
6th Century	Early Medieval Church	The Second Council of Orange (529) accepts Augustine's view of original sin but rejects double predestination, affirming human cooperation with grace.	Council of Orange (529 A.D.)
14th Century	Late Scholasticism	Augustinian determinism resurfaces among Gregory of Rimini and Thomas Bradwardine. They emphasize God's absolute will to fight works-based salvation.	Bradwardine, Gregory of Rimini
16th Century	Protestant Reformation	Luther revives Augustine's doctrine of bondage of the will. Calvin systematizes it into a coherent theology of divine sovereignty and predestination.	Martin Luther (1525), John Calvin (1559)
17th Century	Post-Reformation Europe	Synod of Dort (1618–1619) codifies the Five Points of Calvinism (TULIP) in response to Arminius and the Remonstrants.	Synod of Dort, Jacob Arminius
18th Century	Enlightenment & Evangelical Revival	John Wesley and Jacob Arminius's heirs replant grace in the soil of love, freedom, and holiness.	Wesley, Fletcher, Arminian Methodists
19th–21st Centuries	Modern Theology	Only 7% of the world claims Calvinism, but 30% in the USA (esp. in Presbyterian and Baptist circles). It is challenged by those emphasizing relational love and free will.	John Piper, Joel Beeke, Albert Mohler, John MacArthur, Francis Schaeffer vs C.S. Lewis, William Lane Craig, Alvin Plantinga, Thomas Oden

Appendix 3: Comparison of Grace, Freedom, and Salvation

Concept	Calvinist / Reformed	Arminian / Wesleyan	Catholic / Orthodox
Core Principle	Monergism – God alone acts to save; human will contributes nothing to regeneration.	Prevenient but Resistible Grace – God's grace enables genuine choice; humans may resist or cooperate.	Synergism – Grace and human will cooperate throughout salvation; divine-human cooperation is ongoing.
Human Nature after the Fall	Total Depravity – Humanity is utterly incapable of seeking God or doing good apart from regenerating grace.	Total Depravity Healed by Prevenient Grace – Humanity is powerless until God's universal grace restores the ability to respond.	Wounded Nature – Humanity's nature is damaged but not destroyed; freedom remains weakened yet real.
Role of Grace	Irresistible Grace – God's saving grace effectually transforms the elect; it cannot ultimately be resisted.	Prevenient Grace – Grace precedes faith, enabling repentance and belief; it can be accepted or rejected.	Sanctifying Grace – Grace pervades the entire process of salvation, from initiation to glorification.
Human Freedom	Compatibilist Freedom – Humans act voluntarily, but their choices are determined by God's sovereign decree.	Restored Freedom – Grace restores the will's ability to choose freely between obedience and resistance.	Cooperative Freedom – The will is always free but always dependent on grace; human cooperation is real and ongoing.
Divine Sovereignty	Absolute and Determining – God foreordains all that comes to pass, including human decisions (Eph. 1:11).	Conditional Election – God's election is based on foreknowledge of those who freely respond to grace.	Universal Salvific Will – God wills all to be saved; grace is offered universally, though cooperation varies.
Nature of Election	Unconditional – Chosen solely by God's will, not foreseen merit or response.	Conditional – Based on God's foreknowledge of faith and perseverance.	Corporate and Cooperative – God elects the Church as His people; individuals participate through faith and obedience.
Extent of Atonement	Limited Atonement – Christ died effectively only for the elect.	Universal Atonement – Christ's death made salvation possible for all, effective for believers.	Universal Atonement – Christ's death provides grace for all; full participation requires human cooperation and the sacraments.

Concept	Calvinist / Reformed	Arminian / Wesleyan	Catholic / Orthodox
Effect of Grace on the Will	Transforming and Irresistible – Regeneration precedes faith and guarantees conversion.	Enabling and Resistible – Grace empowers but does not compel belief.	Healing and Cooperative – Grace heals the will and works in synergy with it through life.
Salvation Process	Monergistic – God alone accomplishes salvation from election to glorification (Rom. 8:29–30).	Begins Monergistically, Continues Synergistically – God initiates; humans cooperate by faith and obedience.	Fully Synergistic – God's grace and human response operate together at every stage of salvation.
Perseverance	Perseverance of the Saints – The elect will infallibly persevere in faith.	Conditional Security – Believers can fall away through persistent unbelief.	Conditional Perseverance – Salvation can be lost through mortal sin or rejection of grace.
Goal of Salvation	God's Glory – Manifestation of divine sovereignty and mercy.	Union with God by Faith and Love – Restored relationship and holiness through grace-enabled freedom.	Theosis / Deification – Participation in the divine life through sanctification and communion.

References

Ambrose of Milan. *De Abraham*. In *Saint Ambrose: Theological and Dogmatic Works*. Translated by H. De Romestin, E. de Romestin, and H. T. F. Duckworth. *Nicene and Post-Nicene Fathers*, Second Series, Vol. 10. Edited by Philip Schaff and Henry Wace. New York: Christian Literature Publishing Co., 1896

————. *De excessu fratris Satyri (On the Death of Satyrus)*. In *Saint Ambrose: Select Works and Letters*. Translated by H. De Romestin, E. de Romestin, and H. T. F. Duckworth. *Nicene and Post-Nicene Fathers*, Second Series, Vol. 10. Edited by Philip Schaff and Henry Wace. New York: Christian Literature Publishing Co., 1896.

————. *De fide ad Gratianum Augustum*. In *Saint Ambrose: Theological and Dogmatic Works*. Translated by H. De Romestin, E. de Romestin, and H. T. F. Duckworth. *Nicene and Post-Nicene Fathers*, Second Series, Vol. 10. Edited by Philip Schaff and Henry Wace. New York: Christian Literature Publishing Co., 1896.

————. *De paenitentia*. In *Saint Ambrose: Theological and Dogmatic Works*. Translated by H. De Romestin, E. de Romestin, and H. T. F. Duckworth. *Nicene and Post-Nicene Fathers*, Second Series, Vol. 10. Edited by Philip Schaff and Henry Wace. New York: Christian Literature Publishing Co., 1896.

————. *Epistulae (Letters)*. In *Saint Ambrose: Select Works and Letters*. Translated by H. De Romestin, E. de Romestin, and H. T. F. Duckworth. *Nicene and Post-Nicene Fathers*, Second Series, Vol. 10. Edited by Philip Schaff and Henry Wace. New York: Christian Literature Publishing Co., 1896.

Aquinas, Thomas. *Summa Theologica.* Translated by the Fathers of the English Dominican Province. New York: Benziger Bros., 1947.

Athanasius. *Festal Letters.* In *Nicene and Post-Nicene Fathers*, Series 2, Vol. 4. Edited by Philip Schaff and Henry Wace. New York: Christian Literature Publishing Co., 1892

———. *On the Incarnation.* Translated by A Religious of C.S.M.V. Crestwood, NY: St. Vladimir's Seminary Press, 1998.

Augustine of Hippo. *City of God.* Translated by Marcus Dods. In *Nicene and Post-Nicene Fathers*, Series 1, Vol. 2, edited by Philip Schaff. Buffalo, NY: Christian Literature Publishing Co., 1887.

———. *Enchiridion on Faith, Hope, and Love.* Translated by J. F. Shaw. In *Nicene and Post-Nicene Fathers*, Series 1, Vol. 3, edited by Philip Schaff. Buffalo, NY: Christian Literature Publishing Co., 1887.

———. *Homilies on the First Epistle of John.* In *Saint Augustine: Homilies on the Gospel of John and the First Epistle of John*, translated by John Gibb and James Innes. *Nicene and Post-Nicene Fathers*, First Series, Vol. 7. Edited by Philip Schaff. New York: Christian Literature Publishing Co., 1888

———. *Letters of St. Augustine.* In *Saint Augustine: Letters of St. Augustine*, translated by J. G. Cunningham. *Nicene and Post-Nicene Fathers*, First Series, Vol. 1. Edited by Philip Schaff. New York: Christian Literature Publishing Co., 1886.

———. *On Baptism, Against the Donatists.* In *Saint Augustine: The Anti-Donatist Writings*, translated by R. Stothert. *Nicene and Post-Nicene Fathers*, First Series, Vol. 4. Edited by Philip Schaff. New York: Christian Literature Publishing Co., 1887.

———. *On Holy Virginity.* In *Saint Augustine: Treatises on Marriage and Virginity*, translated by C. L. Cornish. *Nicene and Post-Nicene Fathers*, First Series, Vol. 3. Edited by Philip Schaff. New York: Christian Literature Publishing Co., 1887.

―――. *On Merit and the Forgiveness of Sins, and the Baptism of Infants.* In *Nicene and Post-Nicene Fathers*, Series 1, Vol. 5, edited by Philip Schaff. Buffalo, NY: Christian Literature Publishing Co., 1887.

―――. *On Nature and Grace.* In *Nicene and Post-Nicene Fathers*, Series 1, Vol. 5, edited by Philip Schaff. Buffalo, NY: Christian Literature Publishing Co., 1887.

―――. *Sermons on the Liturgical Seasons.* In *Saint Augustine: Sermons on the Liturgical Seasons*, translated by R. G. MacMullen. *Nicene and Post-Nicene Fathers*, First Series, Vol. 6. Edited by Philip Schaff. New York: Christian Literature Publishing Co., 1888.

―――. *Tractates on the Gospel of John.* In *Saint Augustine: Homilies on the Gospel of John and the First Epistle of John*, translated by John Gibb and James Innes. *Nicene and Post-Nicene Fathers*, First Series, Vol. 7. Edited by Philip Schaff. New York: Christian Literature Publishing Co., 1888.

Basil of Caesarea. *Homilies on the Psalms.* Translated by Roy J. Deferrari. Washington, D.C.: Catholic University of America Press, 1963.

Bauer, Walter, Frederick William Danker, William F. Arndt, and F. Wilbur Gingrich. *A Greek-English Lexicon of the New Testament and Other Early Christian Literature.* 3rd ed. Chicago: University of Chicago Press, 2000. s.v. "παράκλητος (paraklētos)."

Bavinck, Herman. *Reformed Dogmatics.* Vol. 3, *Sin and Salvation in Christ.* Grand Rapids, MI: Baker Academic, 2006.

Bebbington, David W. *Evangelicalism in Modern Britain: A History from the 1730s to the 1980s.* London: Unwin Hyman, 1989.

Bercot, David W. *A Dictionary of Early Christian Beliefs: A Reference Guide to More Than 700 Topics Discussed by the Early Church Fathers.* Peabody, MA: Hendrickson, 1998.

Bloesch, Donald G. *Essentials of Evangelical Theology.* 2 vols. San Francisco: Harper & Row, 1978.

Boniface VIII (Pope). *Unam Sanctam.* Papal Bull, November 18, 1302. In *Denzinger-Hünermann: Enchiridion Symbolorum, Definitionum et Declarationum de Rebus Fidei et Morum.* Edited by Peter Hünermann, 43rd ed. Freiburg: Herder, 2012, nos. 870–875. *(English translation in The Papal Encyclicals 1302–1878*, edited by Claudia Carlen. Raleigh, NC: McGrath Publishing, 1981.)

Bruce M. Metzger, *The Text of the New Testament: Its Transmission, Corruption, and Restoration,* 2nd ed.

Bruce, F. F. *The New Testament Documents: Are They Reliable?* Grand Rapids, MI: Eerdmans, 1981.

———. *The Acts of the Apostles,* 3rd ed., 1990, 269

Calvin, John. *Institutes of the Christian Religion.* Translated by Henry Beveridge. 2 vols. Edinburgh: Calvin Translation Society, 1845.

———. *Institutes of the Christian Religion.* Translated by Ford Lewis Battles. Philadelphia: Westminster Press, 1960.

Canons of Dort. 1619. In *Reformed Confessions of the 16th and 17th Centuries,* Vol. 4, edited by James T. Dennison Jr. Grand Rapids, MI: Reformation Heritage Books, 2014.

Carson, D. A. *Divine Sovereignty and Human Responsibility: Biblical Perspectives in Tension.* Atlanta: John Knox Press, 1981.

Catechism of the Catholic Church. 2nd ed. Vatican City: Libreria Editrice Vaticana, 1997.

Chrysostom, John. *Homilies on Romans.* In *Nicene and Post-Nicene Fathers,* Series 1, Vol. 11, edited by Philip Schaff. New York: Christian Literature Company, 1889.

Clement of Alexandria. *Stromata (Miscellanies).* Translated by William Wilson. In *Ante-Nicene Fathers,* Vol. 2, edited by Alexander Roberts and James Donaldson. Buffalo, NY: Christian Literature Publishing Co., 1885.

Council of Orange (529). "Canons of the Second Council of Orange." In *Decrees of the Ecumenical Councils,* edited by

Norman P. Tanner. Washington, D.C.: Georgetown University Press, 1990.

Daniélou, Jean. *The Theology of Jewish Christianity*. Translated by John A. Baker. London: Darton, Longman & Todd, 1964.

Dutcher, Greg. *Killing Calvinism: How to Destroy a Perfectly Good Theology from the Inside*. Phillipsburg, NJ: P&R Publishing, 2012.

Edwards, Jonathan. *Freedom of the Will*. 1754. Reprint, New Haven: Yale University Press, 1957.

Erasmus, Desiderius. *On the Freedom of the Will*. Translated by E. F. Winter. New York: Nelson, 1969.

Finney, Charles G. *Lectures on Systematic Theology*. Oberlin, OH: James M. Fitch, 1846.

Frame, John M. *The Doctrine of God*. Phillipsburg, NJ: P&R Publishing, 2010.

Gregory of Nazianzus. *Oration 45 (On Holy Pascha)*. In *Nicene and Post-Nicene Fathers*, Series 2, Vol. 7, edited by Philip Schaff and Henry Wace. New York: Christian Literature Company, 1894.

Gregory the Great. *Dialogues*. Book 4. Translated by Odo Zimmerman. New York: Fathers of the Church, 1959.

Irenaeus. *Against Heresies*. Translated by Alexander Roberts and William Rambaut. In *Ante-Nicene Fathers*, Vol. 1, edited by Alexander Roberts and James Donaldson. Buffalo, NY: Christian Literature Publishing Co., 1885.

Kittel, Gerhard, and Gerhard Friedrich, eds. *Theological Dictionary of the New Testament*. Translated by Geoffrey W. Bromiley. Vol. 5. Grand Rapids, MI: Eerdmans, 1967, 800–810.

Lecler, Joseph. Toleration and the Reformation. Vol. 2. Translated by T. L. Westow. London: Longmans, Green & Co., 1960.

Liddell, Henry George, and Robert Scott. *A Greek-English Lexicon*. Revised and augmented throughout by Sir Henry Stuart Jones. 9th ed. Oxford: Clarendon Press, 1940. s.v. "παράκλητος."

Luther, Martin. *De Servo Arbitrio (On the Bondage of the Will)*. 1525. In
   *D. Martin Luthers Werke: Kritische Gesamtausgabe (Weimarer
   Ausgabe)*, Vol. 18, pp. 600–787. Weimar: Hermann Böhlaus
   Nachfolger, 1908.

———. Translated by J. I. Packer and O. R. Johnston as *The Bondage
   of the Will*. Rev. ed. Grand Rapids: Revell, 1957.

———. *Lectures on Romans (1515–1516)*. In *Luther's Works*, Vol. 25:
   Lectures on Romans. Edited by Hilton C. Oswald. St. Louis:
   Concordia Publishing House, 1972, pp. 373–377.

———. *Table Talk (Tischreden)*, No. 3745. In *Luther's Works*, Vol. 54:
   Table Talk. Edited by Theodore G. Tappert. Philadelphia:
   Fortress Press, 1967.

McGrath, Alister E. *Iustitia Dei: A History of the Christian Doctrine of
   Justification*. 4th ed. Cambridge: Cambridge University Press,
   2020.

Metzger, Bruce M. *The Text of the New Testament: Its Transmission,
   Corruption, and Restoration*. 3rd ed. New York: Oxford
   University Press, 1992.

Mill, John Stuart. *An Examination of Sir William Hamilton's Philosophy*.
   4th ed. London: Longmans, Green, Reader, and Dyer, 1872.

Moreland, J. P., and William Lane Craig. *Philosophical Foundations for a
   Christian Worldview*. Downers Grove, IL: InterVarsity Press,
   2003.

Muller, Richard A. *After Calvin: Studies in the Development of a Theological
   Tradition*. Oxford: Oxford University Press, 2003.

Oberman, Heiko A. *The Dawn of the Reformation*. Grand Rapids, MI:
   Eerdmans, 1992.

Oden, Thomas C. *The Transforming Power of Grace*. Nashville:
   Abingdon Press, 1993.

Origen. *De Principiis (On First Principles)*. Translated by Frederick
   Crombie. In *Ante-Nicene Fathers*, Vol. 4, edited by Alexander
   Roberts and James Donaldson. Buffalo, NY: Christian
   Literature Publishing Co., 1885.

Orr, James. *The Progress of Dogma: Being the Elliot Lectures for 1897*. London: Hodder and Stoughton, 1901.

Packer, J. I. *Evangelism and the Sovereignty of God*. Downers Grove, IL: InterVarsity Press, 1961.

Pelagius. *Commentary on Romans*. In B. R. Rees, *The Letters of Pelagius and His Followers*. Woodbridge, Suffolk: Boydell Press, 1991.

Plantinga, Alvin. *God, Freedom, and Evil*. Grand Rapids, MI: Eerdmans, 1974.

Pope, William Burt. *A Compendium of Christian Theology*. Vol. 2. London: Wesleyan Conference Office, 1875.

Schaff, Philip. *History of the Christian Church*. 8 vols. New York: Charles Scribner's Sons, 1882–1892.

Skinner, Quentin. *The Foundations of Modern Political Thought*. Vol. 2. Cambridge: Cambridge University Press, 1978.

Sproul, R. C. *Chosen by God*. Wheaton, IL: Tyndale House, 1986.

———. *What Is Reformed Theology?: Understanding the Basics of the Reformed Faith*. Wheaton, IL: Tyndale House Publishers, 2005 (Kindle version)

Stott, John R. W. *The Cross of Christ*. Downers Grove, IL: InterVarsity Press, 1986.

Swinburne, Richard. *The Coherence of Theism*, rev. ed. (Oxford: Clarendon, 1993).

Tertullian. *A Treatise on the Soul*. Translated by Peter Holmes. In *Ante-Nicene Fathers*, Vol. 3, edited by Alexander Roberts and James Donaldson. Buffalo, NY: Christian Literature Publishing Co., 1885.

The Holy Bible. *New American Standard Bible (NASB)*. La Habra, CA: Lockman Foundation, 1995.

The Westminster Confession of Faith. Edinburgh: Free Presbyterian Publications, 1646.

Virgil. *The Aeneid*. Translated by John Dryden. London: Jacob Tonson, 1697.

Walls, Jerry L. *Heaven, Hell, and Purgatory: Rethinking the Things That Matter Most.* Grand Rapids, MI: Brazos Press, 2015.

———. *Hell: The Logic of Damnation.* Notre Dame, IN: University of Notre Dame Press, 1992.

Walls, Jerry L., and Joseph R. Dongell. *Why I Am Not a Calvinist.* Downers Grove, IL: InterVarsity Press, 2004.

Warfield, B. B. *Calvin and Augustine.* Philadelphia: Presbyterian and Reformed, 1956.

Wesley, John. *A Plain Account of Christian Perfection.* London: Epworth Press, 1766.

Wilson, Ken. *The Foundations of Augustinian-Calvinism.* Tulsa, OK: White Horse Publishing, 2019.

Zagorin, Perez. *How the Idea of Religious Toleration Came to the West.* Princeton, NJ: Princeton University Press, 2003.

www.ingramcontent.com/pod-product-compliance
Lightning Source LLC
Chambersburg PA
CBHW051817090426
42736CB00011B/1528